Palgrave Studies in the Enlightenment,
Romanticism and Cultures of Print

Series Editors
Anne K. Mellor
Department of English
University of California Los Angeles
Los Angeles, CA, USA

Clifford Siskin
Department of English
New York University
New York, NY, USA

Ralph Cohen
John L. Rowlett
Editor

Transformations of a Genre

A Literary History of the Beguiled Apprentice

palgrave
macmillan

Ralph Cohen
Department of English
University of Virginia
Charlottesville, VA, USA

Editor
John L. Rowlett
Independent Scholar
Charlottesville, VA, USA

ISSN 2634-6516   ISSN 2634-6524 (electronic)
Palgrave Studies in the Enlightenment, Romanticism and Cultures of Print
ISBN 978-3-030-89670-6   ISBN 978-3-030-89668-3 (eBook)
https://doi.org/10.1007/978-3-030-89668-3

Cover illustration: Florilegius / Alamy Stock Photo

This Palgrave Macmillan imprint is published by the registered company Springer Nature Switzerland AG.
The registered company address is: Gewerbestrasse 11, 6330 Cham, Switzerland

EDITOR'S FOREWORD

Shortly after founding *New Literary History* (*NLH*) in 1969, Ralph Cohen drafted two working papers in the early 1970s that inconspicuously opened a new horizon on literary study, one that combined theory and history in a compelling way. These two original essays, "The Origins of a Genre" and "Literary Theory as a Genre," unpublished in his journal but now readily available, may serve as a prologue to the kind of thinking Cohen would continue to explore and refine for the rest of his literary life.[1] By the time he had composed the present work, his thinking had moved well beyond Mikhail Bakhtin's and Tzvetan Todorov's successes in shifting "the direction of genre study from classification to its functions in human speech and behavior."[2]

Whereas numerous critics—from Northrop Frye, Rosalie Colie, and Alastair Fowler to Barbara Lewalski, Fredric Jameson, Hans Robert Jauss, Jonathan Culler, Michael McKeon, and many others—had, by the turn of the century, advanced our understanding of literary genres and their mixtures, these works stopped short of arriving at a sufficiently historical conceptualization of genre that attended to its range, its shifting continuities, and its cultural bases. Introducing the first of twin issues of *NLH* (2003) on "Theorizing Genres," Cohen writes: "There have been few attempts to envision genre study as a theory of behavior or as one that can provide an insight into the arts and sciences. This issue and the following one … are an effort to expand the range of genre study as well as to examine its current practices" (v).

The individual and collective aim of Ralph Cohen's literary project was to orchestrate "a generic reconstitution of literary studies."[3] The present work, his literary history of the genre beguiled apprentice, encompasses his vision of just such a project. It is the first study of its kind. Since we continue to confront many of these problematics today—an adequate theory of change, the nature of narrative, a richer understanding of "literature" and the "literary," the literary nature of our humanness, and the shifting generic contexts for interpretation and gender relations—this posthumous work is as fundamental, lively, and useful today as it was when composed in the latter decades of the twentieth century (and perhaps more readily grasped). I note this cognizant of the vast amount of scholarship produced in the last thirty years (much of it introduced in *NLH*) that has made us increasingly aware of the varied and valuable ways genre has been criticized, theorized, and historicized. Yet this study, the sole book Ralph Cohen wrote after initiating the journal, stands alone. In Ralph Cohen's modest words: "This book represents what it describes; it offers an argument that redefines the nature of the literary and does so by attending to historical arguments and those of contemporary theory. Its genre is critical theory and practice, though it is also affiliated with genres like poetry, history, periodical papers, autobiography, and so forth." The identification and analysis of a genre that began as an anonymous ballad, "became" an array of literary genres, and ended up a new literary history demonstrates Cohen's procedure for dealing with a theory of genre as the basis of literary creation, interpretation, and history.

Placing Cohen's work among contemporary critics, mediating its applicability to present critical endeavors, and denominating the currency of its usefulness properly remain the task of critics who find his procedures persuasive and enlightening. Knowledgeable readers of English literature will recognize his contribution as anything but archival. Although it emerges at an earlier moment in the generation of a literary norm that is governed by competing forms of theory, its foundational components, the manner in which they are handled, and its ethical autobiographical features are persistently illuminating, and its long-lasting vision remains a reliable guide, especially useful today to a wide range of scholars practicing genre criticism.

Most of Cohen's published contributions to contemporary theory and literary history came in the form of the theoretical essay, of which he wrote and edited many. Cohen excelled at this short prose form, which he shaped to serve two purposes: to theorize, with deft particularity, critical concepts in need of rethinking; and to teach those concepts, by reading and discussing them transactionally at the personal invitation of a colleague or former student. Consequently, he published few of these essays-as-scripts since they had served Cohen's intensely occasional, pedagogical purpose. He used these conceptualist essays to articulate his major contribution to historical studies, a theorization of genre devoted to describing and explaining two principal systems of generic phenomena: one synchronic, the other diachronic.

On the one hand, his theoretical essays explain how a literary period may be understood as a synchronic system—a hierarchy of generic and discursive forms and their shifting interrelations, from innovation through norm stabilization to norm weakening through forms losing their validity, to their supersession by an immediately succeeding system. In his essay "Historical Knowledge and Literary Understanding" (1978), Cohen refers to a work-in-progress that proposed to describe, theorize, and account for such a synchronic genre system, "a study of literary change from Milton to Keats."[4] This study Cohen never published as a book; rather it took the form of innovative essays, only some published by Cohen, that deal with the emergence, epistemology, exemplification, and supersession of what he called "the Augustan mode."[5] In occasional essays, he demonstrates and develops in detail this literary system of interrelated works, governed by didactic forms, and the manner in which it is supplanted by a generic system governed by lyric forms.

On the other hand, between 1985 and 1987, Cohen published five theoretical essays in which he refers to another project, a multi-period project "proposing a literary history based on a theory of genre and generic transformation."[6] Cohen had begun to formulate these issues around his process theory of genre in the 1970s when he began to envision a working model to test and apply what amounts to a theory of human behavior. These five essays announce his study of the Barnwell ballad that proposed to exemplify how a new literary history might be written as a diachronic history attentive to continuities and changes. This, too, became for him a work-in-progress. These essays, intended for publication as a book, trace, diachronically, the generic transformations of a single genre, the beguiled apprentice, within and across diverse generic systems. The creativity demonstrated by gender critics has been apparent for some time; but in recognizing, naming, describing, and explaining the cultural bases for the transformations of this genre, Cohen deals with gender issues in a generic framework, reminding us of the creativity and self-revelation that belongs to genre criticism as well.

By 1984 he had completed a draft of much of the manuscript, as can be seen from the sudden emergence of the essays dealing with genre theory and the Barnwell ballad, including: "The Regeneration of Genre" (published here for the first time, but delivered in 1984), "Literary History and the Ballad of George Barnwel" (1985), "Afterword: The Problems of Generic Transformation" (1985), "Generic History as New Literary History" (1985), "History and Genre" (1986), and "The Fictions of Rhetoric" (1987); all of which featured Cohen's Barnwell project in order to expose some of the deficiencies of contemporary critical practice and to propose a satisfactory alternative. One of the three published articles that have not been collected among his theoretical essays is reissued here, adapted as part of the book's design.

It is in this book, rather than in his published essays, that Cohen reconceives, describes, analyzes, and demonstrates what a history of genre could look like and what a reconception of narrative implies. His published theoretical essays and the Barnwell history complement and shed light on each other. I have noted that "the lack of a comprehensive source to serve as an explanatory model of [Ralph Cohen's] concepts" might account for "the lack of widespread appropriation of his revisionary theory" (xix), and my recent collection of his essays was designed to constitute such a source. The present history of a genre, a more personal work, provides another. By "more personal" I mean not to suggest that Cohen considered scholarship impersonal. Indeed, in his "Note" to the journal's inaugural issue, he writes: "I have said that *New Literary History* was born out of the personal research in which each of the editors was involved. Its initiation is not, and could not be, impersonal. For us, personal belief and involvement is consistent with, even essential to, effective and reliable scholarship."[7] Yet while clearly indicating the editor's role in connecting personal inquiries to public values, Cohen scarcely ever published in his own journal; and when he did publish essays—like most of the essays mentioned above that are based on or refer to the Barnwell manuscript—they were characteristically placed in a collection of essays or a European journal that constituted expressions of his friendship to the editors (sometimes former students), what we might call public inquiries connected to personal values.

The Barnwell book is a more private instance of the strategy by which Cohen connected personal inquiries with public values. In his introduction, he separates personal inquiries and public values in his writing: "I shall not pursue the line of personal autobiography in terms of family, teachers, and background. Rather, I shall limit myself to those episodes which serve as intellectual autobiography." Withholding the personal from the reader is a private act which veils his recognition of the applicability, to his own personal romance, of the sexual saga of a virgin's seduction by an experienced woman. This recognition shaped his personal behavior and may account for his choice of the Barnwell story as the generic Proteus whose transformations he decided to treat, since other genre possibilities existed.

If this is not the precise corpus Ralph Cohen intended to contribute to the discipline of genre studies, such an important and useful history is nonetheless as reliable and convincing—indeed, as necessary—if edited with fidelity. Cohen's reticence in bringing the study to a close may have had something to do with the fact that he recognized the history he was writing was indeed closely affiliated with Addison's criticism and Percy's editing and their contributions to the genre. Their participation as critics in the genre's unfolding built in transformability of the genre by a theorist. Negotiating his own role in the resurgence of the genre, Cohen can be understood to enact the term *beguiled* in an antithetical sense to that fittingly applied to most previous instances of the genre—namely, a shift from Barnwell's being deluded by trickery and flattery based on the vulnerable pleasures of gender differences, to the genre critic's being charmingly diverted by the pleasant occupation of his own study based on the private pleasures of genre discrimination. Yet from time to time the genre critic makes public some of the pleasures in a published essay, exhibiting a pattern of proffering and withholding, thereby enhancing the pleasure in a kind of intellectual seduction of the reader or listener, whom he is beguiling to learn.

If we consider the Latin *apprendere* and the French verb *aprendre* from which *apprentice* is derived, we can note its dual sense, to *learn* and to *teach*. Consequently, Ralph Cohen—as both scholarly apprentice and intellectual enticer to his students and colleagues and to a scholarly journal and its international community—considered his study of the genre he was identifying as a pleasurable source of both learning and teaching. Hélène Cixous recognized Cohen's openness to difference as a "lucid, patient exercise of a great *force* of nonaggression," an openness she found exhibited by his journal, "a sort of *well-tempered* literary democracy."[8] His paradoxical sense of teaching as learning, borne of the same openness to difference, led to a scholarship of gender neutrality.

Ralph Cohen continued to extend his insights and explore and test conclusions in the generic history he was unfolding, while simultaneously using his theoretical essays to address and think through ancillary issues of explaining change that arose in the literary domain of theory and gender relations. Accordingly, he used the diachronic project as he employed his theoretical essays to frame questions for himself and for the journal that needed broader theoretical attention. In this respect, his theoretical essays and the present book served its author dialectically with the issues of *New Literary History*, what Wolfgang Iser insightfully dubbed "Ralph Cohen's book."[9] This "book" was a periodical series of essays challenging readers to rethink contemporary theoretical issues the editor was so prescient at apperceiving; in turn, collecting and editing the essays had an influence on the editor's own literary history.

This "book" promised its readers to unfold on schedule. Yet the present book was unscheduled. And I must acknowledge that despite all the theoretical thinking the gestation of this book received, it stubbornly resisted being born. One reason for this was Ralph Cohen's assuming an even greater scholarly burden in establishing, at the University of Virginia in 1990, the Commonwealth Center for Literary and Cultural Change, an organization that "requires a forum to share its inquiries with an audience beyond the actual participants"; those inquiries were received in *New Literary History*, which thereafter became a quarterly.[10] In addition to that, after retirement from the University of Virginia, Cohen, rather than completing the Barnwell manuscript for publication, founded and directed the Cohen Center for the Study of Technological Humanism at James Madison University in 2014. This institutional conduct revealed his emerging interest in learning about cognitive studies, an interest that had enveloped his thinking over the last decade of his life. Explorations in cognition and its changes, probing the boundaries of the human in science and technology, interested him because, if his behavioral understanding of genre consciousness as a social technology might be shown, by way of neurological advances, to have a biological as well as a generic basis, a novel interdisciplinary study of human behavior, what he called "technological humanism," might be established. At the close of his life he was once again engaged, as apprentice, in the pleasures of a visionary.

Aside from that, Ralph Cohen, an indefatigable master at the genre of revision, had more or less completed all but the conclusion to the book by 1990, and multiple drafts existed of each of the earlier chapters. There is no question but what the manuscript was unfinished and that it had become more practical to release parts—or the thinking those parts had generated—in the form of theoretical essays that used the single genre he was describing as evidence and control. Besides, since revisions for Cohen constituted "a process of literary self-discovery,"[11] generating revisions preempted completion so long as attempts in different versions remained productive of literary self-knowledge. In this regard, he may have been averse to anything short of posthumous publication lest his product of self-discovery, upon becoming a product, be misunderstood as an act of self-advertisement, a posture he studiously avoided all his life.

Revising as textual correcting, collating, and assembling the chapters to his satisfaction simply for the sake of publication he recognized as a daunting task; and for the editor of *New Literary History* and the educator-at-large, as he became, it was too distracting a task, one that could perhaps better be left to an editorial apprentice. Indeed, establishing the most illuminating, most complete draft of each chapter became the pleasure of the editor. So editing a publishable version that would serve Cohen's vision was a test of the editor's conscientiousness and a wager that the result, whatever its shortcomings, would merit a reprieve from the reader. In deference to the author and in keeping with the genre, no editorial effort has been made to reduce repetitions. The book's two interventions are designed to interrupt the rhythm of the proceedings, change the perspective, rehearse the aim of the project, and take stock of its implications. Though by no means unconversant with Cohen's oeuvre, I have found these interruptions and redundancies illuminating because they sometimes replicate and thereby clarify conceptual dilemmas. Any inconsistencies belong to the editor's limitations.

Recognizing the prescience of Iser's comment, I can add that—alongside the journal Cohen founded and edited for forty years and his collected theoretical essays—we now have four of Cohen's major works of critical theory, only one of which, I might note, he completed.[12] Was completion necessary? In the case of an open genre, completion belongs to the unknowable future of possibilities, our inability to foretell the actualizations of generic history. The genre the critic is rewriting cannot be completed, of course, by the critic, but Cohen's instance of the genre, his analyzing and explaining the genre's interrelations and the social provocations and implications, is done—though unfinished. Treating acts of beguilement and victimization in acts of critical theory and literary history, Cohen converts the received corruption of innocence and the subjugation of women that are characteristic of versions of the genre into his personal reworking of the gender of literary history, the public analogue of which he pursued in his journal. The issues Cohen pursued in *New Literary History*, and the thinkers he selected to publish, reveal his cognizance of their work and serve as public syllabi of his studies and of the issues and courses he was teaching.

Cohen's vision was of an inclusive literary history, a multi-voiced endeavor, aimed at reconceiving historical knowledge and regenerating literary studies, a visionary invitation open to all humanistic scholarship, an enterprise that promises to be much less narrowly conceived than was customary in the twentieth century. In another sense, it is clear from the Barnwell manuscript and from the related essays he published that Cohen wrote as if he expected to finish the book and convert his work-in-progress, born out of the personal research of an apprenticing historian, into a model for writing the history of a genre.[13] With respect to any beguiling pleasures for the author, a work-as-process applies only to the genre critic's lifetime. However, from the reader's standpoint, even if finished with by the author, the same unfinished work-as-product, may beguile literary historians well beyond.

The multiple genres that belong to the history of the Barnwell plot reveal, Cohen notes, "the need to undo history by redoing it in a different genre. And they demonstrate that no undoing can proceed without some continuous doing. Genre members enact the process by which a genre undergoes change so that my own chapters are themselves a contribution to literary history and critical theory." Is the disappearance of Barnwell as a cultural force analogous to the disappearance of sonnet narratives in the seventeenth and eighteenth centuries? Is this the dissipation of a cultural force? Or is it another systemic transformation, a rejuvenation of that force, as the narrative is redeemed by way of a novel combination of history and theory? What Cohen has modeled in this study of genre is a historical procedure to study all literary texts, all texts worthy of study, as a family of forms and their shifting connections and transformations.

Nevertheless, continuity persists. Consider the possibility that Cohen's history of the beguiled apprentice amounts to its renewal, its reformulated function in a new norm in which literary history and genre criticism provide the epistemological conditions for its continuance. In his reinvigoration of the genre, the critic becomes a rebooted apprentice to a scholarly discipline, and the actualization of literary history as a transformation of genres becomes possible. Unless more fiction writers, filmmakers, or television screenwriters see the emergent possibilities of the beguiled apprentice for the twenty-first century, contemporary genre critics may be responsible for this particular history's continued theoretical presence.[14] In any case, with Cohen's example, the horizon of expectation is open for a new group of *literary* genres whose histories can now be created. For these critics, at the very least, one aspect of that continuity is the joy to be taken in the reading, the analysis, the explanations of change. After all, as Iser has reminded us, the work of completing the text has always belonged to the reader. Although rhetorical arguments did not persuade Cohen to complete and publish the sequestered manuscript, the extraordinary insights and implications of his study generated the editor's confidence to deliver these pages to readers with the conviction that a new literary history becomes its own form of persuasion.

Charlottesville, VA   John L. Rowlett

Notes

1. Ralph Cohen, "The Origins of a Genre: Descriptive Poetry" and "Literary Theory as a Genre," *Genre Theory and Historical Change: Theoretical Essays of Ralph Cohen*, ed. John L. Rowlett (Charlottesville: Univ. of Virginia Press, 2017), 36–49 and 50–67.
2. Ralph Cohen, "Introduction," *New Literary History* 34, no. 2 (2003): v.
3. Ralph Cohen, "Introduction: Notes Toward a Generic Reconstitution of Literary Study," *New Literary History* 34, no. 3 (2003): v–xvi.
4. "Historical Knowledge and Literary Understanding," *Genre Theory and Historical Change*, 221.
5. "The Augustan Mode in English Poetry," *Eighteenth Century Studies* 1, no. 1 (1967): 3–32. This essay and "Historical Knowledge and Literary Understanding," should be considered in conjunction with Cohen, "On the Interrelations of Eighteenth-Century Literary Forms," "The Origins of a Genre: Descriptive Poetry," "Innovation and Variation: Literary Change and Georgic Poetry," and "Some Thoughts on the Problems of Literary Change 1750–1800," all but for "The Augustan Mode," collected in Rowlett. In addition, see Ralph Cohen, "On the Presuppositions of Literary Periods," *New Literary History* 50, no. 1 (2019): 113–27; and Rowlett, "Ralph Cohen on Literary Periods: Afterword as Foreword," *New Literary History* 50, no. 1 (2019): 129–39.
6. "Literary History and the Ballad of George Barnwel," in *Augustan Studies in honor of Irvin Ehrenpreis*, ed. Douglas Lane Patey and Timothy Keegan (Newark, NJ: University of Delaware Press, 1985), 13–31; 14.

7. Ralph Cohen, "A Note on *New Literary History*," *New Literary History* 1, no. 1 (1969): 6.

8. Hélène Cixous, "Tribute to Ralph Cohen," *New Literary History* 40, no. 4 (2009): 751; Cixous's italics.

9. Wolfgang Iser, "Twenty-five Years *New Literary History*: A Tribute to Ralph Cohen," *New Literary History* 25, no. 4 (1994): 738.

10. Ralph Cohen, "Introduction," *New Literary History* 21, no. 4 (1990): 777.

11. Cohen, *The Art of Discrimination: Thomson's* The Seasons *and the Language of Criticism* (Berkeley: Univ. of California Press, 1964), 17. Cohen goes on to note that "this [Augustan] concept of 'process' as a form of criticism identified 'criticism' with the poet's literary self-knowledge" (18). So it was with Cohen's revisions of the literary history he was writing, and he privately discovered his individuality within this process.

12. I should note that since interpretation is a genre, Cohen had already written the partial history of a genre in his critical theory, *The Art of Discrimination*, by focusing his narrative of continuity and discontinuity on an "analysis of critical statements and critical activity, spanning more than two hundred years, with regard to a single poem" (3). As his theory of change and of genre criticism developed, Cohen came to see every act of literary writing—not simply that of criticism—as constituting interpretation, or, more precisely, as a genre member articulating an interpretive response, whether particular or general, to the predecessor genre.

    In delivering his own interpretation of the poem in *The Unfolding of* The Seasons (1970), Cohen was responsible for an innovative mutation in the critical reception of the poem. At the same time, he revealed the value and necessity of a literary history that—unlike new critical readings of the poem—set systematic (Augustan) limits on any analysis, understanding, and explanation of the poem as such. After his interpretation of that poem, he returned his attention to *literary* theory, with a particular interest in theorizing genre as a reformulation of a linguistic-based concept of literary criticism, or critical practice, that had been less capacious and more suited to explanations of particular poems.

13. In December 1984, Cohen delivered a presentation at the meetings of the Modern Language Association that he called "Examples of a New Literary History." Among the auditors was Paul Zimmer, Director of the University of Iowa Press, who, "looking for promising work," surmised that Cohen's paper might be part of a book-length manuscript. In a letter dated January 15, 1985, Zimmer invited Cohen to consider Iowa's publishing his manuscript. In response, Cohen replied, January 23, 1985: "my presentation ... is part of a book that I am writing which deals with genre, narrative, and history. In fact, I hope to complete the book by September 1985." Paul

Zimmer was not the sole editor Cohen disappointed by withholding this manuscript for more than thirty years.

14. The genre was rewritten in the twentieth century as *The Beguiled* (1966), Thomas Cullinan's Civil War novel of a wounded Union soldier recuperating at a southern all-girls boarding school. It was subsequently transformed into a southern gothic film by Don Siegel (1971). Sofia Coppola (2017) flips the script, transforming Siegel's southern gothic into a feminist parody, with teenage Alicia as apprentice tease and McBurney as emasculated male. Cohen's reconceptualization of the beguiled apprentice as literary history and Siegel's transformation of the genre into a film indicate the rhizomatic directions a genre can take. Cohen's literary history and the parody of Siegel's film by Coppola are both indicative of a shift in generic systems.

The television series *The Apprentice* and *The Celebrity Apprentice* hold provocative possibilities for enterprising and creative interpreters.

ACKNOWLEDGMENTS

The scholarship that traces the history of a genre over four centuries could not have been accomplished without the prodigious help Ralph Cohen received from the librarians he came to so rely upon. Cohen spent most of his summers of the 1970s and 1980s in the British Museum gathering instances of the Barnwell genre, and to this end he was forever appreciative of their unflagging contributions. I regret that I did not know these librarians and that, without Ralph's personal thanks in print, they must remain nameless in this acknowledgment of their invaluable services.

Also deserving of special appreciation are the amanuenses, three of whom I know well, who surrendered countless hours typing, then later keyboarding, what must surely have seemed an endless manuscript. Barbara Smith and Charlotte Bowen, serving successively as Assistants to the Editor of *New Literary History*, contributed many pages to the proliferating manuscript in the early stages; and Mollie Washburne, now Managing Editor of *New Literary History*, continued producing rewritten versions of the manuscript and confides, having recently welcomed her first grandchild, that she no longer wants to talk about "ole George Barnwell, who was undone by a strumpet." I'm grateful to Mollie for getting to me updated versions of chapters she saved that were not among the manuscript files.

Ralph's and my colleagues who encouraged this undertaking were many. I must thank, in particular, Jeffrey Plank, whose attentive readings were as precise as they were tireless. Cliff Siskin, Jerry McGann, Rita Felski, Chip Tucker, Eddie Tomarken, and Michael Prince each played an important role in encouraging my efforts. Those who knew of my ambition were as skeptical as I that it would come to fruition. Considering how pleased they will no doubt be to read a demonstration of Ralph's generic criticism, I feel emboldened to seek their leniency for the editorial crime of sending forth something they may feel Ralph's demanding insistence on getting it right withheld.

I owe special thanks to Cliff Siskin and Anne Mellor, editors of Palgrave Studies in the Enlightenment, Romanticism and Cultures of Print, who have made this editorial collaboration uncommonly insightful, and to Molly Beck, Senior Editor for Literature, and Jack Heeney, Editorial Assistant, at Palgrave Macmillan for executing seamlessly the book's production. This book also profited from the close reading of a knowledgeable literary scholar who served as an astute external reader. The reader's discerning comments articulating the importance of this publishing event suggest a theoretical framing of Cohen's generic transformations that would argue, shifting emphasis, "not ... for a literary *history* but ... for a *literary* history, one that recognizes the historical dynamics and rhythms of forms as more than just sociological epiphenomena." Indeed, advocates and represents.

All of the papers making up the manuscript of this book have been housed in the Albert and Shirley Small Special Collections Library at the University of Virginia, under the able supervision of University Archivist, Lauren Zuchowski Longwell. Once catalogued, they will be accessible to those wishing to consult the material from which this book has taken shape, as well as letters pertaining to its production and publication. On behalf of future scholars who will benefit from her curatorial care, I thank Lauren.

Over forty-five extraordinary years, Abbie has become all too accustomed to receiving quiet notes of gratitude. She wouldn't have it any other way. Even so, I can't but declare that her abiding love, keen intellect, sense of moderation, and discerning taste have been—like a second nature—richly enabling without my acknowledging it.

Part of Chap. 2 appeared as "Literary History and the Ballad of George Barnwel" in *Augustan Studies: Essays in Honor of Irvin Ehrenpreis*, ed. Douglas Lane Patey and Timothy Keegan (Newark, NJ: University of Delaware Press, 1985). It is here reprinted with permission of Associated University Presses. Chapter 9 appeared in a somewhat different iteration as "Afterword: The Problems of Generic Transformation," in *Romance: Generic Transformation from Chrétien de Troyes to Cervantes*, ed. Kevin Brownlee and Marina Scordilis Brownlee (Hanover, NH: Univ. Press of

New England, 1985), 265–80. Parts of Chap. 12 appeared as "The Fictions of Rhetoric," in *The History and Philosophy of Rhetoric and Political Discourse: Volume II*, ed. Kenneth W. Thompson (Lanham, MD: University Press of America, 1987). Edited versions of the latter two are here reprinted with permission of the publishers. The unpublished conclusion, adapted for the book, was delivered in October 1984 as part of the Patten Lectures at the University of Indiana.

CONTENTS

ABOUT THE AUTHOR

Ralph Cohen (1917–2016), among the most eminent critical thinkers and educators of his time, achieved international distinction as scholar and editor and as classroom teacher and colleague. *New Literary History*, the award-winning journal of theory and interpretation that he founded at the University of Virginia in 1969 and edited for forty years, was a new type of learned journal that introduced the theoretical essay into literary studies, thereby shaping and normalizing the role of theory in writing creatively about literary history and cultural problems. He extended these activist procedures throughout the modern university by initiating, at the University of Virginia, an interdisciplinary research center, the Commonwealth Center for Literary and Cultural Change (1988–1995), which had as its primary aim, he wrote, "the study of change and continuity in individuals and institutions in the arts, humanities, sciences, and social sciences." Cohen's historical scholarship was centered on genres of the British Enlightenment, and his dissertation on Hume's critical theory and his own book of critical theory, *The Art of Discrimination: Thomson's* The Seasons *and the Language of Criticism* (1964), were forerunners of his essays on contemporary history and genre theory. The present book stands as the culmination of a brilliant career that opens new horizons on the future of genre criticism and literary history.

About the Editor

John L. Rowlett received his doctorate in literary studies from the University of Virginia where he was a student of Ralph Cohen's. He served as Program Director of the Commonwealth Center for Literary and Cultural Change at the University of Virginia and as Advisory Editor of *New Literary History*. He edited *Genre Theory and Historical Change: Theoretical Essays of Ralph Cohen* (2017) and is writing about Cohen's literary thinking.

Autobiographical Introduction

During the 1970s I began to write a book that addressed itself to the question, "Why do writers write in particular genres?" Why do writers choose to write a tragedy, a novel, a critical essay, a comedy, a sonnet sequence? Was there something about a genre that connected the writing of a tragedy or other genre with a new view of human experience? What sense would it make then to suggest that every time a writer like Virginia Woolf or Susan Sontag changed the genre in which she wrote, she changed the worldview she held? If the genre did not express a worldview, did this mean that our assumption that each text is its own world is a redundant conception—meaning no more than that each text is what it is?

I want in this introduction to explain how I came to think my question an important one and to indicate the kind of problems it led me to consider. I shall not pursue the line of personal autobiography in terms of family, teachers, and background. Rather, I shall limit myself to those episodes which serve as intellectual autobiography. Before I conclude I shall want to explain my choice of writing this introduction as autobiography and literary theory and how such choice relates to the theory of genre I came to hold. It will, I hope, become apparent that some of our distinctions between public and private explanations need to be erased and that you will recognize in my linkages some of your own generic procedures.

R. Cohen, J. L. Rowlett, *Transformations of a Genre*, Palgrave Studies in the Enlightenment, Romanticism and Cultures of Print, https://doi.org/10.1007/978-3-030-89668-3_1

The question that I posed as a beginning was not, of course, a beginning. Somewhere in the midst of my considerations about genre the question began to assert itself: How and why do writers, given a single narrative, treat it in different genres—narratives of Prometheus, Antigone, Samson, Jesus, Mary, Faust, Queen Elizabeth, Robin Hood, and so forth? What role, if any, does genre play in narration? No text I know of can be treated as though it is mono-vocal; they are all multivocal. Could a theory of genre then assume textual, multivocality as a given? What would such a theory be and why would I want it? In other words, the question with which I began my inquiry was not one question but many. Yet the critics with whom I discussed these inquiries seemed to have only one reply. It appeared that to utter the word "genre" was to preemptively invalidate any inquiry one was to pursue. Genre theory was one siren song that critics had no trouble disregarding.

Jacques Derrida and Paul de Man and many non-deconstructive critics, including Michel Foucault, sought to deny the usefulness of genre theory for literary study. It is, of course, always possible to make a virtue of resisting fashion, as Stanley Fish does, and insist on one's conservatism. But resisting or affirming fashion is not of interest to me. I sought then, as I seek in this book, to understand what texts are and what parts they play in our lives. Surely, up to the mid-twentieth century the identification of texts as "kinds" or "genres" was taken for granted by most critics, even though the concept of "genre" underwent many changes from the time it came to be used as an explanatory device by Greek rhetoricians up to and including the writings of R. S. Crane and Kenneth Burke.

Of course, not all of our contemporary theoreticians—Russian Formalists and Marxists—are prepared to abandon genre. Fredric Jameson, who is probably our most persuasive Marxist literary theorist, sought to retain a genre theory because it permitted him, for example, to reveal the historical changes from realism to modernism in the genre "novel" and to relate genre to developments in capitalist society. Genre theory served to support his belief in a homology between literary structure and economic structure. Another reason for his support of a genre theory was the tradition, initially developed by the Russian formalists and continued by the Prague structuralists, that genres formed hierarchies. Such hierarchies with their dominant genres were used by the formalists to explain the "evolution" of literary history. In our time, a belated formalist, Tzvetan Todorov, has applied a generic view to the study of the "fantastic" and has been pursuing an inquiry into the origin of genres.

It became clear to me that this major contemporary disagreement on genre theory was not a matter of taking sides, of joining one or another of the theoretical claimants. Rather, it appeared at first a disagreement about the area to be covered. Those critics who sought to explain *historical* continuities and discontinuities frequently did so on grounds that were identified with a historical concept no longer producing "effective history," in Foucault's term—a historical concept that could not cope with contemporary, dispersed writing. Foucault argued that genre theories were constituted to explain writings more stable than contemporary texts. Thus, to apply such genre theories to contemporary writing was anachronistic as well as inappropriate. Of course, any genre theory that could not apply to contemporary writing would indeed be of little use to me as an explanatory procedure.

What was taking place in contemporary writing, not merely in contemporary literary writing, was noticed by scholars in many disciplines. Anthropologists like Margaret Mead, Ruth Benedict, Mary Douglas, Victor Turner, and Clifford Geertz found in literary study tools and procedures for describing an interpreting behavior in non-industrialized societies. The sociologist Erving Goffman found in "frame analysis" a genre procedure for dealing with everyday life. Cultural geographers found in literary study the basis for analyzing the function of cultural space. The mixing of genres clearly implied multiple strategies in dealing with human behavior. Geertz called this phenomenon the "blurring" of genres, assuming, mistakenly, that this was a new phenomenon in genre theory. Referring to what he called "blurred genres," Geertz wrote the following:

> This genre blurring is more than just a matter of Harry Houdini or Richard Nixon turning up as characters in novels or of midwestern murder sprees described as though a gothic romancer had imagined them. It is philosophical inquiries looking like literary criticism (think of Stanley Cavell on Beckett or Thoreau, Sartre on Flaubert), scientific discussions looking like belles lettres *morceaux* (Lewis Thomas, Loren Eiseley), baroque fantasies presented as deadpan empirical observations (Borges, Barthelme), histories that consist of equations and tables or law court testimony (Fogel and Engerman, Le Roi Ladurie), documentaries that read like true confessions (Mailer), parables posing as ethnographies (Castaneda), theoretical treatises set out as travelogues (Levi-Strauss), ideological arguments cast as historiographical inquires (Edward Said), and so on.[1]

Surely in the light of such texts my inquiry, "Why do people write in particular genres?" could not and should not be interpreted as assuming genres are fixed. The question, therefore, might be rephrased, "Why in our time do people write in genres that are mixed?" If the question were put this way, it would be apparent that it requires at least a historical answer since "in our time" becomes part of the inquiry. If it was answered, we could come to understand something about the way writing changed from earlier times when it was considered less obviously mixed. And the answer would then undertake to explain why this change in writing took place.

But I had developed an argument that genres, even in Aristotle's *Poetics*, were seen as mixed in the sense that tragedy, for example, included all the parts or elements from epic. The problem was not that genres have now begun to be mixed, but in what way, and for what reasons, are they mixed in different ways at different times?

I should note here two issues that troubled me. The first was that, although Foucault dealt with the historical use of genre theory and its present inadequacy, he did not inquire into the historical changes which the concept "genre" had undergone and could undergo. If he had, he would have recognized the possibility of it undergoing yet another change in our time. The second that troubled me, though perhaps more excusably since it came from an anthropologist, was the study of generic criticism that took "blurring" as a new and modern phenomenon.

Nevertheless, it seemed to me necessary to face the overwhelming question, "What do I mean by genre?" My answer would require some explanation, some demonstration of the changing concepts of genre. Without pursuing this question there would be little likelihood that readers would grasp, or, if grasped, would welcome this inquiry. There were many facets of genre to cover; after all, some genres, like comedy and tragedy, were performed usually in a particular place like a theater. Others, like hymns, were sung in a church, and still others, like broadside ballads, were originally sung and distributed like merchandise in the streets. I therefore proposed a negative strategy: to come to terms with genre, not directly, but indirectly—to face the opponents of genre and to consider the case as carefully as I could. The foremost contemporary case against genre was to be found in Jacques Derrida's essay "The Law of Genre."[2]

In this essay Derrida pointed out that genre presupposed a common trait of membership in a class. Texts were not to be identified, however, by such traits since other traits would identify them as members of other genres, or the same trait could function differently in different texts. In practice, therefore, he was theorizing about the blurred genres that troubled Geertz. Thus the question, "Why do people write in particular genres?" seemed an empty question to such a critic since writers no longer write in known genres.

I was confronted here with an explanatory problem: texts that I wished to explain required some grouping in order to distinguish similarities and differences. Even if I wished to analyze a single text, I had to have at least one other from which it could be distinguished and to which it could be compared. But even as I offer this explanation, I think of genres in terms of written texts and as groupings that serve interpretative purposes. Yet how is it that genres serve interpretative purposes? Were genres not once considered primarily classifications of texts? Were they not seen as necessary for genealogical purposes? They were, but they need not and should not be considered permanently classificatory. In oral societies, genres served to make logical connections and distinctions so that the listener could follow the oral discourse. Francis Cairns points out that generic markers served to distinguish one type of communication from another since such communications showed many secondary elements. Discourses of the same oral genre shared at least one primary trait for purposes of recognition by hearers, such as the praise of a city in a farewell address. Is this then the "law" of genre to which Derrida referred? Or is the "law" of genre that which Northrop Frye discussed when he wrote that "the purpose of criticism by genres is not so much to classify as to clarify … traditions and affinities, thereby bringing out a large number of literary relationships that would not be noticed as long as there were no context established for them"?[3] Is the grouping of texts for purposes of clarifying traditions and affinities that "law" that is to be overthrown? Or is the "law" of genre a reference to that concept which finds "genre" an institution for joining texts in ways that support the current economic and social structure; classes or groupings that, along with other institutions, fall casualties "to the gradual penetration of a market system and a money economy"? In Jameson's terms, "the older generic categories do not, for all that, die out, but persist in the half-life of the subliterary genres of mass culture … where they await the resurrection of their immemorial, archetypal resonance at the hands of a Frye or a Bloch."[4] Here we have a procedure of generic disappearance and reappearance in relation to economic structure, their overthrow dictated by changes in the economic structure.

These changes lead to generic demotion to popular or mass culture. Is the "law" of genre then dependent upon the economic structure?

Let us assume that the "law" of genre has no reference to the actual concepts of genre in history: to what then does it refer? It refers to the assumption that texts cannot belong to one class; rather, they participate in more than one. But what if we assume that a text is combinatory, composed of some past features of a genre and of numerous interrelations with other texts. A genre would then be defined by the manner of combination; would a critic of genre who attacked the hypothesis of a single or multiple "belonging" be attacking a combinatory theory of genre? When Lillian Hornstein discusses *Recent Middle English Scholarship and Criticism*, she notes that "all critics apparently concur that … there will emerge only hazy borderlines where epic, saga, *chanson de geste*, romance, historical romance, *lai*, saint's life, pious legend, fabliau meet and blend."[5] Anyone who watches television knows and recognizes the blend of advertising, narrative, and economic exploitation. The way texts are composed presupposes that blending or blurring are givens and can best be described by noting that which is blended or blurred. It is not that "blending" or "blurring" has suddenly occurred, but that the manner, intent, and extent of blending and blurring have historically changed.

Supposing we put the question this way: If we write of "traces," "supplements," and "contradictions between rhetoric and grammar," are we writing of texts or of parts of texts? What will these analyses tell us if we wish to understand the varied discourses in an epic or even in a sonnet? After all, the notions of "supplement" and "trace" presuppose groupings of parts of texts, and these would be included in any genre theory that granted intertextuality.

Now it should be apparent that the genre theory toward which I was moving would identify texts within a group in terms of their combinatory connections. Any text can thus belong to several genres depending upon the hierarchy the critic establishes for his combinatory aims. But what is important about this procedure is that it can explain why some critics should wish to join texts in a genre and others should wish to deny this. Why some critics like Barbara H. Smith and Maria Corti, for example, should wish to identify certain texts as "literary" and why others like Jacques Derrida and Harold Bloom should wish to deny the distinction between "literary" and "non-literary" texts?

You do, of course, note that I put aside all essentialist definitions of genre. Whenever texts are grouped together to form a class, I assume that the critics are engaging in "genre-izing" or "genderizing." What interested me were the grounds for doing so and what literary consequences followed. Here I was, of course, interested in the defensibility of the arguments, but I wished also to describe the way in which literary criticism or theory developed as a generic instance. Among the aims of my genre theory was one that sought to illustrate the distortions any genre revealed. I knew that to answer why writers wrote in particular genres was to answer the antithetical question, why did they not write in other genres? An answer to my inquiry would have to explain why new genres like the novel and film arose when they did. Why writers ceased to write epics; ceased and then, after a period of absence, resumed writing the sonnet sequence?

You must understand that it was not my desire to mediate among opposing critical factions. I assumed that all critics were writing in genres and that there was thus some inevitable agreement among instances of the same genre—literary criticism or literary theory. This is not the occasion to go into detail on the virgin birth of theoretical positions: phenomenological, deconstructionist, Lacanian, Marxist, Feminist, formalist, generic, and so on. My genre theory assumes that certain elements or features of a genre are shared at any one time by its practitioners. It does not, I repeat, does not deny differences; it argues for a relation between the similarities and the differences.

Still, my inquiry into "genre" must deal with those who reject such a concept (even if their own texts exemplify it), substituting history of ideas or thematic analysis or rhetorical analysis or *écriture* or "discursive formations" as alternatives. The term "text" is surely an effort at leveling literary and non-literary writing, just as alternatives like "writing" or "discursive formations" seek to erase these distinctions. This happens because one assumes an archeological and the other a bibliographical point of view. It is not necessary for me to draw your attention to one of the terms— "literary work"—that these are meant to displace. For in this term the desire to relate mental to physical labor is obvious, whereas "text" wishes to "deauthorize" this relation.

In confronting this problem I sought to inquire into Derrida's and Foucault's desire to conceive of a text as a dismantled whole. Perhaps the very term "whole" is inadequate in describing what they examine: they deal with disjunctions, with dispersions. Yet the very notion of disjunction or dispersion in a text is only to be understood by reference to those passages which have become disjuncted in one text to become conjuncted in another; those dispersed or scattered in one text become assembled or associated in other texts. What then are we to understand by the term "text"? Does it refer to all the sentences of a novel? To representative sentences or phrases? Should we use the phenomenological distinction between text and actualization of the text? What consequences are to be drawn for genre from such assumptions?

Does my generic theory imply that a text is connected with other texts and thus cannot be enclosed, sealed, or fixed in its private world? Yes, it does. Yet does a text not have some kind of closure which is achieved when a reader reads it?

This question about closure may appear to be a long way from the apparently simple inquiry about writing in genres. But I did not find it so. If a genre refers to a class, and a text is a member of the class, it must share one or more traits with some members. Trait-sharing indicates that any text—no matter how many genres it belongs to—is not complete in itself. Does the idea of closure in my genre theory imply that some texts are deliberately anti-generic; that they parody the genre, exaggerate the genre, declass or reclass the genre? When broadside ballads become sophisticated "literature," have we not reclassified a non-literary text to a literary one? Since this implies a distinction between literary and non-literary genres, is this a distinction based only on language or on some social view of genre?

There is, as I have indicated, a disagreement among contemporary critics about texts and "literary texts": there are those who argue that all writings we have are texts in language, and, as Harold Bloom puts it, "I behold no differences, in kind or in degree, between the language of poetry and the language of criticism."[6] Then there are those, stemming from the positions of the Russian Formalists and Prague Structuralists, who insist on important differences in kind and degree between the language of literary and non-literary texts. Today Barbara H. Smith and Wolfgang Iser would subscribe to this position, but I quote one of the founders of Russian Formalism, Roman Jakobson, on the autonomy of the aesthetic function of a literary text. The poetic function or "poeticity" manifests itself, he writes, "when the word is felt as a word and not a mere representation of the object being named or an outburst of emotion, when words and their composition, their meaning, their external and inner form, acquire a weight and value of their own instead of referring indifferently to reality."[7]

Both Bloom and Jakobson would grant that a poem is a social act related to the social structure. Where they would disagree is in the determination that in a poem "the word is felt as a word and not a mere representation of the object being named." For Bloom (and indeed for Paul de

Man) all works can and do acquire a weight of their own and can foreground a text. What then about the texts we call poems? This question is not of particular interest to these critics even though Bloom is primarily concerned with poems. But it does seem to me to require explanation. The very term "text" disengages any particular kind of writing from its kind. An ode, an elegy, an epic, a description, a tragedy—all these are texts. Do we not erase the differences among the kinds by treating them as texts? And do we not erase the fact that the different texts have in the past been referred to as members of one or more specific kinds or genres?

These are two separate questions and it is appropriate to address them in turn. If we erase the differences among the kinds, we do so despite the fact that the kinds are composed of differences. Naming a text a "novel" or "non-fiction novel" or a "mini-series" or a "soap" identifies it and pins down what is unpinnable; in Derrida's terms, genre-naming fixes what is necessarily unfixable, encloses in boundaries that which crosses boundaries. Nevertheless, if we think of people instead of maps, we know that border crossings are common practice in some countries (like our own) and that the reasons for such crossings are social and economic. Every time such a crossing occurs, it places the person in a dual relation, and sometimes dual jeopardy, with his own and with a foreign country. But texts need not have an originating or fixed border. Texts called "novels" may include stories, letters, and poems as their constituents. They may even belong to more than these kinds because they may also be biographies or journalistic reports. The point is that if texts cross borders or boundaries, they must have borders or boundaries to cross; they need group or class names to identify them. If all we have are textual crossings, we can make no distinctions between novels, non-fiction novels, and autobiographies that are also fictions and non-fictions. Genre-naming or -grouping is inevitably both necessary and loose; critics may change the boundaries and the name. But they then continue with other strategies that, nevertheless, involve renaming and remapping.

I seem to have come some way from the time I started to inquire into particular genres, into the reasons for writers selecting a particular generic mixture in which to write. But in my theoretical-autobiographical narrative which concerns itself with my writing of theory, I want to convey to you how the drafting of a text necessarily led me to questions that were unanticipated and that required me to engage in the very boundary crossings that this introduction exemplifies. Nevertheless, I can only explain such crossings by knowing or creating the *names* of the crossed kinds: "Do we not erase the fact that the different texts have indeed been referred to as members of specific kinds or genres in the past?"

If this sounds like the old joke about Noah and the naming of the animals as they entered the ark, it is not unintentional. Naming is a procedure performed by readers and writers, and what one person names another can rename. Some generic names may endure longer than others, but they are all erasable. Take those tragedies in England that were initiated by George Lillo with *The London Merchant* (1731). Lillo called them "plays, founded on moral tales in private life"; in Germany, in the eighteenth century up to the present, these were and are still called "bourgeois" tragedies, and in our time they have been called "dramas of sensibility" and "sentimental tragedies." In each of these classifications or genres, the texts referred to and the features discussed were somewhat different, though there was much overlapping.

In the eighteenth century, Lillo and John Hughes called such plays *"tragedies of private life"* because they wished to see them as an extension of Aristotle's notion of tragedy. Their contribution to tragedy as a genre was to extend the characters and themes of tragedy from affairs of state carried on by the holders of power to the sad and often criminal lives of members of the lower classes. A major genre was used to embrace and enhance a class that had an inferior status. We can note the strategies involved: an undermining of classical tragedy by claiming merely to extend it, the *demotion* of tragedy as a genre form dealing only with aristocratic protagonists to the elevation of commoners as capable of tragic emotions, the promotion of a class previously deemed unworthy of presentation. In Germany the same plays were called bourgeois tragedies to stress the innovative role of this class and the need for it to possess a genre that characterized it. In our time, when the bourgeois were not an innovative class, the classification of many of these plays as "dramas of sensibility" resulted from a desire to attack Enlightenment departures from a classical norm that led, in the views of these critics, to the collapse of twentieth-century values. It was, of course, an attack upon the bourgeoisie. This generic classification of "sensibility" sought to classify a literary tendency assumed to be socially and literarily dangerous, and it thus made possible the attack upon this group of texts in comparison to others that upheld the so-called appropriate values.

Generic classifications such as these deal with whole texts. But texts, it can be argued, are not wholes but rather fragments and, as such, do not require names that imply wholes of a prior time. Any representative passage will, for the de Manian deconstructionist, serve as a demonstration of the inevitable contradiction between rhetoric and grammar. But if texts are fragments of all writing, it is still necessary to distinguish an unfinished poem from an unfinished joke. But mere naming is not enough; for we all have given names (which may or may not classify us) and we all have family names which establish us as members of a patriarchal or matriarchal lineage. We recognize the need for names which constitute us as members of one or more groups. Our government gives us numbers for purposes of identification because for them family trees or any other type of generic joining is of no importance. The induplicability of numbers is the aim. For them we are all accessioned neutrally and equally so that this strategy, by demonstrably numbering all, conceals the actual inequality that some human beings suffer. The purpose of naming a type of writing "feminist literary criticism" or "slave narrative" or "legal brief" is to establish an identity that is socially and literarily related to other identities. "Feminist literary criticism" makes a political assertion that it is for one group and against another, announces that a literary act cannot be dissevered from social action, and rejects the belief that anonymity stimulates fairness. In doing so, the genre of "literary criticism" is enlarged to include interconnections with autobiography, with political manifestos and polemics, with documents containing sociological and historical data. This literary criticism, like other such criticism, merges descriptions of political and institutional power with analyses of textual response. Still, "feminist literary criticism" is related not only to other feminist writing but also to other literary criticism—Marxist, phenomenological, Freudian, and so on— whether written by or for feminists or non-feminists.

If we accept the idea that generic naming serves the purpose of identification by grouping similar texts, that any particular text can be included under more than one name or genre, that grouping makes possible a recognition of interrelations among texts, that group-naming is always teleological, then we can return to the issue of literary and non-literary texts. Whenever texts are denominated "literary" they form a genre, governed by aesthetic principles which serve as the dominant generic components. These aesthetic components are defined by critics as "self-referentiality," as "allusion," as play, as fictionality, as any one of a number of aesthetic principles. The objection to this as a genre can be seen in the attack on such components as insufficiently distinctive, as creating textual differences where none exist.

Those critics who abandon the two-genre system of literary and non-literary texts can, from my treatment of the generic approach, claim that the distinction has lost much of its justification. These two genres were created in the early twentieth century to give to "literature" the status of independent values, affective and cognitive. The Russian Formalists argued that "literary" texts made a special contribution to the culture of a new society. But the maintenance of this distinction has come to serve, in our time, as a bulwark against the introduction of texts that have aesthetic and other values for specific groups. Slave narratives, women's autobiographies, diaries and journals, the writings of factory workers have been denied entry into "literature" because they lack the aesthetic criteria that were established to exclude texts like them. But a theory that cannot grasp the diverse social nature of genres is surely inadequate. And a literary theory that excludes these genres is unable to address the changed consciousness created by them. What is pertinent here is that these works, possessing as they do features which make them significant writings for a group or groups of readers, compel us to reconsider and to rethink not merely our literary values, but the very institutions that purvey these values.

While speaking recently to a West Indian colleague who is engaged in writing a history of West Indian literature, the role of genre theory surfaced. What could such a theory—no matter how combinatory and innovative—contribute to such a history? My colleague pointed out that he was overwhelmed by trivial and unartistic poems and stories and that the authors of these could have no place in his history. What he sought were the best, the finest, the greatest works. I listened to these evaluative terms, and I sympathized with the problem that confronted him. But I did not see the dilemma in his terms. What seemed of issue to me was his writing of a history, in this case the writing of a "literary" history.

From the Aristotelian discussion of history and poetry in terms of particularity and universality, from the seventeenth-century discussions of the truth value of history in comparison with the fictions of romance, from the nineteenth-century discussions of history in comparison with the quantitative data of science to contemporary discussions of history in comparison with the types of narrative, history as a genre has been discussed in terms of its intersections with other genres. To write literary history as a journey among masterpieces is to write a history of literary monuments in a culture. The reasons for writing such a history might be nationalistic—the demonstration to foreigners of the quality of a culture that has been overlooked. Or the history writer might seek to demonstrate the universal quality of his culture as the equal of those in industrialized countries. Or the historian might seek to kindle a nationalistic response in the citizens of his own country by instilling in them pride in their literature. Whatever reasons one might have for writing such a literary history, it would be shaped by the aims one gave to the genre in which he wrote.

It may appear that I have pushed aside the problem of quality by converting it into a generic problem. But I do not think this is the case. Critics have denied the importance of value as an issue—such was certainly the example of Northrop Frye and is the case with many contemporary critics. But the reasons for this were and are to make interpretative procedures primary. I do not deny that some works are better than others; I merely affirm that such a value term—"better"—implies an aim; better for what? For whom? Or, better in what respects and for what and for whom? Evaluative terms become relative to the aims and preferences of the history writer, and those texts are claimed as masterpieces which best serve his purpose or which can be *interpreted* as best serving his purpose.

If I now rephrase my initial inquiry, "Why do writers in our time choose to mix their genres in the ways that they do?" it will become clear that combinatory genres shape our consciousness of how to express our views. This is a position not unlike that of Roland Barthes; but I would add that it implies that certain social reasons indicate why a genre develops as it does. Why would a genre like the biography of an artist, for instance, persist for several hundred years with increasing details, the fiction of artistic continuity, and of origins in genealogy? Ernst Kris and Otto Kurz discuss the biographical relation between Cimabue and Giotto in these terms. In the eleventh canto of Dante's *Purgatorio*, the poet "mentions two of the leading artists of his age and sets one off against the other": "Once, Cimabue thought to hold the field/In painting; Giotto's all the rage today;/The other's fame lies in the dust concealed."

Kris and Kurz point out that the Dante commentators, up to the twentieth century, interpreted these lines as referring to a historically intended contrast between generations, and attempted to establish a connection between the representatives of an earlier and a more modern group of artists. To do this they drew on material which evidently originated in the oral traditions of Florence. ... Cimabue was made the greatest artist of his day, the Ducento, and then, in a report which goes back no further than the early fifteenth century, the teacher of Giotto. Not only does this piece of information have no basis in any tradition traceable to the lifetime of either of the two men, but it is also contradicted by everything that we do know with any certainty of their lives, and particularly of their works. ... The story has long been recognized for what it is—history faking. Here as elsewhere, the popular imagination has tried to link glamorous figures from the past with one another. Such a process of linking, which leads directly to the formation of sagas and legends, make Cimabue into Giotto's teacher. It springs from the urge to provide a genealogy for the achievement of the great man who revived Italian art.[8]

The point is that biography was connected with anecdote and with fictitious history to establish the idea of an artistic tradition, and biography functioned to elevate anecdote into "history," so called.

In the view of the persistence of mixed genres, and in terms of my presentation of a genre problem, it seems to me reasonable to venture some explanations why our generic mixtures are not as before. What James Watson was doing in *The Double Helix*, for example, was to undermine the objectivity of scientific discovery by relating it to personal competition and subjective guessing, just as Norman Mailer's *Armies of the Night* combined autobiographical commentary with formal history in order to undermine the impersonality, the so-called objectivity of history. What we have are mixed genres that undermine the concepts governing claims for writing as "objective" or as "truth-telling"; they undo even though they may redo the strategies of deception.

The generic study that I envisioned led me to strategies of writing that, so far as I could tell, seemed unexplained. Autobiography plays so large a part in generic revision because male and female writers assume that it is more open and honest about "self," about "identity," about events than impersonal narratives. But a renewed presentation of Freudian views, whether in Lacanian or other psychoanalytic programs, reveals again the difficulties of self-knowledge, though not without some developments of the genres in which these are presented.

This introduction would falsify my experiences if I concluded with a neatly resolved solution as to why writers write in the genres that they do. Aside from the fact that in writing this book, I found myself living with the very consciousness I seek to explore, trying to control the inevitable distortion. But I have some speculations to which this introduction has led me, and I share these with you before you read the study that follows.

We mix our forms because we find ourselves having to cope with forces and powers that we only partly understand. We thus mix our genres as we mix our drinks, believing that by ingesting differences we can absorb them. Mixing genres becomes a way of meeting history by consolidation. Those of us who resist consolidation see the mixtures as exemplifying dispersion—the breakup of linear thinking. But the breakup of conglomerates or the merging of corporations into new conglomerates are two sides of the same coin. We may say that the development of corporate structures in which book companies and film companies become part of a multiform business corporation is a mixture. But this mixture, no less than textual mixtures, serves strategies that are forms of concealment as well as exposure. Indeed, one reason for advocating the generic theory I propose in this book is to create the consciousness necessary to explore the implications of generic mixtures.

Generic mixtures are, I have suggested, characteristic of all texts. What we need to understand is the nature of such mixtures as we find them in Swift's *Tale of a Tub* and Mailer's *Armies of the Night*, in Pope's *The Dunciad* and Nabokov's *Pale Fire*. *Mixtures* do not have the political and economic implications of *mergers*. Blurring, blending, mixing, merging, and combining may be similar, but they are not identical processes in cooking or painting or writing. A genre theory which undertakes to explain why writers compose in the genres that they do confronts these inquiries. In doing so, it may help us confront and shape a world larger than the literary world in which we live.

NOTES

1. Clifford Geertz, "Blurred Genres: The Refiguration of Social Thought," *Local Knowledge: Further Essays in Interpretive Anthropology* (New York: Basic Books, 1983), 19–20.
2. Jacques Derrida, "The Law of Genre," trans. Avital Ronell, *Critical Inquiry* 7, no. 1 (1980): 55–81.
3. Northrop Frye, *Anatomy of Criticism: Four Essays* (Princeton, NJ: Princeton Univ. Press, 1957), 247–48.
4. Fredric Jameson, *The Political Unconscious: Narrative as a Socially Symbolic Act* (Ithaca, NY: Cornell Univ. Press, 1981), 107.

5. Lillian Herlands Hornstein, "Middle English Romances," in *Recent Middle English scholarship and criticism: survey and desiderata*, ed. J. Burke Severs et al. (Pittsburg, PA: Duquesne Univ. Press, 1971), 55–95.
6. Harold Bloom, *Agon: Towards a Theory of Revisionism* (New York: Oxford Univ. Press, 1982), 16.
7. Roman Jakobson, "What Is Poetry?" in *Language in Literature*, ed. Krystyna Pomorska and Stephen Rudy (Cambridge, MA: Belknap Press, 1987), 378.
8. Ernst Kris and Otto Kurz, *Legend, Myth, and Magic in the Image of the Artist: A Historical Experiment* (New Haven, CT: Yale Univ. Press, 1979), 23–24.

Bibliographical History of a Genre

THE HISTORY OF THE BARNWELL BALLAD

This is a study of the transformations of an early seventeenth-century ballad entitled "An Excellent Ballad of George Barnwel, An Apprentice of *London*, who was undone by a Strumpet; who having thrice robbed his Master, and murdered his Uncle in *Ludlow*, was hanged in chains in *Polonia*, and by the means of a Letter sent by his own hand to the Mayor of *London*, she was hang'd at *Ludlow*." "The tune is, the Rich Merchant-Man."[1] It analyzes these transformations of the ballad into its various genres and their historical and cultural significance.

This ballad has had an English cultural presence for approximately four hundred years, and my contribution is a generic inquiry (historical and theoretical) into this phenomenon. I seek to understand why this particular ballad exhibits such continuity. Its generic transformations have made it into a chapbook, a life history, a tragedy, a prose narrative of a tragedy, a novel, a short summary of the novel, a memoir, a short summary of the memoir, a revision of the ballad, a parody, a Christmas pantomime, a book of illustrations, a historical novel, and, in the twentieth century, reprintings of the tragedy together with versions of the ballad.

This anonymous ballad is first mentioned as a transfer property in the Stationer's Register in 1625, so that it had an existence prior to this. Its tune is the same as that of Thomas Deloney's ballad "The Rich

Merchant-Man" published to new music in 1594. The initial date of the ballad is sometime between 1594 and 1623. The ballad appeared in several versions during the seventeenth century and in 1700 there appeared a prose chapbook entitled *The 'Prentice's Tragedy: or the History of George Barnwell: Being a Fair Warning to Young Men to Avoid the Company of Lewd Women*. And the ballad was reprinted in this publication. In 1731 the ballad was converted into a tragedy by George Lillo and was acted and published under the title *The London Merchant*. Soon after this tragedy was staged, a chapbook (undated) based on the play was published, *Youth's Warning-Piece; or, The Tragical History of George Barnwell; Who Was Undone by a STRUMPET, That Caused Him to Rob His MASTER, and Murder His UNCLE*. The play went through four authorized editions before Lillo revised the final act and published it as the fifth edition. There were two other authorized editions during Lillo's lifetime and five pirated editions. The number of editions since Lillo's death up to 1990 is too extensive to list here. As for the performances of *The London Merchant*, Emmett L. Avery estimated the total number between 1731 and 1776 as 179 and notes that "its frequency ... averages higher than any other [serious] play except *Jane Shore* and *The Orphan*." Meanwhile, *Youth's Warning-Piece* continued to be reprinted during the century, and in the nineteenth century it was reprinted in 1810, 1815, and 1820.

In 1765 the ballad was edited and revised by Thomas Percy for inclusion in his anthology *Reliques of Ancient English Poetry*, and this edition of the poem was corrected and included in Joseph Ritson's anthology *Ancient Songs and Ballads* "from the reign of King Henry the Second to the Revolution." Percy's Reliques went through five editions between 1765 and 1800 and at least fifteen editions from 1800 to 1900. Francis James Child reprinted Percy's version of the ballad in his *English and Scottish Ballads* in 1859 and Child's edition became the recognized edition for students of the ballad. The Barnwell ballad was burlesqued by James Smith in *Rejected Addresses* in 1812 and was made into a Christmas pantomime in 1837. In 1840 Edward L. L. Blanchard published *George Barnwell* as a historical novel and his version was reprinted in 1841 and 1849. The story of George Barnwell was made into a burlesque of Edward Lytton Bulwer by William M. Thackeray in *Punch* 1847. The woodcuts of the ballad were caricatured by Joseph Crawhall in *Chap-book Chaplets* in 1883. In 1900 an edited version of the ballad was published in the Roxburghe collection, and it is this version to which I frequently refer in this text.

In 1798 the ballad and the tragedy formed the basis of a novel by Thomas Skinner Surr entitled *Barnwell*. This text went into six editions by 1834. Meanwhile, in 1810, there was published (anonymously) a fictional volume entitled "*Memoirs of George Barnwell*; the Unhappy Subject of Lillo's Celebrated Tragedy; Derived from the Most Authentic Source, and Intended for the Perusal and Instruction of the Rising Generation" "By a Descendant of the Barnwell Family." These "memoirs" and the 1817 reprint concluded with discussions of Lillo's play and Thomas Surr's novel. About 1820, Dean and Munday, publishers in London, printed a chapbook (anonymously) based on the *Memoirs* and entitled "The Life and History of George Barnwell; who from the Highest Character and Credit, fell to the lowest depth of Vice through the artful Stratagems of a Woman of the Town: retailing his love for Maria; and the steps which led to his own ruin, and ultimately to the murder of his uncle; his affecting execution, and the death of Maria through a broken heart."

In the twentieth century, *The London Merchant* was published together with Percy's version of the ballad by A. W. Ward in 1903, by Bonamy Dobrée in 1952 and by William H. McBurney in 1965. Editions of the play and the Surr novel appeared in America and translations of the play were published in France and Germany. This listing is not intended to be complete; as for the reviews of and some comments upon the various texts, they are referred to in the following chapters.

What accounts for the persistence of the ballad plot? Despite the various genres into which this plot is enfolded, it has at least three mythic components that seem to persist in human behavior. There is the uncontrollable desire for sexuality—the seduction of a young apprentice by an experienced harlot; a study of virtue seduced by vice. It is also the narrative of the power of one person over another, of a woman over a man; the criminal manipulation of the harlot as she dictates the actions of the youth. This has an ironic relation to trade—merchandising sex for money. Finally, it is the story of crime and punishment, murder and redemption, with an oedipal implication in the murder of a substitute father.

The genres of which this plot is a part undergo many transformations during 400 years; these reveal the cultural bases of genres and the importance of genres for an understanding of writing, speaking, and behavior. Every text has components—a speaker, narrator, or orator; a plot or subjects; a sense of writing or speaking of artistic or musical styles; a location (space); an existence in time; actors or characters; a reader, viewer, listener, or audience. Some of these can exist as performances; others as texts for reading. But all oral, vocal, written expressions are instances of behavior and behavioral constructions. Yet they do not exist as autonomous phenomena. They are understood, heard, viewed, grasped, responded to, and grouped with or distinguished from other presentations.

These instances can only be responded to if we know what they are, and what they are not. If presentations, for example, are written, we need to distinguish them from oral or performed examples. If we distinguish them as ballads, we need to distinguish them from sonnets or chorales. The point is that for thinking, acting, writing, we need to make distinctions if we are to communicate. Such distinctions are based on groupings or open systems. When such systems are comprehensive, like poetry, fiction, drama, we make extensive distinctions (systems within systems)—lyric poetry, eclogues, georgics, epics, dramatic poetry, sonnets, and so forth.

Systems need to be distinguished not only from varied kinds, but from components (*elements* in a system) that form texts. Plots, for example, are not systems, but components of systems. Nevertheless, it is possible for components to be not only elements but small systems such as sonnets or parables within larger systems. And if we think of some presentations or systems as aesthetic objects, they can also serve as information, pleasure, and entertainment in public or private places. The words that composed a ballad with music may have been a transformation from actual events, as Bishop Percy believed was the case with the Barnwell ballad, although no such events have been found. But the production of the ballad as a performance and as a written text became for two centuries embedded in British popular and polite culture, without providing information that could be identified as a particular incident in everyday life.

Genres and Their Provenance

In seeking to understand the processes of transformation, I have been led to confront the issue of genre. Although the Barnwell ballad became a chapbook, a tragedy, a novel, a satire, a biography, an autobiography, a memoir, a historical novel, and so on, and although each requires and receives interpretations and analyses, are these generic names of only peripheral significance? Do they have formal requirements as the sonnet? Structural analysis and formalistic analysis in general have had their unitary principles minimized or deconstructed. Aesthetic objects are recognizably multiple, and their production and reception undermine any assumption that attributes unhistorical or culturally static characteristics to them. Thus the naming biography, autobiography, novel, tragedy may have referred to a series of classified texts for accessibility in a library, but such classification has not proved valid for indicating cultural linkages.

It is thus necessary to ask whether naming functions other than location. One can see at once that the naming of human beings is as much a ritual behavior as it is an identification. There is, despite the identification purpose, considerable difference between a name and a social security number. They belong to different systems of behavior with quite different aims. Identifying a text as a novel or an elegy or a tragedy is to group it with similar texts and distinguish it from others. A text can be grouped in different genres based on the components selected; thus the Barnwel ballad can be grouped with confessional ballads or with prose confessions or with ballads that share the same tune. One particular contribution of genre criticism is that it makes possible a study of members of the group over time, thus making possible a careful study of change in the history of a genre. It also makes possible the study of different linkages among genres since a text can belong to more than one genre.

Moreover, insofar as members of a genre have some traits in common with some previous members, a text is a combination of past and present historical components. Passages from the early seventeenth-century ballad thus appear together with eighteenth-century language in *The London Merchant*. The paradoxical generic issue is that the language of the ballad is the appropriate language for a historical play situated in the time of Queen Elizabeth, but that by being converted into a prose tragedy the language ceases to have the implications of the ballad. The dialogic tradition of the tragic genre and the language of the ballad song alter their implications.

Although this is a study of the mutations and metamorphosis of a ballad, the forms into which it is mutated or metamorphosed are members of genres—chapbooks, tragedy, novel, memoir, parody, song, and historical novel. The ballad is also made into a component of an anthology, in an edited text, into a joint publication with another genre—tragedy, and into the target of critical and interpretative essays. It is desirable, given the intent both in kind and in time of the transformations, that I indicate what I take a genre to be.

To begin with, "genre" is a term which came into use at the end of the eighteenth century when it replaced "kind" or "type" or "style." It was used to refer to "a particular style or category of works of art; esp. a type of literary work characterized by a particular style, form, or purpose" (according to the OED). It was also a style of painting in which scenes of ordinary life were depicted. But medieval and Renaissance uses of "gender" functioned to identify kind, sort, or class. And in grammar, "gender" was the term used to classify words into sexual categories—masculine, feminine, and neuter. The use of "genre" for "gender" may be a consequence of separating the literary and artistic from the sexual implications at the beginning of the nineteenth century by critics who sought to disengage imagination from the cultural implications of everyday life.

"Genre" is, in other words, an open system. The notion of a system implies some order that, in an open system, can be, and is, interrupted by unanticipated components. These serve to enlarge the system which can be altered by changes in vocabulary or content; such changes can be thought of as mutations. But a system can also be made part of a larger system—a poem in a novel—or it can cease to be used and become a fossil. The Barnwell plot, therefore, can be part of a poem, of a tragedy, of a memoir, of a novel. But each of these are also genres in a formal sense. The formal properties of a ballad or tragedy are not dependent upon the plot but are genres that interact with the plot to create a unity or disunity, to create a network within each member of the genre.

Genre applies to a group of texts that can exist at the same or different times. Thus ballads of different kinds constitute a genre; there can be criminal ballads, heroic ballads, religious ballads, and so on. They are grouped together in order to distinguish them from other groups and each of these groups can be further divided: criminal ballads about theft, about murder, about children. Each individual member of a genre may belong to a number of groups, but the basis for composing distinct groups is to make possible explanations of behavior, varied types of pleasure, and in this respect, genres are social constructions; they make possible our understanding of the past precisely because each member of a genre alters the constructional implications of the genre as a whole. Each indicates the added or revised or altered implications of the genre as a historical phenomenon. Thus identifying the genre depends upon identifying the components of the individual texts that compose it. These components are combinatory of the smaller units or even genres that compose it. Thus epigrams, proverbs, sonnets, letters, memoranda, stories, parables, literary criticism, and so forth can be included in larger genres such as novels, tragedies, and epics. Genres are thus significant for the changes they reveal especially in retaining components of the past.

This may not seem particularly significant since any past text when interpreted from a later period is assumed to have value for the present—otherwise why bother with a curiosity? But a genre theory assumes that the writing of criticism and theory are genres that undergo change no less than other genres. Thus the process of editing as historically practiced by Richard Bentley on Milton or Thomas Percy on the ballad of Barnwell assumes a theory of authenticity that permits the editor to revise or adapt a manuscript to meet his, rather than its, conditions of composition. These are rule-governed, and the editor can create the fiction that texts which lack rule-governed metrics or language are interpolations by inadequate editors or amanuenses.

There are several different types of reader response criticism, but the one that has elicited critical support is the argument that readers of a given community respond in the same way. If a community is governed by authoritarian principles, then such response is legislated; it is not a literary response but a political response to protect the responder. But any democratic community permits readers to determine the kind of response genre which they wish to undertake: deconstructive, phenomenological, Freudian or Lacanian, Marxist, pluralist, or cultural. In this respect, the claim of a shared community of responders presupposes that responders share the same genre and that their differences are less significant than their generic unity.

This does not imply that, for example, a poetic text being examined has no effect upon the critical text examining it. What is this effect? If the criticism aims to describe what is taking place in a Shakespearean text, for example, it needs to distinguish between the reading of the text and the performance. A critic may try to master whatever information is available about lexical and metrical procedures. But all such information is presented in an interpretive genre. It is an act of ventriloquism. It is the critic engaged in a self-dialogue, voicing oneself and the other. The use of quotations from the text is selected by the critic and form part of the system being developed or expressed.

The combinatory character of a text does not have to give it coherence. The Barnwell ballad is an example of disorder in its construction, and there is no reason to assume that combinations imply wholeness. The combinatory character of a text permits fragments to be considered as a genre and this is what Addison describes in his discussion of the significance of fragmentary discoveries. Our contemporary critics have begun to recognize the combinatory character of texts. Thus Nina Baym describes

Moby Dick as a novel that in turn is a "sermon; short story; occasional, scientific, political, and moral essay; satire; dictionary; encyclopedia; drama, dramatic monologue; manual; travelogue; character; tall tale; and prophecy."[2]

Although this description may blur the distinction between component and composition, it does show an awareness of the combinatory construction of a text. It is, moreover, less important to agree that this is a novel than to inquire into the kind of behavior such combinations imply. The genre—whether novel or anatomy or miscellany—makes the particular construction a resistance to, or an alteration of, a received genre. Even if it is the initiation of a new genre (and we need more than one example for a genre to be identified) it would still be generic. And the reason is—all writing is generic. Genre is not another critical or theoretical point of view; it is a description of every kind of writing.

Throughout this study I refer to *narrative*. Considerable disagreement exists about the uses to which the term is put. Narrative can be used as a synonym for epic, or novel, or plot. Such uses make it a genre or part of a genre. But narrative is sometimes considered a genre irrespective of whether one discusses a poem as a "narrative," a tragedy as a "narrative," a novel as a "narrative," or a short story as a "narrative." Such a view of genre disregards or subordinates the formal features that compose a text. It posits a metaphysical or other absolute that supposedly underlies all members of the genre. Such a theory of genre is antithetical to the version I offer, and it provides insufficient determination for the literary history I am proposing.

I shall use "narrative," therefore, as the name of a part of, a feature of, a genre and shall make distinctions of continuity and change by attending to the language of specific texts. Since I shall be discussing a plot that has survived despite centuries of change, I shall, in my own statements, extrapolate the series of actions that persist. These will then permit me to distinguish how the language and other textual features are continued or discontinued. It should be noted that the statements are an abstraction offered in the words of the critic-historian. They are intended to make distinction apparent, not to identify actual continuities.

The term *genre* came into use in English at the end of the eighteenth century. The term "kind" preceded "genre," but it did not imply the purity, the coherence, the unity that described "genre." In the nineteenth century "genre" as a concept reflected in art and literature the hostility to combinatoriness that characterized in social life the horror of miscegenation and the scandal of class mixtures. It represented the fiction that texts which did not fit specific generic requirements were obviously inept or inadequate or dangerous. This view of genre was obviously related to sexual repression, and it affected the artistic production even of those writers who like Rossetti were not deterred from undertaking mixtures. The point is that in our time, the purity of genre is neither practiced nor defended, even though it lives on in the formulas of romance and westerns.

The writings and performances that are now produced are directly—intentionally or not—against unitary order. They disregard existing views of temporal order, disregard conventionally public versions of place, of dress, of purpose and behavior. The unfinished, the fragment replaces the coherent whole in texts by Harold Pinter and Tom Stoppard, by Italo Calvino and Julian Barnes. Critics who find genre crucial to contemporary study derive their concern from the failure of received views of genre. The received views controlled behavior. Take the example of African-Americans and the exposure of so-called legal and economic equality as a way of imposing subordination through the legal language of equality. The mixture of genres was thus an exposure of false claims and the rejection of generic purity was revealed as the rejection of forms of control and oppression. A rejection of genre as inherited practices was identified by feminists as patriarchal, and they undertook to develop a new view of genre that would undo the implied order they found oppressive. The attack on the canon was connected with the discovery of innumerable texts that were governed by practices that had been ignored or disregarded. It was necessary to reformulate the kind of behavior that generic constructions produce. It thus became apparent that generic constructions seemed unrelated to the changes taking place in society although such changes took place in and through genres. A theory of genre that would explain not only continuity and change but transformations was necessary.

Genre and Its Kinds

"Genre" refers to a group of texts that form a system. There is no name for each member text of a genre and I have referred to them as "members" to contrast them with the combinatory components that constitute a text. Each member of a genre can belong to more than one genre. The reason for this is that "genre" is a particular kind of open system. The members form a network and generic networks have different degrees of comprehensiveness. A sonnet or an ode constitutes two systems, but they are part of a system called poetry. Poetry is part of a system called literature and literature is part of a system called writing. Each system is based on distinctions that relate and yet differentiate it from other systems. And within each system the range of sonnets or orders of poetry or literature or writing are directed at distinctions that are viable at a particular time.

Thus each member of the genre sonnet or ode or ballad may have characteristics that distinguish it from other members of the genre while they still possess sufficient features to make its membership viable. Genres within poetry, for example, are identified to distinguish them from prose. They therefore contain genres, such as sonnets which are rule-governed by line numbers, by rhyming and metrical arrangements, that are far more rigid than free verse. But the purpose of using the generic distinction called "poetry" is to distinguish it from the genre called "prose." And this procedure can accommodate a new genre called "poetic prose" which is used to establish distinctions which include features of prose and poetry.

If we assume that genres are systems that include lesser systems of comprehensiveness, it is self-evident that members of one genre are inevitably members of a larger system and are thus members of more than one genre. But if we conceive of genre members as texts that are independently dependent, we can see that formal features of a genre can only explain relatively few features in a genre like tragedy or epic or novel in contrast to less comprehensive systems such as proverbs, epigrams, limericks, residential telephone directories, or cooking recipes.

Literary texts are not merely formal combinations. Formal properties are interrelated with some other features of the text as product. Formalists tend to confine genre to kinds of literature, but genre as a system involves the analysis of character or of diction or of thought or ideas. In the study that I undertake, the character of Barnwell as presented in the ballad, tragedy, novel, memoirs, and numerous chapbooks is defined by the language describing his thoughts and behavior in the different texts. The system of seduction in which the apprentice is involved represents a behavioral pattern with conflicting variations. Not only does Barnwell become a genre over some three hundred years but so, too, does Millwood, the victimizing seductress.

The treatment of characters as representations of behavior over time clarifies the assumption on an open system. Although the characters of Barnwell and Millwood undergo changes in behavior in the different genres, it is possible to analyze the conceptions of behavior as these provide variations resulting from the formal features of a genre as well as the cultural changes the language undergoes. It is not surprising that Dickens should refer to Barnwell in the *Pickwick Papers* and that Thackeray should use the name for a satirical portrait of his contemporary.

The thoughts and ideas that are generic are well known even though they are not identified as such. Lovejoy's *The Great Chain of Being* is an example of an idea that he traces as a system from classical times to the nineteenth century. Here again the variations are many, but the idea has sufficient stability to be recognized. For Lovejoy the actual expression (the formal trait) is connected with forms of discourse that indicate the changes. One might note that Trilling's objection to Lovejoy's method was his failure to consider the impact of the traits of the different genres in which this genre was placed.

The initiation of the genre of the beguiled apprentice and the victimizing seductress occurred in the early seventeenth century. The speculation by Percy that it was based on an actual incident has not been verified, but the story of a woman who exercises sexual power over a youth has reference to Venus and Adonis. The filiation of the story can be found in Eve's temptation of Adam. But the genre has a beginning in the sexual pleasure that Barnwell finds in Millwood.

THE SOCIAL STRUCTURE OF GENRE

Genre is the name given to a number of texts that are classed together so that general remarks can be made about them. Thus to the extent that any text is a social construction, genre composed of texts must also be a social structure. Thus each text that constitutes the genre tragedy is situated in time and place, and those features of the tragedies *Oedipus Rex* and *Hamlet*—such as performance, scenery, characters who engage in dialogue and are the leaders of the state and who are involved in murder—relate to the very different times which these features represent, yet they still constitute a basis for similarity. The different features such as different plots, diction, and chorus do not deny the transmission which the similar features represent. Historically, therefore, the Elizabethan play challenges the spectator to recognize the stability of the transmitted features and the instability of their interpretive uses.

Genre, therefore, through its members offers a basis for historical distinctions that are precise. They also indicate linkages among different genres. Edward Said calls these filiations. What is the nature of the social structure of the same work produced in London and later in the states? If the situation contributes to the social implications of a text, does it lack the resonance of a society which has a king or queen and one in which these do not exist? Which components become the basis for interpretation? And this is made still more difficult when a translation of a text is produced or published. What happens to *The London Merchant* when it is translated and produced in Germany or France?

The social construction of *The London Merchant* as a dramatic performance targets a particular audience in London insofar as the merchant's guild underwrites two performances every year for apprentices between 1747 and the century's end. If we do not now have any evidence of the impact it had upon apprentices, we do know that when the anonymous *Memoirs* was published the concern for the corruption of the youth of the metropolis was at least as great as when Richardson published his conduct book, *The Apprentice's Vade Mecum*, in 1733.

The nature of genre as a social structure is that its components are texts that form a system sufficiently open so that there exists some formal membership within the system. Such formal membership or filiation should be distinguished from association with or affiliation to a genre. In the latter case connections with other systems or genres are apparent and these form a network of genres. Thus a confession can be affiliated with criminal narratives or sermons, criminal biographies, biblical proverbs that come from the allusions or components of different members of the genre. Critics of genre seek to explain genre by referring to the various genres as communication systems. And this seems to be the case with disciplinary texts from recipes to reproductive technologies. These seem to be sufficiently nonlingual for readers to assume a stringency of rule-governed productions that can reduce the possibility of misinterpretation. In these cases genres replicate the knowledge that is necessary to keep the discipline within specified bounds. Every effort to expand the discipline or inquire into the implications of its boundaries inevitably requires the introduction of components that cause a reordering of the discipline.

But communication is only one function of genre. Roman Jakobson in his well-known discussion of language lists six, including communication. What genre does is to make distinctions in the uses of language. Genres provide the discourses and practices which seek to sustain it. Thus certain writings such as the Bible or the constitution or the forming myths embodied in epics are given hierarchical dominance that endure over considerable periods of time. But other writings in a society indicate ways of thinking and feeling that gradually undergo change. Thus the changes in a genre like tragedy by altering the characters involved from kingship to middle class and criminals suggest class changes and the consequences they entail. Members of a genre can suggest shifts in power and authority without overthrowing the social order. But even when the social order is overturned—as in the American Revolution and the French Revolution—and certain new genres are developed, older genres continue with new affiliations or associations. Because genres can become more or less comprehensive, more or less inclusive of components, they can deal with greater or lesser changes in the practical economy of a society. Since texts can involve contradictions in their combinations, so genres can have members oppose earlier generic components. In this respect, the term "literature" can include for Dr. Johnson all kinds of writing, but for Wellek and Warren only those texts that are "imaginative." The construction of a genre like "literature," governed by these exclusionary claims, is sustainable because, as a social construct, it becomes powerful in the academy, if irrelevant outside it.

What accounts for the persistence of the Barnwell ballad plot? Despite the various genres into which this plot is enfolded, it has certain components that persist in all but the burlesques. The plot has two characters: a youthful male virgin and an experienced harlot who seduces him. Uncontrolled sexuality is a commodity that has a cash value. The youth is apprenticed to a merchant whose trade or exchange can prove to be advantageous or dangerous to the individual. Thus there is the strumpet who is also engaged in merchandizing—sex in exchange for money; in transformations of the ballad the strumpet uses sex for revenge on patriarchal corruption of women and the state or for personal survival and empowerment. Then the ballad plot has an oedipal component. Barnwell murders his uncle who is a substitute father. Whether the murder is the consequence of Barnwell's extravagance or Millwood's desire for power through familial destruction, the murder serves to assert Millwood's power over Barnwell; it climaxes his progress in criminality; in the ballad it also serves as his continued pursuit of pleasure. Finally there is the scene of punishment or escape, redemption or despair.

These components undergo a double process. They are shaped into a particular genre by one or more persons who construct it by revisiting, revamping, or reconceiving a past form or initiating a new one. This is not a rule-based procedure but one that develops by practice, the genre revealing itself in the making. When a text is read, heard, seen, the responses to it are formulated, felt, and expressed by practices that have been generically constructed. What such responses attend to are defined by past experiences of explanation or interpretation. Each text can thus be seen as a challenge to one's generic imposition, each imposition an intrusion that selects from the whole.

A structure is identified by what it is and one aspect of this is what it includes and excludes from the past. Genres that exist at a particular time indicate the comprehensiveness as well as the limitations of that time. Thus the discontinuance of genres like that of the sonnet after Milton up to the mid- and late eighteenth century, up to the sonnets of Charlotte Smith and William Lyle Bowles, indicate a neglect of the rule-governed short form in poetry while innovating the much freer short form in prose—the periodical papers. The resumption of the production of sonnets by Wordsworth, Coleridge, and the second generation of "Romantic" writers indicates an attraction for those aspects of Elizabethan writing that captured the personal moments of freedom within highly confined limits. The sonnet becomes in Wordsworth's hands, for example, more Miltonic than Shakespearean. It becomes an example of public action and vision that remains controlled by the rule-governed form.

The inference I draw is that any time span cannot adequately be defined by the genres that are innovated but requires, rather, an understanding of those that are inherited, those that can be inherited but are not, and those that are innovated. It is for this reason that discussions of the origins of the novel are inevitably inadequate when traced to and interpreted by cultural assumptions. New genres are derived from old, as Fielding explained in his identification of the kind of text *Joseph Andrews* was. Those components or genre members that are selected for generic innovations possess cultural implications quite different from their source genres. These become affiliations while the new genre members develop filiations.

The grounds for the initiation of new genres rather than the alteration of received genres can represent the reshifting of class or status or gender relations. Such reshiftings cannot lead to the innovation of merely one genre, but they affect the interaction of all genres. The origin of the novel, the origin of ballad opera, the origin of periodical papers, the shift in the concept of tragedy, dialogue, encyclopedias, and dictionaries, these are some of the innovations and transformations that take place in the early eighteenth century. The emphasis on the origin of the novel since Ian Watt's *The Rise of the Novel* has distorted the rise and fall of other genres that had a simultaneous existence. The combinatory composition of satire has been correctly seen by Claude Rawson as the inherited genre that assumed importance as a model for characterizing the political and economic shift that was taking place. The novel, the periodical papers, the magazines and journals that develop in the eighteenth century become instances of the short forms collected together whether by travel or by moving from one action to another, the model of which is *Rasselas*.

We live at a time when a major transformation in the retrieval and distribution of knowledge is taking place. The genres of research, of construction and dissemination of knowledge, of the education or training of citizens in the accumulation of knowledge, in the physical notion of the book or painting—all are being systematized to replace the received behavior. But received behavior still exists and its practices continue. We are witness to and participate in a conflict of genres. It is a conflict that can be described as a resistance of received genres to be colonized by new systems of behavior. Ways of thinking, feeling, and organizing experience are in conflict and the practice of new genres will have to make room within their systems for some of the dissonant values of the older genres. This study of narrative, ballad, genre, and history is an effort to describe the behavior of such transformations.

NOTES

1. Note the spelling of "Barnwel": after *The London Merchant*, "Barnwell" becomes the standard spelling and I have followed that spelling throughout unless citing the exact title.
2. Nina Baym, "Melville's Quarrel with Fiction," *PMLA* 94 (1979): 918.

Ballad, Texts, Tunes, Material Culture

GENRE AS COMBINATORY COMPOSITION

Sometime between 1594 and 1624 there was composed a ballad entitled "An Excellent Ballad of *George Barnwell*." The basis for the dating is that the Stationers' Register lists the poem as a transfer property in the latter date, so it is likely that it was in existence before that date though no earlier copy has been found. The earlier date is based on the music for the ballad that is taken from the tune for Thomas Deloney's "A Rich Merchant Man," registered on "the 22nd March 1594." Since the music for the ballad is identified as "an Excellent New Tune" it provides the earliest possible date for the Barnwell ballad.

Although we have significant bibliographical information and Deloney's ballad has survived, the "new Tune" written for it has not. The music historian C. M. Simpson remarks, "Despite the popularity of Deloney's ballad and the frequent use of the tune associated with it, no music has survived which can be completely identified."[1] Thus although the ballad of George Barnwell is a song, we can only identify aspects of performance from what we know of street ballads in the early seventeenth century and from the text of the ballad itself.

The dating for the ballad is admittedly complicated by the fact that no music now exists for Deloney's ballad and no extant copy of the Barnwell ballad provides the music. But the mere fact that the same music was used

© The Author(s), under exclusive license to Springer Nature Switzerland AG 2021
R. Cohen, J. L. Rowlett, *Transformations of a Genre*, Palgrave Studies in the Enlightenment, Romanticism and Cultures of Print, https://doi.org/10.1007/978-3-030-89668-3_3

for two contemporary ballads that tell contrary stories indicates that the Barnwell ballad might be an ironic or parodic reference to the Deloney ballad.

Whether it is or not, the relation of the Barnwell to the Deloney ballad indicates the complications that can arise in identifying a genre member. The same music, the use of ballad stanzas, the subject of love, the form of presentation, the naming of the two poems as ballads—all indicate that they were considered at the time of publication as instances of a genre. But if Barnwell parodies the Deloney ballad, it is a member of the genre called parody. Both are also ballads about criminals. The term "subgenre" is frequently used to describe genres that are subdivisions of larger genres, and this procedure supports the generalization that genres are formed from other genres.

The significance of this procedure is that it can direct our attention to the differences which a particular example introduces in comparison with previous instances of a genre. It also explains why a text can be identified as belonging to more than one genre. This multigeneric character of a ballad provides insight into a reader's choice of genre-naming and it also explains the kind of interrelations among genres that readers identify at a particular time. The grounds for difference, for deciding that a text is either a parody or a confession or a criminal ballad or all three, presuppose a theory of genre in which texts provide the possibility of multigeneric decisions. Why one genre rather than all should be selected depends on the varied cultural and other assumptions with which a reader operates. I aim, in this work, to explore how such varied decisions arose and have continued to arise in interpreting and evaluating the Barnwell narrative.

In *The Rise of the English Street Ballad, 1550–1650*, Natascha Würzbach offers a tentative "pragmatic genre definition" of the street ballad for this time frame. The literary ballad has a presenter who refers to self, to the listeners, to the outside world "from entertainment and instruction to advertising techniques."[2] It includes references to various kinds of songs: humor, parody, satire, and so on. These are developed in structural procedures (229) that are specific to the presenter even though they may occur in other genres. Ballad is a "collective" term that has diverse genre types (231). The "constitution of the street-ballad text makes it possible to convey and process information in a way suited to an audience situation having the particular disturbance factors connected with street-ballad rendition" (232). The "street-ballad communication situation contains, apart from genre-specific characteristics of a literary medium, components of a journalistic medium which are all the more significant in that they represent an innovation for that period [1550–1650]" (234).

The Barnwell ballad begins as a confession spoken by Barnwell, but as the ballad proceeds it changes from first to third person. Since Barnwell was hanged in Poland, it is apparent that the ballad is a construction by one or more narrators who use the first person for artistic purposes. Since Barnwell becomes a criminal, together with his whore, and a murderer, the ballad belongs to the genre criminal ballads. The ballad can be interpreted as a confession or criminal ballad or parody. What is important in generic study is to demonstrate that the confession didactically provides the moral import, while the criminal ballad undercuts the moral by indicating the pleasures of whoring and partying. The punishment of the two criminals derives from their betrayal of each other. Barnwell's punishment is the result of being condemned for a murder in Poland. That he can escape punishment remains a distant possibility. As for parody, its idealized version in the Deloney ballad is ironically reversed in the Barnwell ballad. Whatever generic choice or choices we make in interpreting this ballad, a close reading leads the responder to acknowledge its multigeneric character.

The Ballad of George Barnwell is an early seventeenth-century narrative of a young, lower class merchant's apprentice seduced by his vision of "upper class" finery and then by the sexual manipulations of the whore whom he takes to represent it. The handkerchief, the language, and the dress of the harlot are the fragments of material culture that first attract the youth. The handkerchief is a not unknown sign of intimacy in Elizabethan literature and the exposure of Millwood's feelings emboldens Barnwell to touch her, to take her hand. Millwood feigns feelings of affection but Barnwell is genuinely moved, a youth incapable of telling true sentiments from false. He reverses his refusal to stay for supper, knowing that this act is his first disobedience to his master. He begins by identifying class and status with these trappings, and the sex becomes another aspect of this culture since it, too, has to be paid for. From this stems the descent into criminality—since the pleasures of sex are dependent upon his payment of their cost—embezzlement, parricide. The passion for sex and the passion for money to pay for riotous living enclose a relationship devoid of the merchant or his family whom he robs and whom he jealously resents; a relationship of criminality untouched by moral scruples or personal respect. It is a relationship that disrupts itself and is not without some analogy to the disruptive forces of the higher society of which this is a criminal part.

The Barnwell ballad alludes only implicitly to the biblical injunction to avoid strumpets, but the opening confession declares, "Take heed of Harlots then, and their inticing trains/For by that means I have been brought, to hang alive in chains" (5–6). Yet this very avoidance, this initial innocence is responsible for Barnwell's incapacity to distinguish between a strumpet and a woman of quality. When he visits Millwood for the first time, he does so because she promises important news: "In faith, my boy," quoth she, "such news I can thee tell,/As shall rejoice thy very heart, then come where I do dwell" (13–14). When he sees her, he is overwhelmed by her appearance:

> I went to *Mrs. Milwood's* house and thought on little harm:
> And knocking at the door, straightway herself came down,
> Ruffling in most brave attire, her Hoods and silken gown:
> Who through her beauty bright, so gloriously did shine,
> That she amaz'd my dazzling eyes, she seemed so divine.   (26–30)

At the outset the ballad deals with the dilemma of an innocent, youthful apprentice who has no guide by which to recognize the manipulations of an experienced harlot. The sexual seduction that follows leads to pleasures that Barnwell comes to enjoy. Barnwell's narration attributes his seduction not only to the physical presence of Millwood, but to her kind words and embraces.

> Thus I, that ne'r before of Woman found such grace,
> And seeing now so fair a Dame, give me a kind imbrace:
> I supt with her that night, with joys that did abound,
> And for the same paid presently, in money twice three pound.   (59–62)

The "Rich Merchant Man" tells the story of a merchant from Chichester who having murdered a German in a quarrel in "Emden Town" is bought to the scaffold for hanging.[3] He readily and openly admits his guilt and apologizes for his deed. He also offers to recompense the widow and her children. The merchants of the town offer a thousand pounds to pay any woman who will marry the prisoner, an act that, according to tradition and law, would set him free. Four women offer to marry the Englishman, but he rejects them because he doubts the genuineness of their love. Nevertheless, he asks that they divide his own thousand pounds equally among them for their generous gesture. But then a fifth woman speaks up offering to live or die with him.

> "And die within mine armes,
> If thou wilt die," quoth shee;
> "Yea, live or die, sweet Englishman,
> Ile live and die with thee."
> "But can it be," hee said,
> "That thou dost love mee so?"
> "'Tis not by long acquaintance, sir,
> whereby true love doth grow!"
> *A sweet thing is love*, etc.   (136–144)

The same music accompanies the ballad of George Barnwell that tells the story of a young merchant's apprentice who falls in love with a strumpet Mrs. Millwood who seduces him and leads him to rob his master and murder his uncle. When Barnwell can no longer provide her with money, she betrays him to the authorities. Learning of her betrayal, Barnwell escapes to "Polonia" but not before writing to the authorities confessing his crimes and the involvement of Millwood. Millwood is hanged and although Barnwell felt some pangs of conscience, he apparently murdered again for he was hanged in "Polonia" for murder. The title of the black letter ballad reprinted in the Roxburghe Collection reads as follows: "An Excellent Ballad of *George Barnwel*, An Apprentice of *London*, who was undone by a Strumpet; who having thrice robbed his Master, and murdered his Uncle in *Ludlow*, was hanged in chains in *Polonia*, and by the means of a Letter sent by his own hand to the Mayor of *London*, she was hang'd at *Ludlow*." The full title of the ballad in the Houghton Library is "An Excellent Ballad of GEORGE BARNWELL Who was undone by a Strumpet, that caused him to Rob his Master, and murder his Uncle." Neither ballad is dated, although the latter was printed and sold by L. How in Petticoat Lane and the former was "printed for F. Coles, T. Vere, J. Wright and J. Clarke."[4] This latter seems a revision of the former and I shall use it for my quotations when I do not use both.

The Barnwell ballad can be read as either an ironic or a parodic criminal narrative linked to Deloney's "A Rich Merchant Man," despite some significant differences. The music is the same in both, but the characters of the Barnwell ballad are not rich; rather they are marginal—a whore and merchant's apprentice; these steal the money of others, and live riotously upon it. The rich merchant man places true love above the value of money; in the Barnwell ballad the characters buy and sell love for money.

Generically speaking, the author of "A Rich Merchant Man" was a known ballad writer whose ballad structure can be characterized by its relation to Deloney's other work. The Barnwell ballad is anonymous, and in its two versions there are narratorial shifts that indicate multiple authorship or authorial difficulty in managing a first-person confessional narrative. Another difficulty resides in the ambiguous moral attitude that the ballad reveals with regard to Barnwell. Although he is an innocent apprentice, he is overwhelmed by the apparent finery of the strumpet as well as by her extravagant professions of love.

> A handkerchief she had,
> all wrought with silk and Gold,
> Now for to dry her trickling tears,
> before her Eyes did hold.
> This thing unto my sight,
> was wondrous fine and strange,
> And in my soul an inward thought,
> it wrought a sudden change.

In the later version it reads:

> A handkerchief she had, all wrought with silk and gold,
> Which she to stop her trickling tears against her eyes did hold.
> This thing unto my sight, was wondrous rare and strange;
> And in my mind and inward thoughts, it wrought a sudden change.   (49–53)

The shift from "in my soul" to "in my mind" would seem to indicate a revision in which the thinking process is identified with "mind" rather than "soul" and would thus indicate a late seventeenth-century revision. But the assumption that Barnwell makes in both editions is that the material object, the handkerchief, leads him to believe that the outward shows are indicative of the inward qualities. This naïve view is finally overturned when Millwood believes he has no more money for her. When she discovers that he still has some, she changes her tune. It is at this time that Barnwell recognizes her deceit, but knowing this he is nevertheless unable to reject her.

The crisis arrives when the merchant asks his apprentice to deliver their accounts. Barnwell, having embezzled "almost" or "above" 200 pounds, flees to Millwood for protection. It is at this point that the narrator intervenes in the third person and declares an end to the first part of the ballad. Generically, what takes place is a pause in the performance. The ballad can be understood to function as street theater, the two parts serving as two acts.

The speaker, hawker, ballad seller, and narrator thus turns from actor—the confessor George Barnwell—to the merchandizer. He separates himself from the character he has been acting and declares:

But how she us'd this Youth, in this his extream need,
The which did her necessity so oft with money feed:
The second part, behold, shall tell it forth at large,
And shall a Strumpet's wily ways with all her tricks discharge.   (95–98)

SEXUALITY AS MATERIAL CULTURE

The second part resumes with the speaker in the confessional voice:

Here comes young *Barnwel* unto thee, sweet *Sara*, my delight,
"I am undone, except thou stand my faithful friend this night.
Our Master to command accounts, hath just occasion found,
And I am found behind the hand, almost two hundred pound:
And therefore, knowing not at all what answer for to make,
And his displeasure to escape, my way to thee I take.   (99–104)

But Millwood refuses to shelter him, calling him a "Prentice boy." When Barnwell points out that he embezzled money to satisfy her every wish, "Quo' she 'Thou art a paltry Jack, to charge me in this sort,/Being a Woman of credit good, and known of good report'" (115–116). But when Barnwell proposes to leave, he announces that he has twenty pounds to seek safety elsewhere. She then claims her rejection was merely a joke. Barnwell finally recognizes her duplicity but is unable to resist his sexual attraction: "Thus I that was with Wiles bewitch'd, and snar'd with fancy still,/Had not the power to put away, or to withstand her will" (135–136). In the earlier version it reads:

So i was with strong frauds byassed,
and snar'd with fancy still;

And had no power to go away
nor to withstand her will.

The ballad thus deals with Barnwell's overriding sexual desire for Millwood, a sexuality that cannot be controlled by reason or by moral awareness. If at first Barnwell did not understand Millwood's manipulations, he does now, and yet is unable to control his sexuality. In fact, this knowledge of Millwood's manipulations releases him to participate joyfully and completely in her view that life is for sensual delight and that money is what makes it possible: "For without money, *George*," quo' she, "A man is but a beast" (153).

What is important about this shift in Barnwell's attitude is that it expresses the pleasures one takes in the joys that successful criminality brings. Although the ultimate consequences of this behavior lead Millwood to throw Barnwell out of the house when the money runs out, the ballad as moral warning leaves open the possibility that if Millwood did not betray Barnwell, he could have remained unpunished. Instead, he betrays her in turn. Barnwell misinterprets the viciousness of Millwood in seeking to keep her "good" reputation by reporting him, but she misinterprets his capacity for revenge.

What they share, however, are the sensual delights that money can bring. No moral awareness of a future life surfaces in the ballad. If living without money is to live the life of a beast, the choice between hanging and bestiality may not be as difficult to make as the didactic warnings imply.

> Then wine and wine I called in, and cheer upon good cheer,
> And nothing in the world I thought for *Sara*'s love too dear:
> Whilst I was in her company, in joy and merriment,
> And all too little I did think, that I upon her spent.

> "A fig for care or careful thought, when all my gold is gone,
> In faith, my girl, we will have more, whoever it light upon:
> My father's rich, why then," quoth I, "should I want any gold?"
> "With a [rich] father indeed" (quoth she), "A Son may well be bold."
> (137–144)

In the earlier version these lines read as follows:

> A fig for care and careful thoughts,
> when all my Gold is gone,

In faith my Girl we shall have more,
who e're i light upon.
My father's rich and then said i,
shall i want store of Gold;
For with a Father a son said he,
may veryly make bold.

It is Barnwell who suggests a carefree attitude to familial behavior—making bold with his father, robbing his sister, and robbing and murdering his uncle. Although Millwood agrees with him, it is Barnwell who assumes the active role in deciding to pursue his family for money that is not rightly his. It is during this conversation with Millwood that the ballad shifts from the first person to the third once again, but this time the shift continues to the end in the passage that begins: "Nay more than this, an Uncle I have, at *Ludlow* he doth dwell,/He is a Grazier, which in wealth, doth all the rest excell./E're I will live in lack" (quoth *he*)" (my emphasis).

The narrator's extensive intervention at the end of the poem, therefore, appears in both versions and seems to have an ideological function. It removes the viciousness of Barnwell's acts by avoiding any detailed recitation of the murder. It also, however, makes no mention of contrition or sin in the murder and robbery. The narrator merely remarks, "And how he had his Uncle slain, to her [Millwood] he plainly told" (176).

"Tush, 'tis no matter, *George*," quo' she, "So we the money have,
To have good cheer in jolly sort, and deck us fine and brave."
And thus they liv'd in filthy sort, till all his store was gone,
And means to get them any more, I wis poor *George* had none.
And therefore now in railing sort she thrust him out of door,
Which is the just reward they get that spend upon a Whore.   (177–182)

The narrator disregards the parricide that Barnwell has committed. Neither familial disloyalty nor sinfulness nor brutal violence is mentioned as the transformation in George's behavior. The deserved punishment for George is his rejection by Millwood. The moral that the narrator conveys is the self-interest that governs harlots. When George can no longer provide her with money, she betrays him as thief and murderer to the police, a betrayal that has as its aim the preservation of her self-alleged "good report" (116).

The ballad makes reference to Barnwell's family, but no such reference exists for Millwood's. She mentions a brother, but it is unclear whether this is a lie or a fact, since she is seeking to declare Barnwell her intimate friend. Her self-deception, "Being a Woman of credit good, and known of good report" (116), implies that she has managed publicly to maintain a reputation as a decent woman despite living off the money provided by others, even as in this case, money that has been embezzled. The two parts of the ballad provide a scenario of presentation, the first part of which makes Millwood the aggressor and the second of which reveals Barnwell as cognizant of her manipulation of him; however, he accepts this manipulation, even accedes to it.

The performance of the ballad should be likened to street theater. The evidence is unspecified, but the oral performance probably accounts for the two versions of verse. The rhythm can be interpreted as four iambic feet followed by three-foot lines with the second and fourth lines rhyming, or it can be interpreted as seven-foot iambics rhyming as couplets. There is an elementary frequency in the use of end words, as "said he," "quoth she," or "thee," "me," "he." Moreover, the frequency of repetitions in the printed ballads attest to its oral performance as does the frequency of printer's errors in spelling in different editions. The language of the ballad is a mixture of Barnwell's initial religious assumptions with Sarah Millwood gloriously shining through her beauty. His declaration, "she seemed as divine," and his frequent repetitions of simple rhymes, like me/he, she/he, and phrases, such as "in saddest sort" (74), "in secret sort" (93), "in this sort" (115), "in such sort" (126), "in jolly sort" (178), "in filthy sort" (179), and "in railing sort" (181), reveal a simple-minded as well as inarticulate narrator (or narrators). There is, in other words, a mixture of bits of religious language with the imprecise language of the street, including such slang as "A fig for care or careful thought" (141), "I'le rob the churl and murder him!" (150), "why man I do but jest" (128), "or else the Devil take all" (134).

The relation of this ballad to drama is apparent in the frequency of quoted dialogue between Millwood and Barnwell. The performer would have to attend to the varied tones and emotional responses of the two characters. Among uses of the term "ballad" in the sixteenth century was that of a song for dancing as well as a song accompanying a narrative. Shakespeare's references to ballad include both. Ballads were early linked to popular street entertainment, but they were also products for sale and the sellers were ballad-mongers. To the extent that a ballad like Barnwell was performed as street theater, its composition included features from drama. In this respect ballads contained discourse features of sophisticated dramatic genres. But in the development of generic forms it is apparent that such ballads as Barnwell possessed sung dialogue that later became sources for ballad opera. The shift of a marginal genre to a primary feature of a new genre initiated more than a hundred years later in *The Beggar's Opera* (1728) reinforces the argument that smaller genres can fit into larger and serve to challenge the hierarchical conception of genre.

The institutions of justice—the constable and the mayor of London— become instruments of manipulation first by Millwood and then by Barnwell. The characters betray each other, not knowing even how to best preserve themselves for and from each other. Millwood is hanged but George escapes to "Polonia." There he once again commits murder and is "hang'd in chains" (194), the end of a youth who has become a habitual criminal.

The Barnwell ballad is about a harlot and its didactic message is "Take heed of Harlots then, and their inticing trains" (5) and "Lo, here's the end of wilful youth, that after Harlots haunt,/Who, in the spoyl of other men, about the streets do flaunt" (195–196). The ballad is, therefore, related to discourses on harlots and sexuality just as it is related to discourses on apprentices and their behavior at the beginning of the seventeenth century. What the ballad deliberately avoids is situating the events in terms of history or of family or of motivation other than the individual sexuality of Barnwell and the monetary exploitation of sex by Millwood.

Indeed, the moral might be read as a warning to choose one's prostitutes more carefully. For Barnwell and Millwood are untouched by religion or justice. Embezzling, stealing, and even murder go undetected or unapprehended until the culprits implicate each other. The advice of avoidance is undermined by the fact that innocence prevents Barnwell from recognizing a harlot when he is approached by one, and when he finally recognizes her duplicity, he is too deeply enmeshed in sexuality to extricate himself. The social implications of his behavior and that of Millwood's are to be found in the manipulation of society illegally so that one can have pleasures which are unearned.

The ballad is ostensibly about the wiles of a prostitute in seducing an apprentice, but the seduction involves the allusion to classical references— to sexuality in the reference to Venus and Adonis and to Argus in hiding from the constable:

For say thou should'st pursued be, with twenty hues and cries,
And with a warrant searched for with *Argus'* hundred eyes:
Yet in my house thou shalt be safe, such privy ways there be,
That if they sought an 100 years, they could not find out thee.   (155–158)

The prostitute has found a way to live joyfully by seduction and exploitation without sacrificing her reputation. Her death is the result of not knowing that she has made Barnwell into a criminal with a will like her own. Readings of the ballad in the ways I have suggested indicate that criminals, like non-criminals of the time, behave in similar fashion—manipulating others for wealth or power. The ideological interpretation of this text can thus be read not only as a warning against harlots but as a warning to be more careful in selecting them. It can be read as an example of sexuality as a drive more powerful than moral or religious injunctions. Such sexuality overrides family traditions and work obligations. And it can be read as revealing the pleasures that sex can provide, although there is always the risk with prostitutes of betrayal and punishment.

These readings cannot be derived from commentaries made in the seventeenth century, but generic alterations of the text can provide interpretive clues. The first is the rewriting of the ballad as a prose chapbook at the end of the seventeenth century. It is appropriate, therefore, before turning to a late seventeenth-century prose version, to consider what such a transformation involves. As members of genres, texts have a historical existence which, however recoverable—in part or wholes—depends on generic resurrection. Thus the absence of the "tune" in the Barnwell ballad may nevertheless permit us to explain why such a loss occurs, or more importantly, how a generic procedure can reveal a literary history that, like the "tune," has disappeared from sight. This study of the generic procedure provides an example of a literary history that answers the question: Is literary history possible? The literary history of the Barnwell plot leads to a consideration of a history of diverse genres that remain related by the component of the plot. In this respect, literary history requires a recognition of the similarity of plot which, because of its insertion into different genres, is reshaped by them.

The Ballad of George Barnwel is shaped by the "tune" as well as by the method of construction applicable to ballads of this time. The loss of the "tune" may make the repetitions more subject to parody or irony than the interpretation I propose, but the performance in parts, the role of a narrator who addresses the audience, the repetitions that serve to remind the listeners of the moral consequences that the participants ignore, the use of language that moves from naivety to vulgarity—all these are characteristic of broadside ballads that are directed at an audience that walk the streets of London. The Barnwell ballad is the beginning of a history that became a series of literary transformations. The first is the rewriting of the ballad as a prose chapbook at the end of the seventeenth century. This begins the 400-year series of rewritings that form the basis for this generic analysis, since the ballad is transformed into different genres.

If we consider that a text is composed of elements that include not only formal features such as rhyme, rhythm, versification, rhetorical features such as voice, and devices of expression, of allusion, quotation, and the nature and order of character and events, then every text is combinatory. Terms that critics invent to describe texts as blurring genres, as monologic or dialogic, as mixing or hybridizing, as constructing or deconstructing themselves are efforts to describe texts as particular forms of combination. But any performance, description, criticism, or analysis of a text is itself a combinatory text. This relationship to which reader-response critics have justly drawn attention, the interaction of the two genres, or generic crossing, needs to be distinguished from a relationship in which the genres are of all the same kind, as criticism of criticism, or of different kinds, as criticism of a ballad. The inevitable intervention of the critic into a text is the examination of one genre by means of another. To analyze a broadside ballad from a critical and historical perspective is to engage in contention, admiration, mediation, from one generic perspective upon another: it involves a crossing of some one type to that of another.

I read the Barnwell ballad as the advice to avoid lewd women not because of some religious or moral concern, but because it can lead to criminality and punishment. The ballad is about an innocent youth who cannot distinguish false statements of love from true, or his moral obligation not to defraud his master. Although Millwood makes herself the victim of seduction, the youth embraces the values of sexual and sensual pleasures of Millwood. The ballad reversed the seduction of the innocent girl and suggests the threat that the prostitute has for the patriarchal norm. It reveals the class relation between the possession of money and the pleasures of bed and board. What becomes significant in this analysis are the means by which the change in Barnwell takes place: how innocence becomes reduced and how, once Millwood's deception is exposed, Barnwell is unable to free himself from his seduction. The ballad can also be read as a parody of the patriarchal order since Millwood possesses power over the innocent youth. Her example, however, is ultimately followed by Barnwell, and in writing a confession that condemns her, he exercises power while seeming to surrender it.

The ballad offers a story of the ultimate punishment for subversive behavior. Barnwell is an apprentice who robs his master and destroys the opportunity apprenticeship offers. He destroys the familial order by treating his father and sister as subservient to his own needs and murders his uncle who entertains him as a valued guest. But this disordering of social and family norms is offset by pleasures both sexual and sensual. The "good cheer" in which Barnwell participates is disrupted by Millwood whenever he ceases to provide her with money. The moral is not to avoid harlots, one might say, only the avaricious ones.

In my analysis of "An Excellent Ballad of George Barnwel" I have invaded it in order to demonstrate a method of generic criticism. The inferences I draw from the ballad pertain to the antithetical nature of the same terms and phrases, to the duplicity that seduction involves by contributing to one's own seduction, to the uncontrollable feelings for which there is not at this time in this history any other explanation than that a seduction leads to a replication of the values of the seducer. Yet neither seduced nor seducer, the apprentice and the prostitute, are models of behavior. They are negative examples of the temptations and corruptions that exist in the everyday life in the early seventeenth century. As a historical document, the ballad, without literary resurrection, seemed destined to share the same fate as its music—to disappear from all historical account.

NOTES

1. C. M. Simpson, *The British Broadside Ballad and Its Music* (New Brunswick, NJ: Rutgers Univ. Press, 1966), 603. There are numerous discussions of the ballad and its music in books and essays by B. H. Bronson and Cecil Sharp. For a useful and concise statement, see M. J. C. Hodgart, *The Ballads* (New York: Norton, 1962), chapter 3.
2. Natascha Würzbach, *The Rise of the English Street Ballad*, 1550–1650, trans. Gayna Walls (Cambridge: Cambridge Univ. Press, 1990), 228; hereafter cited in text.
3. "A rich Merchant man," entitled *A most sweet Song of an English Merchant, borne at Chichester* in *The Roxburghe Ballads*, ed. Wm. Chappell, 8 vols.

(London: Printed for the Ballad Society by Taylor and Co., 1871), 1:320–25. According to the editor, "The first entry of the ballad on the books of the Stationers' Company seems to be one to Abell Jeffs, in March, 1594, and the earliest copy now extant to be in the Roxburghe Collection (1:104–5), from which we reprint. ... The ballad seems to have passed through so many early editions that, even the following, the earliest now extant, is in a very corrupt state" (319).

4. *An Excellent Ballad of George Barnwell* ... (London: Printed and sold by L. How; in Petticoat-Lane, 1741–1762?). The Houghton Library edition does not use line numbering. A transcription of the text can be retrieved from the English Broadside Ballad Archive, University of California, Santa Barbara, https://ebba.english.ucsb.edu/ballad/34458/xml (accessed March 27, 2020).

Companion Genres: From Ballad to Chapbook

At the end of the seventeenth century (the British Library catalogue lists the date tentatively as 1700), there was published the first prose narrative of the Barnwell story. It was a chapbook entitled *The 'Prentice's Tragedy: or, the HISTORY of George Barnwell: Being a Fair Warning to Young Men to Avoid the Company of Lewd Women*, and together with the prose narrative the chapbook included a version of the earliest ballad, here called *An Excellent Song of George Barnwell, an Apprentice in the City of London, who was undone by a Strumpet, who caused him thrice to rob his Master, and to Murder his Uncle in Ludlow, etc. To the Tune of, The Merchant, etc.*[1]

The practice of treating a common narrative in two different genres was not infrequent in the seventeenth century, as the production of some of Shakespeare's plays attests. But publishing them together, both being genres of low esteem, is less frequent. In this instance, what we have is a ballad composed at the beginning of the century and a short prose version published near or at its end. This practice permits analysis of the cultural changes that have led to the treatment of shared events, the invention of new events, and the neglect of some of the old.

But before entering into intertextuality, it is important to note the rationale of chapbooks since the term refers to the mode of distribution rather than to the genre of the product. Chapbooks could include

© The Author(s), under exclusive license to Springer Nature Switzerland AG 2021
R. Cohen, J. L. Rowlett, *Transformations of a Genre*, Palgrave Studies in the Enlightenment, Romanticism and Cultures of Print, https://doi.org/10.1007/978-3-030-89668-3_4

dialogues—for example, "A Dialogue between Honest John and Loving Kate with their Contrivance for Marriage, and Way to get a Livelyhood"; short biographies—for example, "The History of the Learned Friar Bacon"; collections of songs and catches—for example, "The Lover's Magazine; or Cupid's Decoy"; and short rewritings or summaries of published works such as that of the Barnwell ballad.

Chapbooks usually ran to twenty-four pages and the prose narratives were frequently divided into chapters. The relation between the genres in the Barnwell narrative is that the prose short story provides an interpretation of the poem. It functions the way that a modern critical interpretation of a poem in our time relates to the poetic text. Every prose *critical* text that interprets or analyzes a poem is an example of one genre commenting on another. The interpretation belongs to a different genre from that of a poem. As a consequence, an interpretation of a poem is more like other interpretations than like the poem it analyzes. A prose interpretation of a poem or song is guided by premises of criticism as a genre. When it seeks to annunciate the premises of the poet, it is as an outside commentary intervening in the text. No matter how careful and attentive a critic is in constructing the intentions and practices of a poet in the composition of a poem, the response—even if it is reasonable, perhaps even persuasive—can only approximate in one genre what is developed and conceived in the language structure and feeling of another. One can only approximate in prose what has been thought and felt in poetry.

This is not meant to imply that genres are self-enclosed entities; my argument rejects such assumptions. But genres can and do possess discourses that are shared with other genres. Moreover, such sharing alters as a result of time often leading to the initiation of new genres. Some genres seem much closer at one time than another because of discourse affiliations or of plot structure or of ideological implications. I have argued that a text can belong to more than one genre, and *The 'Prentice's Tragedy* is not only a short prose fiction, but a criminal biography and a critical interpretation. The short criminal biography has been studied in detail by Lincoln B. Faller, and he suggests some general structural principles governing the genre in the seventeenth and eighteenth centuries.[2]

But the publication of the chapbook together with the poem which forms the basis of its plot is an example also of critical interpretation within the same discourse class. The chapbook belongs to folk and popular literature just as the ballad does. The conjunction suggests that within popular literature there exist contradictions, oppositions, a broad diversity of interpretations, actions, and genres. The comparison implies that popular culture is as complex as high culture, and indeed can be intertwined with it as in *The Beggar's Opera*.

This is apparent in *The 'Prentice's Tragedy*, which not only abandons the poetry and song of the ballad, but makes Millwood into a vicious gang leader who abases Barnwell even while he is still bringing her money. The murder of Barnwell's uncle is deliberately changed from the ballad.

Millwood not only accompanies Barnwell, but when he knocks his uncle off his horse, Millwood alights and cuts his throat. *The 'Prentice's Tragedy* is not a dramatic tragedy no more than it is a history in the classical sense. Rather, "tragedy" is used in the sense of the unfortunate fate of a young man who is seduced and eventually becomes involved in murder and is hanged. And it is a "history" in the sense that it reveals a series of events leading to his death. It is a short fictional biographical narrative told by a narrator who sees Barnwell's parents and his master as models of behavior and who makes the harlot into an inhumanly vicious woman who takes equal pleasure in tormenting her victim, engaging in sexual acts, and profiting from these actions. Although Millwood's behavior is intended to warn young readers, there is a statement that indicates the difficulty in seeking to prevent youths from succumbing to temptation: "But, alas, there is nothing certain in this World, Temptations are powerful; so that the Wisest at all times, are not proof against them" (p. 4).

Placing a short biographical fiction beside a ballad that provides an originating plot draws attention to the absence of music and poetry in the rewriting. The mode of presentation changes from the street theatricals to that of reading in the home. The shift in presentation does not eliminate the ballad as a form that can be sung in the home, but it does indicate that popular literature now readily finds its place in the sites where people read as well as those in which they congregate to hear. In the ballad Millwood asks Barnwell to come to her home when she greets him: "'In faith, my boy,' quoth she, 'such news I can thee tell,/As shall rejoice thy very heart, then come where I do dwell'" (13–14). But in the prose version she explains why he should come to her home: "*I know you and all your Family exceeding well; and therefore one Request I must ask of you;* (giving him thereupon one gentle Kiss.) *What is that?* (said he.) *Why, my dear pretty Boy,* (reply'd she,) *because I cannot sully my Reputation to go into an Ale-house, or Tavern with thee, I would desire you to come to my House, for I have something to tell you that is extraordinary*" (p. 5).

The reference to Barnwell's family and to the house as the proper venue for personal messages indicates a shift in the audience of the chapbook. Its impact is through its presence in the home. By comparison with the ballad, the prose fiction begins with quotations from Proverbs about harlots and their dreadful consequences: "And indeed *Solomon* rightly warns Youth from it [the snare of a Harlot] as from the greatest Curse that can befal them, and commands them to pray to GOD against such Temptations" (p. 3). And in support of the importance which the family now possesses, the chapbook identifies Barnwell's parents as industrious, rich, and honest and living in the County of Hereford. They apprenticed him to a London merchant "promising themselves the greatest Comforts in their old Age imaginable from such a hopeful Son ... and to add to this, their care was likewise to provide him a rich Wife, when it was convenient for him to marry" (p. 4). Barnwell not only accepted these values but for two years as an apprentice was a model of appropriate behavior.

The juxtaposition of the two genres reveals what the later text locates as gaps in the earlier. The reference to Barnwell's parent (only his father) in the first version occurs but once in Barnwell's resentful remark: "'My father's rich, why then,' quoth I, 'should I want any gold'" (143). The later version fills gaps in the earlier version which exemplify its ideological interpretation. In this particular case the family as a unit applies to Barnwell's parents; its antithesis is Millwood's gang of criminals. The kindness of the first two groups is contrasted with the viciousness of the second. The point is that explanation or interpretation can readily locate gaps in the original narrative, and these are filled by the ideological assumptions provided by the interpreter. There remain, however, elements of plot or of previous generic members of the genre (short prose fiction) that contrast with or resist the introduction of ideological gap-fillers. These refer to Barnwell's youthful naivete, to his embezzlement of his master's funds, and to his culpability and complicity in his uncle's murder. Whatever interpretation the narrator gives to acts, they cannot be explained merely by pointing to Barnwell's victimization.

Barnwell in the prose fiction is not only given a devoted family but one that completely conforms to the desire for class elevation and for treating their son as an investment in his future as well as their own. In this respect the invention of Barnwell's family supports in a legal sense the commercialization of values that Millwood's behavior supports illegally.

Placed against the achievement of commercial success are both romance reading and classical mythology, which emphasize sexuality. Romances provide a false view of upward mobility by indicating that a shoemaker, for example, can marry a princess. Like Barnwell in the ballad, the prose Barnwell is overwhelmed by Millwood's beauty and by his assumption of her divinity. Indeed one might note that the biblical language of Cherubims and sensual delights would seem to indict the use of the Bible and biblical discourses that create false images.

The language of the ballad is frequently in marked contrast to the didactic language of the prose fiction. After Barnwell sups with Millwood and pleas to see her soon again, the ballad reads: "O stay not too long, my dear, sweet *George* have me in mind!"/"Her words bewitcht my childishness, she uttered them so kind" (65–66). The prose fiction reads: "*if you will be gone, pray have me in your mind, and be not long absent from me, that I may not only restore you your Money, but dispence such Favours to you, as you shall desire.* Upon this, and many endearing Kisses, they parted, she to laugh in her Sleeve at the Woodcock she had catched, and he home with six Pounds short of his Master's Cash" (pp. 8–9). The colloquial idiomatic language is often followed by didactic pointing: with "hugging himself in his supposed good Fortune" (p. 9), this was what "she angled for" (p. 10), "This made him ready to leap out of his Skin" (p. 11), "to Bed they went, to play out their old Game at Ticktack" (p. 12).

The narrator's didactic intervention is present even in the scenes which derive from the original. When Millwood comes to the door to meet Barnwell, she wears "a varied Dress, the finest he thought, that ever he had seen in his Life, her Face he fancy'd to be a Cherubin's [sic], it was so set off with curious Paints, and his Smelling was charmed with the Scent of Essences, so that he stood abashed, scarce thinking her Mortal, till taking him by the hand, with a fauning Compliment of, *Welcome my dear George, now I see you are a Man of your Word*" (p. 6).

The prose version adds a new dimension to the narrative. When George returns home he narcissistically regards himself in the mirror. The self-admiration in which he indulges offers a sophisticated insight into his self-analysis. It suggests, even though it does not develop, a much more analytical character than either the ballad or the other parts of the prose fiction demonstrate: "he went home and looked a hundred times in the Glass, fancying himself the beautifullest of all the Youths in the City; many things run in his thoughts, sometimes he doubted she flattered him, then again, her feigned Coyness made him believe she was really enamoured" (p. 5).

The material objects that so impressed Barnwell loom much more important in indicating the merchandizing role of Millwood. Her house and the objects in it provide art for seduction. Although the chapbook narrates Barnwell's seduction and its consequences, it is Millwood's procedures for his victimization that dominate the story. Her success in seducing the young and having created a gang that is engaged in robbery and other unlawful behavior has provided her with an expensive house that contained expensive trophies and paintings:

> [H]e found out her House, which had a very spacious out-side, and was as well answerable within, witnessing the Spoils and Trophies of many simple Youths whom she had ensnared. ... She conducted him into her Parlour, and there for a time left him to dispatch some other Gallants she had above Stairs. ... Being thus left alone, he began to cast his eyes on the Pictures, which were suitable to the trade of the Owner, for on one hand he espied *Venus* and *Mars* naked, embracing each other in *Vulcan's* Net, which he laid to catch them when they were at the height of their stolen Pleasures; on the other hand a Satyr ravishing a Nymph; and again *Jupiter* transformed into a Bull, running away with *Europea* to deflower her, and many other such like Fancies to incite and stir up to Amorous Delights. (p. 6)

The narrator sees Millwood's behavior as creating a consistent and unified pattern of immorality. Not only does Millwood expose "her delicate white Breasts naked" (p. 7) in order to entice Barnwell, but her house, her paintings, and her practices all serve to enhance seduction for money. This late seventeenth-century text sees sexuality as a form of commerce. Millwood uses Barnwell's love in order to victimize him. This victimization even includes a comic scene. When Barnwell is in bed with Millwood, three "Ruffians" rush in and bind and gag Millwood, while a frightened Barnwell tries to hide under the bed covers. They "began to talk of throwing them out at the Window; this redoubled his Fright for fear of having his Neck broke, so that roaring out, they thought the Plot was betrayed, seemed affrighted, and immediately made their Escapes, though you may be sure not without his Cloaths, and all the Money he had left" (p. 11). This was of course a plot initiated by Millwood, the "avaritious Strumpet" (p. 12). Barnwell lost not only money at her home, but rings and other objects of value sent him by his parents; he lost these in gaming and laying wagers, though Millwood often claimed to lose as well. The importance of these additions to the ballad is that they provide details that exemplify the "Strumpet's wily ways with all her tricks" (98).

Without the comparison with the ballad, there would be no knowledge that the role of Millwood had been redesigned. The prose text includes lines taken from the ballad; thus the text contains discourse elements from different times. Arguments for situating a text historically need to indicate not only intertextual elements from different genres as here, but that such elements frequently are discourses from different times and situations. Take for example the passage in the poem which occurs after Barnwell suggests that he has a rich uncle and would be willing to rob and murder him. In the ballad Millwood says,

> For say thou should'st pursued be, with twenty hues and cries,
> And with a warrant searched for with *Argus'* hundred eyes:
> Yet in my house thou shalt be safe, such privy ways there be,
> That if they sought an 100 years, they could not find out thee.   (155–158)

In the prose text this occurs after Barnwell and Millwood have killed the uncle, Barnwell having knocked him off his horse and Millwood having slit his throat. They take his money and live riotously upon it, although Barnwell's "Conscience being much startled at the guilt of so bloody a Fact"; "but she encouraged him, saying, *If a hundred Hues and Cries came, she had such places in her House to hide him in, that tho' they searched an Age they could not find him*" (p. 16). The prose version contrasts Millwood's heartlessness with Barnwell's uneasy conscience, though he is as implicated as she. In the poem an early promise is later broken; the prose version uses the passage to encourage Barnwell after the deed is done and thus makes especially vicious Millwood's thrusting him out of doors.

At least three quarters of a century elapses between the publication of the original ballad and the prose version. This version—with its including of passages that are sometimes direct quotations, at other times indirect or incorrect quotations—poses a question about the relation of past discourses to the present rewriting. It seems reasonable to assume that the later version is intended as a modernization of an early seventeenth-century work. Its attempt to create a middle-class family, its portrayal of Millwood as gang leader and wealthy entrepreneur, its deliberate misogyny in converting Millwood into a woman warrior, all indicate the social changes with regard to prostitution and criminality. The original seduction has become part of a corporate venture. The use of quotations from the original seems intended to note the changes that such quotations have undergone.

Publishing the prose fiction and the ballad together provides the basis for assuming that each is a construction. Whether there was or was not a basis in reality for the events described, the two texts make clear that their mode of presentation was a construction and that the compositions provided different conceptions of the subject. The third-person narrator not only added information about places and times, but altered key events. Millwood goes with Barnwell and is the one who cuts the uncle's throat. And although Barnwell escapes to "Polonia," the narrator writes, "he was Condemn'd abroad on suspition of another Murther, which he deny'd to the last, saying, *However it was Just with God for his Sins*" (p. 16). And he is hanged in chains when dead, unlike the living death in the ballad. The narrator deliberately adds Barnwell's assertion of his innocence of murder in "Polonia," but accepts his punishment for this crime because of his guilt in the other. Thus God's justice is done in ways too mysterious to fathom.

Publishing the two genres together may have proved a profitable venture since later chapbooks often follow this model. This chapbook adds a third genre—illustrations. There are five badly designed woodcuts—the frontispiece shows Millwood taking Barnwell's hand. The second depicts a meeting between Millwood and Barnwell at what might be the entrance to her house. The third contains two scenes on her horse, one depicts a gaming table with men and women playing while others observe the game from a balcony, and the adjacent scene seems to be after the game. The fourth depicts Barnwell in bed with Millwood. And the fifth, apparently unrelated to the narrative, shows a farmer carrying two dead rabbits with a pack on his back and a walking stick.

Although the illustrations are inept, they convey an attitude to Millwood that is not found in the ballads. She is a harlot in both, but in the prose version she is the leader of a gang of thieves as well, and she operates her whorehouse as a business. She has a maid as wicked as herself and she initially solicits money from Barnwell by inventing stories about a vintner's bill and about a silk broker who has called out the bailiffs to arrest her without warning. When Barnwell comes to visit her, she conducts him "into her Parlour, and there for a time left him to dispatch some other Gallants she had above Stairs" (p. 6).

Millwood has become a merchant and when she goes with Barnwell to rob and murder his uncle, she impersonates the wife of the merchant to whom he is supposedly still apprenticed. This disguise constitutes another of the changes that take place in the prose fiction. The one authorized change is the move of Barnwell from his home in Herefordshire to

London. But when he moves from adherence to established religious and social behavior to immoral and criminal behavior, he becomes both the perpetrator of criminality and the victim of it. The ballad has Millwood throw Barnwell out when the stolen money is gone:

> And thus they liv'd in filthy sort, till all his store was gone,
> And means to get them any more, I wis poor *George* had none.
> And therefore now in railing sort she thrust him out of door,
> Which is the just reward they get that spend upon a Whore.   (179–182)

But in the chapbook, after the money is gone, Millwood puts Barnwell on new projects, making him another member of her gang. And when these fail and they involve her in monetary losses, she hates him and beats him. Then she turns him out "in a bitter frosty Night": "However, this ill-gotten Money being squandered away, she put him on new Projects, but they not succeeding, and so becoming a little chargeable to her, she not only hated but miserably beat him, breaking his Head and Face with the Tongues in a pitiful manner; and so, according as his Folly deserved, turn'd him out of Doors in a bitter frosty Night" (p. 16).

The prose fiction adds a viciousness to Millwood's commercial sexuality that makes her more violent, even misanthropic. When Barnwell reviles her for ingratitude, she calls him "Thief and Murtherer, ordering her Maid to fetch a Constable to apprehend him" (p. 16). Barnwell escapes by sea but "being stinged and tortured in Conscience," he first directs letters to his Master and to the Lord Mayor of London confessing his robbery and murder "for the sake of this wicked lewd Woman" (p. 16).

The printing of the two genres together indicates the complicated nature of context. Just as the absence of music delimits the interconnection between "A Rich Merchant Man" and "An Excellent Ballad," so the notion of context is enhanced by the presence of the source and its prose revision. The numerous incidents that are added to the plot in the prose version function to explain the "wiles" of a whore, but they also serve to provide a narcissistic view of Barnwell unavailable in the first-person confession. The generic context would be completely missed if one had no knowledge of the quotations from the ballad that appear in the prose version. The practice of including quotations from classical texts in Renaissance texts has been frequently commented upon. But the relation of a text to earlier members of its own genre or, as here, to instances from a different genre with the same plot, has infrequently been considered as a normal procedure of contextual analysis. In the Barnwell example, the later version reveals a contemporary association of the text with the development of commerce, and with the contemporary assumptions of the immorality of romance reading and of viewing mythological paintings.

There is a relation between the short prose version and the attack on the lasciviousness of contemporary drama by eighteenth-century theater critic Jeremy Collier. The causes of moral corruption are identified with the reading of romances and the seduction and adultery revealed in contemporary drama. The method of arguing, moreover, begins to be joined in the presentation of short prose narratives as they appear in chapbooks and in periodical papers. Indeed, Barnwell is described as having read many romances in which a queen marries a commoner; consequently, his vulnerability is attributed in part to his reading.

NOTES

1. *The 'Prentice's Tragedy: or, the HISTORY of George Barnwell: Being a fair Warning to Young Men to avoid the Company of Lewd Women.* Printed by W. O. and sold by the Booksellers of Pye-corner and London-bridge (n.d.; the British Library suggests 1700), 1–24. Pages 1–16 of the chapbook comprise the prose fiction, and pages 17–24 reproduce a version of the ballad as the source of the narrative. Chapbook pages cited in text.
2. Lincoln B. Faller, *Turned to Account: The Forms and Functions of Criminal Biography in Late Seventeenth- and Early Eighteenth-Century England* (Cambridge: Cambridge Univ. Press, 1987).

Intervention 1: Initiating Genres—Addison's Ballad Criticism and Its Parody

THE SPECTATOR AS GENRE AND GENRES

The Spectator, written primarily by Joseph Addison and Richard Steele, was not the first periodical paper, but it became the model for such papers in the eighteenth century. Each *Spectator* paper was a physical object, a single folio, double-sided and limited to a short prose piece. To disregard these physical dimensions is to ignore the relation between the text as physical object and the low place it held in the hierarchy of genres. In *Spectator* 529, published November 6, 1712, Addison addressed this issue humorously, indicating first how the physical size of a text gave a particular status to its author: "I have observed that the Author of a *Folio*, in all Companies and Conversations, sets himself above the Author of a *Quarto*; the Author of a *Quarto* above the Author of an *Octavo*; and so on, by a gradual Descent and Subordination, to an Author in *Twenty Fours*" (No. 529).[1] Addison remarked that minute pocket-authors have beneath them writers of pamphlets, or works that are only stitched. "As for the Pamphleteer, he takes place of none but of the Authors of single Sheets, and of that Fraternity who publish their Labours on certain Days, or on every Day of the Week. I do not find that the Precedency among the Individuals, in this latter Class of Writers, is yet settled" (No. 529). And it was to this class that the periodical paper belonged. Addison pointed out ironically that when his first copies were gathered into two volumes, "I

© The Author(s), under exclusive license to Springer Nature   59
Switzerland AG 2021
R. Cohen, J. L. Rowlett, *Transformations of a Genre*, Palgrave
Studies in the Enlightenment, Romanticism and Cultures of Print,
https://doi.org/10.1007/978-3-030-89668-3_5

naturally jumped over the Heads not only of all Pamphleteers, but of every *Octavo* Writer in *Great-Britain*, that had written but one Book" (No. 529).

Whatever pleasure we may take in Addison's wit, we can note that he was aware that material production of a text could be seen as an index of status. His own "elevation" through the octavo volumes, however ironically intended, indicates that a change in the physical shape of a genre, even though the content remained the same, could lead to a formal change in naming the genre. Addison suggests ironically that the basis for hierarchy may have been economic—that the publication of the same contents in sheets, then quarto volumes, then octavo volumes, and so forth might have been a hierarchy established by paper manufacturers and publishers: "Whether these Rules, which have been received time out of Mind in the Common-Wealth of Letters, were not originally established with an Eye to our Paper Manufacture, I shall leave to the Discussion of others" (No. 529). But whether or not the paper manufacturers were originally responsible for the textual hierarchy, the present use of it by publishers was obviously connected with profit-making. It should be noted, however, that Addison himself was concerned about the number of papers published and was obviously intent on increasing subscribers as well as readers.

The lowly role of the periodical paper in the hierarchy established by the learned was resisted by Addison, especially on the basis of his conception of the significance of short forms in educating women and other members of his audience. In expounding his views, he made a significant case for the periodical paper as multigeneric. The basis for his argument was that writings "in distinct Sheets, and as it were by Piece-meal" (No. 124) actually improved the quality of writing and communication. Long books required dull passages for which even "severe" readers make allowances, but writers of "distinct Sheets" must not be dull. Including his own periodical papers in his remarks, he wrote: "We must immediately fall into our Subject, and treat every Part of it in a lively Manner, or our Papers are thrown by as dull and insipid: Our Matter must lie close together, and either be wholly new in itself, or in the Turn it receives from our Expressions" (No. 124). Addison did not deny that some papers "may be made up of broken Hints and irregular Sketches." Nevertheless, "it is often expected that every Sheet should be a kind of Treatise, and make out in Thought what it wants in Bulk: That a Point of Humour should be worked up in all its Parts; and a Subject touched upon in its most essential Articles, without the Repetitions, Tautologies and Enlargements, that are indulg'd to longer Labours" (No. 124).

Addison considered the writing of periodical papers as an ideal genre for communicating thought to the world. Short printed forms, "our common Prints" (No. 124) "would be of great Use, were they thus calculated to diffuse good Sense through the Bulk of a People, to clear up their Understandings, animate their Minds with Virtue, dissipate the sorrows of a heavy Heart, or unbend the Mind from its more severe Employments with innocent Amusements. When Knowledge, instead of being bound up in Books, and kept in Libraries and Retirements, is thus obtruded upon the Publick; when it is canvassed in every Assembly, and exposed upon every Table" (No. 124), then knowledge would be readily available to all.

The periodical papers of Addison and Steele were multigeneric. Not only were they formal genres governed by the material conditions of publication, but they were genres in terms of their intellectual structures. The papers included theoretical discussions such as those on true and false wit; they included examples of literary criticism in the papers on *Paradise Lost*. They could include fictional narratives such as "The Vision of Mirza." Even as individual papers they could include such short genres as inscriptions, usually in Latin at the head of a paper, or letters from correspondents.

For example, the run of *The Spectator* from 1711 to 1712 constituted an anthology of short essays on religious, social, literary, philosophical, and related subjects. The papers provided examples of serial publication in the papers on *Paradise Lost* and the papers on the pleasures of the imagination. These served as instances of what Addison called piece-meal publication. As a genre this type of publication was an example of publication in parts that proved valuable for the economics of publishing. Indeed, the essays dealing with Roger de Coverly and the Club indicated the interrelation of periodical genres with the structure of incidents in the novel.

One of the important contributions to an understanding of genre as a social artifact has to do with Addison's comic awareness of the disposability of single sheets. The lowly genre of the periodical paper became part of the domestic economy. Addison noted that single sheets were often used to light one's pipe or to line baking dishes. What was left of the genre was no more than a fragment. Nevertheless, those fragments could still be read and Addison refers to such activities as "accidental Readings" (No. 85) in which he "sometimes found very Curious Pieces, that are either out of Print, or not to be met with in the Shops of our *London* Booksellers" (No. 85).

Although Addison is not interested in theorizing the implications of a textual genre that becomes a household object, part of a domestic economy, he does by his comic example demonstrate the transition from one kind of genre to another. The textual sheet used to line a baking dish is obviously connected with baking, and what is left to read after the pie is done is a fragment of the textual genre, the whole having served as a quite different genre.

The intersection of a textual genre with a social activity interpreted as a genre—a baking convention—reveals how textual genres can interrelate with non-textual genres. But it also reveals how lowly textual genres can become fragments, that is, pieces of a generic entity that become entities themselves. Such fragments, according to Addison, enabled the reader to inquire into their pasts. He writes: "I once met with a Page of Mr. *Baxter* under a *Christmas* Pye. Whether or no the Pastry-Cook had made use of it through Chance, or Waggery, for the Defence of that Superstitious *Viande*, I know not; but, upon the Perusal of it, I conceived so good an Idea of the Author's Piety, that I bought the whole Book" (No. 85).

The fragment illustrates the procedure by which a member of a genre—in this instance a religious text—is reduced to a small piece of the whole and reveals how this reduction can, by its membership in such reductions, become an instance of another kind of genre—that is, the fragment becomes an entity in itself. If we think of periodical papers as short forms which are not fragments but which contain ideas and subjects found in scholarly works, we realize that the genre provides a source of knowledge that is an alternative to texts often cumbersome and boring and impenetrable to ordinary readers of periodical papers.

Fragments become important to a society in search of its national identity and it is not surprising that reliques, ruins, and remains become significant fragments in seeking to establish a "literary history" for Britain. Fragments arise as a result of the interaction of textual and non-textual genres, but ballads and similar short genres often cover a wall in a coffee house or country home. The generic instances become a form of collage; they serve as decorative art as well as separate, individual textual entities. Addison writes: "I can't, for my Heart, leave a Room before I have thoroughly studied the Walls of it, and examined the several printed Papers which are usually pasted upon them. ... The Piece that I am going to speak of was the old Ballad of the *Two Children in the Wood*, which is one of the Darling Songs of the Common People, and has been the Delight of most *Englishmen* in some Part of their Age" (No. 85).

The use of one genre—the ballad or the periodical paper—to serve as decoration in a room draws attention to the role of place in generic inter-relations. Ballads can be sung in the streets, used as linings for baking dishes, or hung as decorations on walls. But as Addison makes clear, the place in which a short genre is found need not deprive it of its textual character. The place in which a textual genre is read or found—whether a library or cell or bed or classroom or monument or human skin—provides an insight into the social character of generic interrelation.

It is significant that a wall decoration should lead Addison to a discussion of a genre that was unacknowledged as a "literary" text. "Two Children in the Wood" was actually the second ballad that Addison undertook to discuss in *The Spectator*. The first was the ballad of "Chevy-Chase" that he analyzed in papers 70 and 74 on May 21 and May 25, 1711. "Two Children in the Wood" appeared in paper 85 on June 7, 1711.

THE SOCIAL BASIS OF ADDISON'S BALLAD CRITICISM

The periodical paper was a new though not highly valued literary genre when Addison undertook to claim for the ballad of "Chevy-Chase" the highest generic form—the epic. This claim was based on a number of arguments, some of which Addison made overtly. Others were implicit in the generic interrelations that Addison described in essays apparently unrelated to the ballad propositions.

Just as he saw the periodical papers as alternatives to scholarly tomes, so he saw the ballad as a genre that could please all readers who were not already corrupted by the writings of such artificially constructed poems as those of Martial and Cowley. These he identified as authors responsible for offering readers "a wrong artificial Taste" (No. 70). He wrote: "an ordinary Song or Ballad that is the Delight of the common People, cannot fail to please all such Readers as are not unqualified for the Entertainment by their Affectation or Ignorance" (No. 70).

Addison argued that if the multitude approved of a work, even though the multitude was a "rabble," the text had to have in it some special aptness "to please and gratify the mind of man":

> When I travelled, I took a particular Delight in hearing the Songs and Fables that are come from Father to Son, and are most in Vogue among the common People of the Countries through which I passed; for it is impossible that any thing should be universally tasted and approved by a Multitude, tho' they are only the Rabble of a Nation, which hath not in it some peculiar

> Aptness to please and gratify the Mind of Man. Human Nature is the same
> in all reasonable Creatures; and whatever falls in with it, will meet with
> Admirers amongst Readers of all Qualities and Conditions. (No. 70)

The basis for treating the ballad of "Chevy-Chase" as a heroic poem or
epic was also based on parallels with passages in the *Aeneid*. He compared
the Latin with the English, finding that they were equally poetic. This
procedure served him as a basis for elevation since it provided a historical
demonstration of the artistic value of ballad poetry. It served also to support his view that ballads such as "Chevy-Chase" were based on nature, as
was the composition of the *Aeneid*.

Addison did not attempt to elevate "Two Children in the Wood" into
an epic. But he did wish to urge that it was "a plain simple Copy of Nature,
destitute of the Helps and Ornaments of Art" (No. 85). He even granted
that there was "a despicable Simplicity in the Verse" (No. 85). But this did
not prevent it from pleasing "because the Sentiments appear genuine and
unaffected, they are able to move the Mind of the most polite Reader with
Inward Meltings of Humanity and Compassion" (No. 85).

These arguments for ballad elevation were seriously questioned by John
Dennis and parodied by William Wagstaffe. But there is another approach
to Addison's criticism which can take its direction from his discussion of
the moral of "Chevy-Chase." He identified the moral with the dangers of
dissention among the factional leaders in a society. This he took to be the
moral of the *Iliad*. The English victory over the Scots led eventually to a
harmonious union. The political implications of "Chevy-Chase" for his
time were the importance of the harmonious union of the two countries.
The sad experience of a bloody war, however unfortunate, led eventually
to a nation unified and powerful.

The relation between the ballad and the epic that Addison was seeking
to bridge through the assumptions of a universal of human nature was
analogical to that of the different nations, between the poor and the
wealthy, between those with natural advantages and those dependent
upon importing them. Economic structures can thus function as genres in
which the models of established genres are claimed as the basis for raising
lower genres even though the procedure distorts the very character of the
lower forms. Economically, the less advantaged countries become the
"beneficiaries" of the superfluous stock of the more advanced countries.
They thus serve the same nationalistic aims as the elevation of genres.

Before Addison published his first critical essay on "Chevy-Chase" he preceded it with an adulatory essay on the Royal Exchange. It began: "There is no Place in the Town which I so much love to frequent as the *Royal-Exchange*" (No. 69). The term "exchange" referred to supposedly fair and equitable trading transactions, and the "exchange" was the place in which transactions involving distant countries were arranged by merchants who remained at home. Addison praised the nationalistic extension of Britain's economic power, the harmony of private and public interest between his own more advanced country and those less advanced. Merchants bring into their own country whatever is wanting and carry out whatever is superfluous. "Nature," he wrote, "seems to have taken a particular Care to disseminate her Blessings among the different Regions of the World, with an Eye to this mutual Intercourse and Traffick among Mankind, that the Natives of the several Parts of the Globe might have a kind of Dependance upon one another, and be united together by their common Interest" (No. 69).

Addison described commercial behavior in the imagery of moral and political benevolence; he used the language of commercial reciprocity to invoke a harmony between distant wealthy nations, between Britons and "Mohametans," Britons and "Inhabitants of the frozen Zone." He touted the merchant as one of the most useful members "in a Commonwealth," although previously merchants like Shakespeare's merchant of Venice were aristocrats, not commoners. The "mutual intercourse" that Addison referred to was not found in any one Nation:

> If we consider our own Country in its natural Prospect, without any of the Benefits and Advantages of Commerce, what a barren uncomfortable Spot of Earth falls to our Share! ... Nature indeed furnishes us with the bare Necessaries of Life, but Traffick gives us greater Variety of what is Useful, and at the same time supplies us with every thing that is Convenient and Ornamental. Nor is it the least part of this our Happiness, that whilst we enjoy the remotest Products of the North and South, we are free from those Extremities of Weather which give them Birth. (No. 69)

The argument that countries are insufficient for themselves forms the justification for establishing relations with others; it also provides justification for exploitation under the guise of necessary and desirable harmony for the countries involved. If native countries do not share the Christian religious view of universal harmony, it is apparent that they lack the civilizing awareness that they need. Christian societies thus needed to overcome whatever political, military, or religious barriers that resisted their civilizing process. Thus the *Aeneid* constituted a model for overcoming a primitive people. "Chevy-Chase" is the sad but noble model of Christian England at war with Christian Scotland, but it led to the peace and harmony that was earned through bloodshed.

GENERIC REVERSION AND THE RESISTANCE
TO BALLAD ELEVATION

The ballad genre did not exist in classical writings and Addison's attempt to elevate its status was twofold: to appeal to its durability among its audience (the common people) and to show by illustration that particular ballads met the recognized standards of criticism for established genres. The audience that he addressed were the readers of *The Spectator*, and to these he apologized for his frequent quotations (in the "Chevy-Chase" papers) from the Latin: "I shall only beg Pardon for such a Profusion of *Latin* Quotations; which I should not have made use of, but that I feared my own Judgement would have looked too singular on such a Subject, had not I supported it by the Practice and Authority of *Virgil*" (No. 74). Addison did not discuss the song-character of the ballads, but he placed his two examples within the genre that he practiced— the short periodical paper. He argued that these poems, despite their lack of classical precedent, nevertheless possessed qualities found in the *Aeneid* and in Horace's *Odes*. The rejection of Addison's criticism occurred almost at once. The rejection took two forms—one critical and one parodical. The first attacked his claim that "Chevy-Chase" met the requirements of an epic poem. The second ridiculed by means of parody the claims for elevation.

Soon after the publication of the papers on "Chevy-Chase," "H-C Esq." inquired of John Dennis if the periodical papers were intended as a jest or as serious criticism.[2] In a letter obviously intended for publication, Dennis replied satirically: "His Design is to see how far he can lead his Reader by the Nose."[3] Hooker believes that Dennis assumed the essays were written by Steele with whom he was at the time feuding, and this accounted for the hostility of his analysis. But what is of significance for generic study is Dennis's criticism itself.

His letter, though written in 1711, was not published until 1721, but it belonged with the short form that characterized the periodical paper. It was an instance of criticism—actually, criticism of a criticism—rather than a criticism of a poem as was Addison's. Despite Dennis's attack on Addison's attempt to treat "Chevy-Chase" in sophisticated terms, he shared with Addison a rejection of the Gothic manner of writing and a belief in noble simplicity. Addison argued "that the Sentiments in that Ballad ['Chevy-Chase'] are extremely natural and poetical, and full of the majestick Simplicity which we admire in the greatest of the ancient Poets" (1: 74). And he remarked that there were passages in which the poet, like Virgil, was directed "in general by the same Kind of Poetical Genius, and by the same Copyings after Nature" (1: 74). Dennis wrote:

> As for Simplicity, of which the Spectator boasts so much, the foresaid *Rapin* has remarkably told us, in his Twenty Seventh Reflection, that the Simplicity of Thought and even Simplicity of Expression in great Subjects is not incompatible with the greatest Pomp and Magnificence. For Simplicity of Thought and Simplicity of Expression is nothing but such Thought and such Expression, as Nature in such and such Cases voluntarily suggests and dictates to us. (2: 35–36)

Dennis did not disagree with Addison about majestic simplicity. But he felt it necessary to indicate that Addison was not original in his remarks. What he did disagree about was whether "Chevy-Chase" provided an example of it. The ballad, he declared, had some of the qualities that Addison attributed to it. Dennis wrote: "Now tho' the Subject of that Song is noble, yet there being nothing figurative in it, 'tis plain by consequence that there is nothing great, nothing noble in it; no Magnificence, no Vehemence, no Painting, no Poetry. To compare any of the Passages in it to *Virgil* is ridiculous" (1: 37). Dennis then quoted a passage about which Addison had written: "What can be more sounding and poetical, resemble more the majestick Simplicity of the Ancients, than the following Stanzas?" (1: 74):

> *The Hounds ran swiftly thro' the Woods*
> *The nimble Deer to take,*
> *And with their Cries the Hills and Dales*
> *An Eccho shrill did make.*

Vocat ingenti Clamore Cithaeron
Taygetique canes, Domitrixque Epidaurus equorum:
Et vox assensu nemorum ingeminata remugit.
Georgics, III, 43–45

Of these lines Dennis declared, "What is there in the first but what is vile and trivial? What Ploughman, what Tinker, what Trull is not capable of saying the like? But that of *Virgil,* where he gives Voice to the Mountains, and Voice, Consent and Soul to the Words, is so bold, so figurative, so pompous, so harmonious, that a Man must be *Virgil* himself to say it" (2: 37). Dennis's attack is on the absence of figurative language. The ballad's lines could be written by any ploughman, tinker, or trull. For him the reader's common language was unfit for poetry. It lacked the figures, passion, and moral quality of poetry. (Hooker, Dennis's sympathetic and reliable editor, believes that Dennis "despised" ballads.)

The dismissal of ballads as instances of the genre poetry raises the question of genre naming. If ballads are not poetry, they must be members of some other genre, namely, songs. But is there any way of mediating between critics who disagree about the genre of a group of texts? Addison argued that common readers could judge what poetry was unless their tastes had been corrupted. And their judgments were reliable because human nature was everywhere the same; thus common judgment that approved of ballads was an adequate basis for approval. Dennis did not argue about the universality of human nature; he argued that criticism required knowledge to determine the artistry of poetry. Poetry was composed by learned and inspired artists and criticism had to possess learning in order to interpret poetry.

In one sense Addison was arguing that the responses of readers indicated that ballads were poetry. But in another sense, he set out to match these responses with the analyses provided by major critics of his time. The learning he displayed in this task was unpersuasive to Dennis and others. But the point Addison was making was that unlearned responses were nevertheless supported by learning. He was thus urging that the lowly ballad was governed by nature—by the most sophisticated critical tests. His claims for "Chevy-Chase" as epic were exaggerated, but his claim was not to be denied.

The issue between Addison and Dennis is not merely an issue of literary criticism. It is a disagreement about the nature of genre. Dennis's conception of poetry as a genre is holistic. Poetry is moral, figurative, and learned.

It is not subject to interrelation with other genres. It is not subject to historical change that would lessen or increase the exclusivity of its genre. It serves, therefore, to support an absolutistic separation within a hierarchy not subject to change. Dennis rejects Addison's view of genre as composite, a view that permits him to argue that though there may not be figures or sophisticated diction in a poem, its sentiments may move the reader and it is the reader's response that determines the effectiveness of a poem. However limited Addison's argument may be—his argument for the value of the ballad as poetry—it is based on the assumption that poems as material objects interact with the moral and aesthetic aspects of people's lives. Dennis's insistence that the reading of poetry requires learning and that without such learning it cannot be properly appreciated posits exclusivity as a value. It is not necessary to argue that such a view of genre supports a social view that resists change. Addison's argument for the elevation of ballads is based on a generic approach that makes it possible for some features of the ballad to relate to those of received forms, thus urging an interrelation that undermines a rigidity of genre.

That more than these conceptions of genre was implied in the writings of Addison's contemporaries is obvious when applied to the interpretation of ballads. In contrast to Dennis's conception of exclusivity, there was the argument of inclusiveness. In the "Preface" to his collection of ballads published in London in 1723, Ambrose Philips identifies the *Iliad* and the *Odyssey* as ballads sung by Homer: "somebody thought fit to collect all his Ballads, and by a little connecting 'em, gave us the *Iliad* and *Odyssey*."[4] Virgil, Anacreon, Horace, Pindar are all considered ballad makers; even Cowley, whom Addison used as a vicious poetic model, is included. The attempt to elevate ballads by identifying their composition with the works of ancients confused orality with ballad making. Philips argued for the importance of ballads as stimulus for the writing of history: "several fine Historians are indebted to *Historical Ballads* for all their Learning. For had not Curiosity, and a Desire of comparing these Poetical Works with ancient Records, first incited them to it, they never would have given themselves the Trouble of diving into History" (vii).

Philips claimed that historical ballads, like "Chevy-Chase," stimulated the curiosity of historians to undertake research to verify the historical references. What was ancillary in one genre became primary in another. Philips did not pursue this inquiry, although it seems he had reference to inquiries into Greek history resulting from the readings of the *Iliad* and *Odyssey*. But he did touch on generic problems that became important in the eighteenth century; was poetry that made reference to history to be judged on its factual accuracy? And were anonymous poems like ballads authentic examples of "natural" and sophisticated art or naïve and simple-minded compositions?

PARODY: THE RIDICULE OF ADDISON'S BALLAD CRITICISM

Parody is the imitation of a generic practice in order to ridicule it; it includes discourses from the target text in order to undermine them. The key example of anti-Addisonian parody was William Wagstaffe's essay *A Comment upon the History of Tom Thumb* published in 1711.[5] William K. Wimsatt Jr. noted that it appeared "perhaps within a week or two of the third guilty *Spectator* (June 7) [No. 85]."[6]

In the prefatory biography of William Wagstaffe in *Miscellaneous Works of Dr. William Wagstaffe*, the anonymous author declares that the aim of the "Chevy-Chase" parody "was to evince that a Man of quick Parts and ready Wit might sometimes extend his Thoughts on Criticism too far; and if Men of Learning were once to give into that way of Writing, they might indeed please some Persons of a vulgar and superficial Taste; but the graver part of Mankind, and those of sounder Judgment, would be apt to think they might have imployed their Talents after a more useful and instructive manner" (xi–xii).

The actual title of the Tom Thumb ballad was "Tom Thumbe, His Life and Death: Wherein is declared many Maruailous Acts of Manhood, full of wonder, and strange merriments, Which little Knight liued in King *Arthurs* time, and famous in the Court of *Great Brittaine*."[7] "Begot and borne in halfe an houre" through Merlin's magic, named after the size of a thumb, Tom undergoes a series of childish adventures, is swallowed and regurgitated first by a cow, then by a giant, and finally becomes a hero at King Arthur's court. It is a ballad of heroic elevation of a figure lowly born and of minuscule size who becomes a hero. Tom Thumb has elements of a fairy tale at its beginning and end; although he is swallowed, he creates such discomfort in the stomachs of the cow and the giant that he is dis-gorged by them. The giant spew him into the sea where he is caught by a fish which eventually is caught and sent to King Arthur.

> Which lusty fish was after caught
> and to king Arthur sent,
> Where Tom was found, and made his dwarfe,

whereas his dayes he spent,
Long time in lively iollity,
belou'd of all the court,
And none like Tom was then esteem'd
among the noble sort.   (176–183)

"Tom Thumb" is a fairy ballad and the commentary ridicules the generic blindness that treats it as historical fact: "There is another Matter which deserves to be clear'd, whether this is a Fiction, or whether there was really such a Person as *Tom Thumb*. As to this, my Friends tell me, 'Twas Matter of Fact" (8). Wagstaffe develops his parody by treating the ballad as an example of "natural" art requiring maturity of judgment. The narrator remarks that

> however it may have been ridicul'd, and look'd upon as an Entertainment only for Children, and those of younger Years, [it] may be found perhaps a Performance not unworthy the Perusal of the Judicious, and the Model superiour to either of those incomparable Poems of *Chevy Chase*, or *The Children in the Wood*. The Design was undoubtedly to recommend Virtue, and to shew that however any one may labour under the Disadvantages of Stature or Deformity, or the Meanness of Parentage, yet if his Mind and Actions are above the ordinary Level, those very Disadvantages that seem to depress him, shall add a Lustre to his Character. (5–6)

The procedure is to treat a fairy story as a natural narrative and to do so with assurance: "The Design was undoubtedly to recommend Virtue." The irrelevance of virtue to being regurgitated is to treat Addison's criticism as generically inappropriate. The interpretation of mind and action as "above the ordinary Level" is to interpret the marvelous as natural. Parody seeks to keep genre practice to its received conventions.

The selection of "Tom Thumb" for parody rests not merely on the ridicule of heroic claims of diminutive stature and common class, but also on elevated moral pretensions. The disproportion that is here used to ridicule criticism of ballads was connected with the mock-heroic genres used by Pope and Swift, Gay and Garth, in their ridicule of political and social behavior in court, courtship, criticism, and commerce. The genres of parody, satire, and mock-heroic could easily include procedures from each other. Thus it was not surprising that Wagstaffe's "Comment" should begin with an ironic praise of artistic discovery—the recognition of newly retrieved texts that had been long buried: "Indeed we have had an

Enterprising Genius [Addison] of late, that has thought fit to disclose the Beauties of some Pieces to the World, that might have been otherwise indiscernable [sic], and believ'd to have been trifling and insipid, for no other Reason but their unpolish'd Homeliness of Dress" (4).

Generically, Wagstaffe uses the procedure of the parody to imitate the historical claims of ballad criticism by speculating that its author is probably "the most ancient of our Poets" (7). Spurious historical claims are converted into facts and cautions are given about the need for knowledge in using "authentic" editions of the text. The procedure of quoting from Addison's essays and following his comparisons of the ballad with fragmentary references from well-known Latin poems are more than imitations; the parody is self-evidently a construction.

Parody as a genre is intertextually intertwined with satire; both are examples of varieties of incident that form a composite structure: "There are Variety of Incidents, dispers'd thro' the whole Series of this Historical Poem, that give an agreeable Delight and Surprise" (6). The parody involves ridiculing historical inferences from unreliable linguistic usages and notes. One of the most parodic examples is based on Wagstaffe's ridicule of the materiality of artistic production. He finds the attempt to situate an author in the process of composition as totally irrelevant to the accomplished text. Wagstaffe did not entertain the possibility that generic selection—like his own parody—is intertwined with material circumstances, although he came from a family that were supporters of King Charles.

Parody, because of its relation to its target text, is a member of the genre it is ridiculing. Parody of Addison's practice in "Chevy-Chase" needs to be understood as an example of literary criticism, but its criticism is comically exaggerated so that it also becomes a member of the comic genre—parody. The generic procedure is to undermine a practice that is considered malpractice. Parody implies that the social function of the target text has been perverted. The implicit claim of the parody is that the hierarchical difference between a childish ballad and a sophisticated epic has been erased. Parody implies that a generic practice undermines the received practice of a genre; it thus becomes a different genre from what it deconstructs.

Wagstaffe parodies certain material assumptions by reference to their genres. He remarks on the practice of commentatory verses preceding the text claiming that they were written by another in praise of his accomplishment, "but my Bookseller told me the Trick was so common, 'twould not answer. Then I propos'd a Dedication to my Lord *such an One*, or Sir *Thomas such an One*; but he told me the Stock to be rais'd on Dedications was so small now a Days, and the Discount to my Lord's Gentleman, etc. so high, that 'twould not be worth while" (35). The direct financial advantage connected with particular genres is obvious, as was the connivance of author and publisher.

But there are other material relations in the writing of criticism that Wagstaffe satirizes. One refers to criticism in which the situation of the writer is considered pertinent to the kind of writing that follows from it. The plan and subject of composition are interrelated in such criticism. Wagstaffe ridicules these critical procedures because they claim to discover meanings that are irrelevant to the meaning or not even conceived by the original authors:

> And certainly, a Critick ought not only to know what his Author's Thoughts were, when he was Writing such and such Passages, but how those Thoughts came into his Head, where he was when he wrote, or what he was doing of; whether he wrote in a Garden, a Garret, or a Coach; upon a Lady, or a Milkmaid; whether at that Time he was scratching his Elbow, drinking a Bottle, or playing at Questions and Commands. These are material and important Circumstances so well known to the *True Commentator*, that were *Virgil* and *Horace* to revisit the World at this time, they'd be wonderfully surpris'd to see the minutest of their Perfections discover'd by the Assistances of *Modern Criticism*. [32–33]

"Modern criticism" in 1711 is not unrelated to postmodern criticism of 1995. Contemporary criticism that argues for situation-based art insists, as Addison did, on the materialist basis of artistic construction. Wagstaffe's parody represents the traditional view that the received genres uphold the moral values of court and country. Addison may represent middle-class values rather than aristocratic authority, but his writings on genre are more radical than the conventional essays in which postmodern critics denigrate it. Here, again, the nature of the genre in which he wrote cannot be overlooked in evaluating his contribution to eighteenth-century thought.

In concluding his "Comment" on Tom Thumb, the narrator becomes autobiographical. The formal critic is replaced by a grub street hack: "I was persuaded by a Friend to write some Copies of Verses, and place them in the Frontispiece of this Poem, in Commendation of my self and my

Comment, suppos'd to be compos'd by AG. FT. LM. RW. and so forth. *To their very worthy and honour'd Friend* C.D. upon his admirable and useful *Comment* on the History of *Tom Thumb*; but my Bookseller told me the Trick was so common, 'twould not answer" (35).

The parody moves from its ridicule of Addison's practice to a satire on the parodist. From being a parody of malpractice, it becomes a satire on the author himself. The genres parody and literary criticism are seen as the hack works of a writer interested in the financial gain of his work, not in the principles of criticism he wishes to defend. In this respect, the economic basis for writing indicates the corruption of the enterprise. What was moral irony, a parody of malpractice, becomes in the end an example of the treachery of writing. What appeared as authentic literary criticism and parody of false values concludes with a statement about how best to profit from writing.

In deriding the hack and in a bitter statement about the material basis of composition, the bookseller explains that most money can be made by treason or heresy which will lead to censure and burning by the common hangman. Such writing will prove much more profitable than either the "Comment" or Addison's ballad criticism. Not moral but immoral writing is profitable—and immoral in attacking state and church. Not malpractice but treason and heresy. The consequence is that genre is irrelevant when one's life is irrelevant: "But if, continues my Bookseller, you have a Mind it shou'd turn to Advantage, write Treason or Heresy, get censur'd by the Parliament or Convocation, and condemn'd to be burnt by the Hands of the common Hangman, and you can't fail having a Multitude of Readers, by the same Reason, *A notorious Rogue has such a Number of Followers to the Gallows*" (35–36).

NOTES

1. Addison, Joseph, and Richard Steele, *The Spectator*, ed. Donald F. Bond, 5 vols. (Oxford: Clarendon Press, 1965), 4: No. 529. Donald Bond notes that Peter Motteux had a similar passage in the *Gentleman's Journal*, Feb. 1692/3, pp. 37–38 (footnote 3 of *Spectator* 529).
2. E. N. Hooker identifies the correspondent, "H—C—Esq," as Henry Cromwell.
3. John Dennis, "To H—C—Esq; Of Simplicity in Poetical Compositions, in Remarks on the 70th *Spectator*," in *The Critical Works of John Dennis*, ed. Edward Niles Hooker, 2 vols. (Baltimore: Johns Hopkins Univ. Press, 1943), 2:29; hereafter cited in text.

4. Ambrose Philips, "The Preface," *A Collection of Old Ballads*, 3 vols. (London: Printed for J. Roberts, 1723), 1:iii–iv. The full title is: "A Collection of Old Ballads. Corrected from the best and most Ancient Copies Extant. With Introductions Historical and Critical, or Humorous."
5. William Wagstaffe, *A Comment upon the History of Tom Thumb*, in *Miscellaneous Works of Dr. William Wagstaffe*, 2nd ed. (London: Printed for Jonah Bowyer, 1726); hereafter cited in text.
6. William K. Wimsatt Jr., *Parodies of Ballad Criticism (1711–1787): William Wagstaffe, A Comment Upon the History of Tom Thumb, 1711; George Canning, The Knave of Hearts, 1787* (Berkeley: Univ. of California Press, William Andrews Clark Memorial Library, 1957), iv.
7. "Tom Thumbe, His Life and Death" (London: Printed for John Wright, 1630) in *Remains of the Early Popular Poetry of England*, collected and edited, W. Carew Hazlitt, 4 vols. (London: John Russell Smith, 1866), 2:175–92.

From Ballad to Tragedy: The Processes of Generic Conversion in *The London Merchant*

THE DILEMMA OF GENERIC CONVERSION

The conversion of the ballad of George Barnwell into a tragedy posed a serious artistic dilemma. The genre of the ballad was a poem that was a confession, a criminal narrative that combined moral statements, dialogue, and description. It dealt with two characters: a lowly apprentice and an avaricious harlot. Tragedy, as George Lillo identified it, dealt with characters who were of the highest class and who were involved in affairs of state. The dilemma was to keep the plot of the ballad without creating a tragedy that parodied the genre.

Lillo sought to accomplish this by several procedures that would make it appropriate for tragedy. The apprentice was given a master, the merchant Thorowgood, who was involved in affairs of state and who expressed the moral values of love of country and of commerce. The apprentice is thus trained in these values. Millwood the harlot is made into an intelligent woman who, as a result of having been seduced and discarded, is a woman warrior. Although still avaricious, she seeks revenge against men. She victimizes the innocent because she has been victimized, and she identifies herself as the enemy of the state. Thus from being an avaricious whore she becomes a vengeful misanthrope.

These changes make it possible for the ballad to be the subject of tragedy, but tragedy was written in blank verse or rhymed verse. Lillo wrote

R. Cohen, J. L. Rowlett, *Transformations of a Genre*, Palgrave Studies in the Enlightenment, Romanticism and Cultures of Print, https://doi.org/10.1007/978-3-030-89668-3_6

The London Merchant in prose but with some lines, usually at the end of an act, in couplets. By this tactic he indicated that he was altering "tragedy" by extending its discourse without abandoning an awareness of its received expectations. It also kept alive the relation to the ballad as poetry, adding however the everyday prose of common people. Nevertheless, in components like the soliloquy of the scenes of repentance, the diction rose to the level of blank verse.

In accommodating the ballad to tragedy Lillo had to increase the number of characters. The ballad, when it had dialogue, was limited to exchanges of Barnwell and Millwood. Tragedy dealt with the primary actors and members of their retinue. Lillo made Barnwell a member of the merchant's "family," which included the merchant's daughter Maria and another dutiful apprentice, Trueman. Millwood was given two accomplices, her maid Lucy and her servant Blunt. Thus the play deals with two moral groups which represent antithetical moral attitudes toward the state and the individual.

It is the combinatoriness of the Barnwell ballad that provides a dilemma. In the ballad, Millwood betrays Barnwell to the constables. He in turn betrays her to the mayor and his master. This instance of mutual betrayal is an example of generic criminal behavior: the informing upon another in order to save oneself. Millwood is tried and convicted but Barnwell escapes to Poland. Tragedy, as Lillo received it, required punishment not escape. Lillo revised the ending so that Barnwell does not betray Millwood or give evidence against her. Rather, he confesses and repents and goes to his death with a belief in God's mercy. Millwood, however, is in despair, loathing life but afraid to die.

The conversion of an early seventeenth-century ballad into an eighteenth-century tragedy leads Lillo to place his tragedy in the time of Queen Elizabeth. But the moral didacticism of the play inappropriately uses the didacticism of the ballad for a tragedy of the same time. The result is that the genres of eighteenth-century criminal narratives fit more closely the concept of tragedy in *The London Merchant* than do the tragedies of Shakespeare, Marlowe, or their contemporaries.

The conclusion of the tragedy was not a conversion of the ballad, but a construction of new events. The redemptive conclusion connected tragedy not only to the criminal biography but to the sermon. As Lillo explained in the "Dedication," he wanted to demonstrate that tragedy could support the lawfulness of the stage. The final act, therefore, which included the redemptive genre, altered the nature of tragedy. Thus the combinatory characteristics of Lillo's tragedy altered the genre of tragedy, as Lillo himself explained.

The dilemma of generic conversion arises for a writer as a result of the different constituents of the genres involved. An early seventeenth-century criminal ballad contains discourses unfit for an eighteenth-century tragedy. The selectivity of the author in choosing to convert constituents of the ballad is interconnected with the audience one seeks to influence by moving or persuading them. The dilemma that this phenomenon presents is the contradictory possibilities such fusion creates.

In altering the nature of tragedy by adding characters and scenes and altering the constituents of the genres involved, the continuity of the ballad's plot no longer has consistent implications. Any continuity of the didactic injunction to avoid lewd women becomes futile when one cannot tell a lewd from a virtuous woman. And a ballad that dealt with the seduction of a young man through his pleasures in sexuality is altered in the tragedy when his love genuinely goes beyond sexuality. Generally, the constituents of the ballad get reinterpreted in the combinatory characteristics of a tragedy. Tragedy, on the other hand, undergoes transformation as a result of the alteration of its characters as they conform to constituents of the genre such as soliloquy, affairs of state, the passion of true love, and the comfort of divine mercy.

Prefatory Genres: The Prologue, the "Dedication," and "Dramatic Personae"

Although the "Dedication" of *The London Merchant* preceded the "Prologue" in the publication of the tragedy in 1731, the performance of the play in the summer of 1731 had no such introductory genre. Dedications only appear in published texts, not in performances. As genres, they embrace patronage by flattering the patron, embellishing his or her abilities as models of art and virtue. Lillo's play was published soon after its successful opening at the Theatre-Royal, and the author dedicated it "To Sir John Eyles, Bar. Member of Parliament for, and Alderman of the City of *London*, and Sub-Governor of the *South-Sea* Company."[1]

Swift, in *A Tale of a Tub* (1704), had ridiculed the self-serving of prefatory genres and Wagstaffe had continued the ridicule, associating the practice with the malpractice of ballad criticism. Lillo's "Dedication," although avoiding egregious flattery, did not completely avoid it. Most of the "Dedication" is devoted to an explanation and justification of Lillo's view of tragedy as presented in *The London Merchant*. His "Dedication," in addition to including panegyrical discourse, was also an exercise in literary criticism.

Although a member of the conventional genre known as "Dedication," the discourse was being altered to relate directly to the text of *The London Merchant* under consideration. That text opened with England under Queen Elizabeth threatened by a potential war with Spain. The throne appealed to the merchants of London to try to prevent the Italian bankers from giving Spain a loan that would have led to war. The merchants persuaded the Italians to break their contract with the Spaniards. Sir John Eyles had been appointed Sub-Governor of the South-Sea Company "at a Time when their Affairs were in the utmost Confusion, and their Properties in the greatest Danger" (ix). He too helped restore faith in commercial enterprises.

There were, moreover, numerous other interrelations between the "Dedication" and the specific tragedy to which it was appended and to the "Prologue" which followed it in the text. The "Dedication" sought to revise the value of tragedy by identifying this in purely utilitarian terms: "the more extensively useful the Moral of any Tragedy is, the more excellent that Piece must be of its Kind" (iii). The implications of this value hypothesis paralleled Addison's justification of ballad value: ballads were valuable because masses of people—the rabble and others—were moved by them. Lillo altered the ends of tragedy so that its utilitarian aspect would be morally appropriate to and in the service of the commonwealth. He defined the end of tragedy as "the exciting of the Passions, in order to the correcting such of them as are criminal, either in their Nature, or through their Excess" (iv).

The London Merchant was based on the ballad of George Barnwell; it was, therefore, a play based on criminal passions and behavior. What Lillo needed to do, if he was to make a case for a new kind of tragedy, was to justify making the chief protagonists a young apprentice and an experienced whore; he had to justify the use of characters from everyday life in tragedy. To do so he argued that dealing with the circumstances of the generality of mankind was more pertinent to move people than the misfortunes of those drawn from those of "superior Rank" (v). He declared: "Plays, founded on moral Tales in private Life, may be of admirable Use, by carrying Conviction to the Mind, with such irresistible Force, as to engage all the Faculties and Powers of the Soul in the Cause of Virtue, by stifling Vice in its first Principles" (vi).

There is, unfortunately, no basis for determining whether *The London Merchant* stifled vice in those who viewed it. Lillo quotes Hamlet "The Play's the Thing,/Wherein I'll catch the Conscience of the King" as support for his belief that tragedies expose and thus control criminal tendencies. Lillo writes, "Such Plays are the best Answers to them who deny the Lawfulness of the Stage" (viii). The concept of the "Dedication" is to persuade those who argue for the immorality of the stage that tales of private woe serve the very moral values for which they argue. *The London Merchant* was the test case: "Considering the Novelty of this Attempt, I thought it would be expected from me to say something in its Excuse; and I was unwilling to lose the Opportunity of saying something of the Usefulness of Tragedy in general, and what may be reasonably expected from the farther Improvement of this excellent Kind of Poetry" (viii).

The "Dedication" as a genre was based on the need for patronage, and Aaron Hill, in his "Dedication" to *The Fatal Extravagance*, wrote that "'tis both natural and necessary, for Poets, to court the favour of the great." Lillo, though still courting the favor of Sir John Eyles, nevertheless provided a literary theory as part of the "Dedication." He altered the genre by introducing into it a discussion of literary theory. It represented one of the future directions of prefatory genres once patronage ceased to be "natural" and "necessary." The "Dedication" was replaced by the "Introduction" or "Preface" or "Foreword" that served as combinations of autobiography, literary theory, summary of contents, and other associated genres.

The procedures by which the "Dedication" was undermined involved the development of author's rights and the cessation of patronage. But Lillo's "Dedication" indicated a generic procedure by which the praise of the patron was not overlooked. It did, however, make it a minor part of the genre. Lillo's procedure here was characteristic of his desire to alter the character and end of tragedy. By adding discourses not previously part of the genre, he changed the construction of the genre. The "Prologue," however, as an introduction to the performance, sought to assure the audience that what they were to see had support from some of the most eminent Restoration dramatists and from the moving reception of the ballad for the past hundred years.

The "Prologue" and "Epilogue" were identified with dramatic performances and were often composed by writers other than the author. They thus served to indicate the combinatory nature of the performance and the text. Other genres like periodical papers, poems, and the novel were also combinatory forms indicating the collaborative professional enterprise of writing and performing. Ballads were inevitably part of this collaborative generic enterprise since their texts underwent oral changes in the performance. Thus it was not unusual that Lillo composed the "Prologue" and that Colley Cibber, whose daughter-in-law played Maria, composed the "Epilogue." The unusual aspect of the tragedy was not that the "Prologue" was composed in heroic couplets but that the play was predominantly in prose.

Although the "Dedication" insisted on the "novelty" of this tragedy based on private life, the "Prologue" that was spoken at the performance sought to minimize the novelty. Lillo acknowledged that although tragedy formerly dealt with "Scenes of Royal Woe," there were some playwrights who dealt with humbler situations.

> Upon our Stage indeed, with wish'd Success,
> You've sometimes seen her in a humbler Dress;
> Great only in Distress. When she complains
> In Southerne's, Rowe's, or Otway's moving Strains.
> The Brillant Drops, that fall from each bright Eye,
> The absent Pomp, with brighter Jems, supply.   (13–18)

Is the listing called "Dramatis Personae" a genre? As a list it appears to be a component of drama, but not itself a genre. But it we consider the listing as a genre like the "Dedication" or the "Prologue," it can be understood as a system. In the first edition of *The London Merchant* the "Dramatis Personae" was placed after the "Prologue" and directly before Act I, Scene i. It was divided into two parts, the first entitled "Men" and below them "Women." After "Women" it added "Officers with their Attendants, Keeper, and Footmen." Below that "SCENE London, and an adjacent Village."

The procedure under "Men" and "Women" was to list the character alongside the name of the actor playing the part; for example, "Thorowgood,—Mr. Bridgwater"; "Millwood,—Mrs. Butler." Not only did the listing suggest a hierarchy, but it distinguished between imaginary persons of the tragedy and the actual persons who were assuming roles.

In twentieth-century versions of the "Dramatis Personae," A. W. Ward (1906) reprints the cast listed in the first edition, but appends in brackets "[Jailer. John]." In the edition of the play published in *Understanding Drama* by Cleanth Brooks and Robert B. Heilman in 1946, the "Dramatis Personae" lists only the characters in the play and it does not divide them

into "Men" and "Women," nor does it include the "Dedication."
Moreover, the "Dramatis Personae" precedes the "Prologue" whereas in
the original version the listing followed both the "Dedication" and the
"Prologue." In the most comprehensive edition, that of 1965, edited by
William McBurney, the "Dramatis Personae" follows the "Dedication"
but precedes the "Prologue." McBurney retains the listing of "Men" and
"Women," but puts the actors of the first performance in a note and adds
an identifying description for each character. And because he includes the
addition of the final scene from the fifth edition, he adds the character of
"Executioner."

The manner of listing the members of the cast and the characters they
play makes perfectly clear the distinction between the parts that actors play
and their real existence. It also serves to advertise the participants in a
profession. Members of the audience interested in seeing the Cibber family would be able to know them as members of a company. Placing the
"Dramatis Personae" after the "Dedication" and "Prologue" made it part
of the text and thus a component of the drama. In performance, the
"Dramatis Personae" was followed immediately by "Act I, Scene i."
Omitting the names of the actors indicates that one is providing a reading
text; the name of actors such as Garrick or Mrs. Siddons would indicate
particular acting techniques and interpretive approaches associated with
them. When these are omitted, the list becomes merely a component, not
a genre, just as the omission of the "Dedication" denies access to the kind
of interpretation and generic alteration of this genre and of tragedy that is
essential for an understanding of Lillo's self-conscious revision of the
nature of tragedy.

When the listing precedes the "Prologue" but follows the "Dedication,"
it indicates that the "Prologue" is part of the genre of tragedy (as well as
a genre of its own). The listing of the cast separates what is considered a
genre that is not involved in the performance of the drama. As part of the
reading text, however, the "Dedication" insists on the connection of the
drama to the social environment of patronage. *The London Merchant*'s
authorial statement of intention relates the play to the society outside the
theater. It becomes for the reader a guide to the reading of the tragedy.

These examples of genre members and their interrelation also indicate
a characteristic of generic change. Within a generic system like that of
"Dedication" or "Prologue," each instance resists, continues, alters, or
adds to components with a genre. In this respect generic continuity can be
understood as an example of transference. Every instance within the same

genre can be seen as transferring some of the same components to the new instance. The nature of the additions can be a resistance to the received components, as in Lillo's "Dedication," or a stereotypical use of generic components, as in his "Prologue." Freud treats the subject of transference in terms of the relation of patient to therapist. So, too, the relation of reader or viewer to a text constitutes a relationship that needs to be studied in terms of transference.

None of the dramatists mentioned in the "Prologue" had composed a prose tragedy with protagonists who were either a whore or a youthful apprentice. Lillo referred to the ballad as the source for his tragedy and correctly identified it as having a history of a hundred years, and he described the responses to it as marked by tears. He was in part seeking to persuade the audience that the ballad had been treated as a tragic song. If the apprentice was seen as a tragic figure in the original poem, he was not in the prose version of 1700.

> Forgive us then, if we attempt to show,
> In artless Strains, a Tale of private Woe.
> A *London* Prentice ruin'd is our Theme,
> Drawn from the fam'd old Song, that bears his Name.
> We hope your Taste is not so high to scorn
> A moral Tale, esteem'd e'er you were born;
> Which for a Century of rolling Years,
> Has fill'd a thousand-thousand Eyes with Tears.   (19–26)

Critics who treat *The London Merchant* as a sentimental play have ample evidence in the "Prologue." But there is no such evidence that this view was present at the original performance. In fact, the reverse seems to have been the case. Theophilus Cibber who produced the play explained that the wits of the town brought the ballad to the play in order to ridicule the performance:

> The old ballad of George Barnwell (on which the story was founded) was on this occasion [the first night] reprinted, and many thousands sold in one day. Many gaily-disposed spirits brought the ballad with them to the play, intending to make their pleasant remarks (as some afterwards owned) and ludicrous comparisons between the antient ditty and the modern drama. ... But the play, in general, spoke so much to the heart, that the gay persons before mentioned confessed, they were drawn in to drop their ballads, and pull out their handkerchiefs.[2]

That handkerchiefs were pulled out—if indeed they were—reveals that the wits' expectations of the ballad were defeated and that the tragedy succeeded in providing a genre that won their approval.

The Social Basis of Generic Conversion

Traditional tragedy, as Lillo noted in the "Dedication" and "Prologue," dealt with affairs of state. He did not wish to abandon this traditional role of tragedy since it related behavior to the moral values of a society. His solution was to make the merchant a significant figure who dealt with state matters. The opening scene of the play is a conversation in which the merchant, Thorowgood, explains to his apprentice Trueman that he and other London merchants have persuaded the Genoese bankers to break their contract with the Spanish court that intended to use the funds to prepare an armada to invade England.

The merchant explains that "honest Merchants, as such, may sometimes contribute to the Safety of their Country, as they do at all times to its Happiness" (I.i). Barnwell is thus included under the moral obligation to the state and to the role of the merchant: "if hereafter you should be tempted to any Action that has the Appearance of Vice or Meanness in it, upon reflecting on the Dignity of our Profession, you may with honest Scorn reject whatever is unworthy of it" (I.i).

To remove the character of Millwood from that of a vulgar, avaricious harlot, Lillo rewrote her as a highly intelligent woman who was seduced when young; as a consequence she regards the male sex as her enemy. In the desire for revenge she sees herself as behaving like the enemy of England in the New World: "I would have my Conquests compleat, like those of the *Spaniards* in the New World; who first plunder'd the Natives of all the Wealth they had, and then condemn'd the Wretches to the Mines for Life to work for more" (I.iii).

Millwood's reference to commerce and colonization represents a view in opposition to the moral value of commercial exchange espoused by Thorowgood. His account of the method of merchandise and its practice claims that it is founded in reason and the nature of things: "it has promoted Humanity, as it has opened and yet keeps up an Intercourse between Nations, far remote from one another in Situation, Customs, and Religion; promoting Arts, Industry, Peace and Plenty; by mutual Benefits diffusing mutual Love from Pole to Pole" (III.i).

The play opens with a scene of instruction. Thorowgood instructs Trueman in the importance of commerce. It establishes the didactic behavior of the merchant and his belief in the mutual love that governs trade. But this genre of instruction is based on an irony; the enmity between Spain and England. The behavior between England and Spain is not one of mutual love, nor is the behavior of the merchant to the Genoese bankers. He and his colleagues persuade the bankers to break the contract they made with the Spanish court. For the safety of England, the merchant's patriotism initiates representations of love that undo the conventional conflict between love and duty in Restoration tragedy. The source ballad has Millwood feign the feeling of love for Barnwell so that he can provide her with money; in the first scene of the play Thorowgood refers to Queen Elizabeth in terms that identify her love for her people as an "Exchequer": her "richest Exchequer is her Peoples Love, as their Happiness her greatest Glory" (I.i).

When Millwood first invites Barnwell to her house, she confronts him with the question: "What then are your Thoughts of Love?" Barnwell replies: "If you mean the Love of Women, I have not thought of it at all.—My Youth and Circumstances make such Thoughts improper in me yet: But if you mean the general Love we owe to Mankind, I think no one has more of it in his Temper than my self.—I don't know that Person in the World whose Happiness I don't wish, and wou'd n't promote, were it in my Power.—In an especial manner I love my Uncle, and my Master, but, above all, my Friend" (I.v).

This is Millwood's scene of instruction and Barnwell's reply. It defines his self-conscious love of human beings and his ignorance of sexual love. It also emphasizes his love for the men in his life: his uncle, his master, and his friend Trueman. Male bonding is what Millwood grants; what she seeks to do is to evoke in Barnwell a love so passionate that it will eclipse all others. Thus it will be through love that he will betray those he loves. Thus he will serve her revenge as well as her economic needs.

Lillo describes in his "Dedication" the end of the tragedy as "the exciting of the Passions, in order to the correcting such of them as are criminal, either in their Nature, or through their Excess" (iv). Millwood, through feigning love for Barnwell, established in him an excess of love that has criminal consequences. In this respect, the excess of love is a form of enthusiasm, a behavior that generically relates to the violent factionalism and viciousness that lead to divisiveness and violence in society. Thus his revision of tragedy makes it into a combinatory genre that reveals the illegality and tragic consequences of excess, even when it applies to love.

Millwood's explanation has no analogy in the ballad, and it identifies the contradictions in a society, especially in the maxims of everyday life. The maxim that a woman without virtue is capable of any action no matter how vile does not reveal that men seek to undo the virtue they claim to admire. As a revenge character, Millwood is aware that she has no other course of action to correct what has been done to her. The aim of Lillo is not to change society, only to prevent people from breaking the law. But as he indicates in the last act, only in heaven are justice and mercy the same.

Millwood's aim is revenge, by doing what men have done to her in the beginning—to feign love for Barnwell, to initiate him into sex, and to make him provide her with money. This involves making him a thief and it thus nourishes her revenge. Her feigned love is thus used as a tactic of corruption. Millwood explains her procedure to Lucy:

> *Mill*: It's a general Maxim among the knowing Part of Mankind, that a Woman without Virtue, like a Man without Honour or Honesty, is capable of any Action, tho' never so vile: And yet what Pains will they not take, what Arts not use, to seduce us from our Innocence, and make us contemptible and wicked, even in their own Opinions? Then is it not just, the Villains, to their Cost, should find us so.— But Guilt makes them suspicious, and keeps them on their Guard; therefore we can take Advantage only of the young and innocent Part of the Sex, who having never injured Women, apprehend no Injury from them. (I.iii)

In making Millwood a revenge character, a victim who becomes a victimizer, the seduction of Barnwell becomes a gender as well as a personal act. Her revenge is directed at all men and Barnwell becomes her victim because he is a tool in that revenge. But the play is not merely a revenge play. It also is about Barnwell's uncontrollable sexuality. In this respect, the imagery of harmonious love expressed in commercial exchange of trade that characterizes Thorowgood's philosophy is called into question by the language and imagery of risk in shipping. It is at the point of submitting to "wild Desire" that Barnwell soliloquizes about the risks that a merchant takes:

> *Barn.* I wou'd not,—yet I must on.
> *Reluctant thus, the Merchant quits his Ease,*
> *And trusts to Rocks, and Sands, and stormy Seas;*
> *In Hopes some unknown golden Coast to find,*
> *Commits himself, tho' doubtful, to the Wind,*
> *Longs much for Joys to come, yet mourns those left behind.*   (I.viii)

The love that now envelops Barnwell is "guilty love" and to it he has added breach of trust and theft. In the process of altering the character of Barnwell as merchant's apprentice, Lillo made him into a youth who believed completely in Millwood's love for him: "She who loves me with such a boundless Passion; can Cruelty be Duty? I judge of what she then must feel, by what I now indure. The love of Life and fear of Shame, oppos'd by Inclination strong as Death or Shame, like Wind and Tide in raging Conflict met, when neither can prevail, keep me in doubt.—How then can I determine?" (II.iii).

The merchant sympathizes with Barnwell's suffering at being absent from home for a night but nevertheless offers him both pardon and love: "If my Pardon or Love be of moment to your Peace, look up secure of both" (II.iv). The love that Maria feels for him without him knowing it results in her restoring the funds that Barnwell stole from her father. Thus love leads her to become an accomplice with Trueman in manipulating the accounts. Implicit in this action is the manner in which true love can lead to criminal acts, no matter how well intended.

It is Maria who repeatedly analyzes her own situation in terms of love and duty. First her responsibility to her father is seen as a duty that she intends to obey even if it pains her to do so. But Barnwell rejects this view of a father. Maria, in musing on love, soliloquizes on the person who is torn by conflicts between love and duty (III.ii). But although the play contains allusions to heroic tragedy, it is a study of the conflict between false and true manifestations of love.

Lillo's definition of tragedy as expressed in the "Dedication" is "the exciting of the Passions, in order to the correcting such of them as are criminal, either in their Nature, or through their Excess." In basing his play upon a ballad which dealt with circumstances that involved ordinary people who became criminals, he did not abandon some of the assumptions that governed contemporary tragedy. He not only returned the relation of tragedy to affairs of state, but had to give his characters motives that would not demean the conflicts in which they were involved.

Barnwell, therefore, could not come to enjoy the lust he felt since he was committed to the values for which the merchant stood. What Lillo does is to make him self-conscious about his criminality but, as a result of its excess, unable to control it. In the scene in which he contemplates the murder of his uncle, he reveals that his uncle served as his father. The murder is thus the destruction of the family, of the impiety that supplants paternal love. When one compares this scene with that in the ballad, the issue of love, of love as vicious and destructive, becomes apparent. The original reads as follows:

> "Nay more than this, an Uncle I have, at *Ludlow* he doth dwell,
> He is a Grazier, which in wealth, doth all the rest excell.
> E're I will live in lack" (quoth he) "And have no coyn for thee,
> I'le rob the churl and murder him!" "Why should you not?" (quoth she).   (147–150)
> ....
> And so carousing in their cups, their pleasure to content,
> *George Barnwell* had in little space his money wholly spent.
> Which being done to *Ludlow* then, he did provide to go,
> To rob his wealthy Uncle then, his Minion would it so: (159–162)
> ....
> Directly to his Uncle then, he rode with might and main,
> Where with good welcome, and good cheer, he did him entertain:
> A Se'nnight's space he stayed there, until it chanced so,
> His Uncle with fat Cattel did unto a Market go.
> His Kinsman needs must ride with him, and when he saw right plain
> Great store of money he had took, in coming home again,
>
> Most suddenly within a Wood, he struck his Uncle down,
> And beat his brains out of his head, so sore he crackt his crown;
> And fourscore pound in ready coyn, out of his Purse he took,
> And coming into *London* strait, the country quite forsook.   (165–174)

In the tragedy, Barnwell soliloquizes before the murder:

the World is punish'd and Nature feels the Shock, when Providence permits a good Man's Fall!—Just Heaven! Then what shou'd I be! for him that was my Father's only Brother, and since his Death has been to me a Father, who took me up an Infant, and an Orphan; rear'd me with tenderest Care, and still indulged me with most paternal Fondness;—yet here I stand avow'd his destin'd Murderer:—I stiffen with Horror at my own Impiety;—'tis yet

unperform'd.—What if I quit my bloody Purpose, and fly the Place! [*Going,
then stops.*]—But whether, oh, whether, shall I fly!—My Master's once
friendly Doors are ever shut against me; and without Money, *Millwood* will
never see me more, and Life is not to be endured without her:— She's got
such firm Possession of my Heart, and governs there with such despotick
Sway;—Aye, there's the Cause of all my Sin and Sorrow:—'Tis more than
Love; 'tis the Fever of the Soul, and Madness of Desire.—In vain does
Nature, Reason, Conscience, all oppose it; the impetuous Passion bears
down all before it, and drives me on to Lust, to Theft, and Murder. (III.v)

The kind of tragedy that Lillo was creating depended on showing that
the noblest feelings, when carried to excess, could become criminal. It was
important that there should be a range of behavior so that the kinds of
"love" that people felt could be distinguished. The Christian concept of
love is identified with Thorowgood's philosophy and practice of trade.
The method of merchandise "is founded in Reason, and the Nature of
Things—… it has promoted Humanity, as it has opened and yet keeps up
an Intercourse between Nations, far remote from one another in Situation,
Customs and Religion; promoting Arts, Industry, Peace and Plenty; by
mutual Benefits diffusing mutual Love from Pole to Pole" (III.i).

Thorowgood explains: "It is the industrious Merchant's Business to
collect the various Blessings of each Soil and Climate, and, with the
Product of the whole, to enrich his native Country" (III.i). The concept
underlying the good merchant's behavior is patriotism that is identified
with "mutual love" referring to the trading partners in the "late found
Western World." Mutual love is thus utilitarian in a social sense. At the
very opening of the play, Thorowgood explains that there is a relation
between the profession of merchant and personal behavior. Speaking to
Trueman, he declares: "if hereafter you should be tempted to any Action
that has the Appearance of Vice or Meanness in it, upon reflecting on the
Dignity of our Profession, you may with honest Scorn reject whatever is
unworthy of it" (I.i).

In *The London Merchant* personal love undermines this professional
credo. The society has used love to seduce and corrupt women and has
thus led to the corruption of the innocent apprentice by a vengeful woman.
The merchant's credo requires the consent of the colonies they exploit in
order for "love" to be "mutual." Millwood, when she is apprehended,
accuses men of creating a society in which self-interest governs behavior.
She accuses men: "Men of all Degrees and all Professions I have known,

yet found no Difference, but in their several Capacities; all were alike wicked to the utmost of their Power. In Pride, Contention, Avarice, Cruelty, and Revenge, the Reverend Priesthood were my unering Guides" (IV.xviii). Thorowgood remarks to her, "What a Pity it is, a Mind so comprehensive, daring and inquisitive, shou'd be a Stranger to Religion's sweet, but powerful Charms" (IV.xviii). But here the play undermines Thorowgood's naïve view of religion. Millwood answers him by saying, "Whatever Religion is in it self, as practic'd by Mankind, it has caus'd the Evils, you say, it was design'd to cure. War, Plague, and Famine, has not destroy'd so many of the human Race, as this pretended Piety has done; and with such barbarous Cruelty, as if the only Way to honour Heaven, were to turn the present World into Hell" (IV.xviii). Thorowgood is for the first and only time in the play made to recognize that his society is not based on mutual love. He replies, "Truth is Truth, tho' from an Enemy and spoke in Malice. You bloody, blind, and superstitious Bigots, how will you answer this?" (IV.xviii).

Lillo's merchant operates within the moral values of the society. He seeks to win the respect of the aristocrats and, if possible, to marry his daughter to one of them. Millwood's attack on religion leads him to suggest to Barnwell in prison a divine whose judgment and integrity he trusts. He is interested in seeing that Barnwell has the opportunity to beg for divine forgiveness. From this divine Barnwell, facing death, declares, "I've learn'd the infinite Extent of heavenly Mercy; that my Offences, tho' great, are not unpardonable; and that 'tis not my Interest only, but my Duty to believe and to rejoice in that Hope,—So shall Heaven receive the Glory, and future Penitents the Profit of my Example" (V.ii).

Millwood's feminist attack on society and Barnwell's redemptive rejoicing are inventions of Lillo. They form part of his construction of tragedy as a Christian genre. The process of conversion that I have been describing can be identified as invention. In order for Millwood to be given tragic dimension, it is necessary that the figures of Thorowgood and Trueman— the possessors of "proper" values—should grant her a mind comprehensive, daring, and inquisitive. She remains, however, unredeemed, unwilling to have the succor of religion. Christian love is not the love she can embrace. In the last act of the play, she is identified as a woman in despair. But in "Scene the Last" in the revised ending of the fifth edition, her last statement as she goes to her death, is "Encompassed with horror, whither must I go? I would not live—nor die! That I could cease to be—or ne'er had been!"[3]

THE FUNCTION OF GENERIC COMPONENTS

Among the processes that mark the conversion into drama are the use of "asides," "acts," "scenes," soliloquies, dialogue, acting or stage directions, and particular conventions that are identified with the writing and performance of comedy, tragedy, tragicomedy, and so on. Some of these belong to the published text such as the "Dedication" and the indication of "scenes." The silent reading of the play and the observation of its performance are two different kinds of genre and generic behavior. Not only does the first permit reversals, repetitions, interruptions, but it does not involve a set time that operates successively and a particular place from which the performance is viewed. It is not necessary to point out that the playhouse invokes a particular scene and stage setting that changes as architecture, costumes, and concept of acting change. The proscenium stage is a genre, as acting, whether modeled after Garrick or Stanislavsky, is a genre. That genres operate within more comprehensive genres is a practice that I have discussed in detail in "Prefatory Genres."

In converting the ballad to a tragedy, Lillo altered some of the first-person confessional statements as spoken by Barnwell to the youths of England to those spoken by Millwood to her maid, a shift from the victim's account of his innocent behavior to that of the victimizer who indicates her manipulation of the victim. Barnwell narrates his polite conversation with Millwood; Millwood treats her conversation as an example of her artful skill in seduction. The ballad states:

> As I upon a day was walking through the street,
> About my master's business, I did a wanton meet:
> A dainty gallant Dame, and sumptuous in attire,
> With smiling looks she greeted me and did my name require.
> Which when I had declar'd, she gave me then a kiss,
> And said, if I would come to her, I should have more than this.
>
> "In faith, my boy," quoth she, "such news I can thee tell,
> As shall rejoice thy very heart, then come where I do dwell."
> "Fair Mistriss," then said I, "If I the place may know,
> This evening I will be with you, for I abroad must go,
> To gather money in, that is my master's due,
> And e're that I do home return, I'le come and visit you."   (7–18)

The play states:

Mill: ... having long had a Design on him; and meeting him Yesterday, I made a full Stop, and gazing wishfully on his Face, ask'd him his Name: He blush'd, and bowing very low, answer'd, *George Barnwell*. I beg'd his Pardon for the Freedom I had taken, and told him, that he was the Person I had long wish'd to see, and to whom I had an Affair of Importance to communicate, at a proper Time and Place. He named a Tavern; I talk'd of Honour and Reputation, and invited him to my House: He swallow'd the Bait, promis'd to come, and this is the Time I expect him, [*knocking at the Door.*] (I.iii)

This scene, which introduces Millwood, has filiations with ironic genre components of Restoration comedy in which characters preen themselves for male visitors. William McBurney draws attention to the humor in Millwood's opening remarks: "Millwood's 'How do I look today, Lucy?' with the reply, 'Oh, killingly, madam! A little more red and you'll be irresistible,' and Millwood's 'Now, after what manner shall I receive him? ... I must take care not to put him out of countenance at first,' must have sounded familiar to those spectators who, a month earlier and in the same theater, had heard Congreve's Lady Wishfort ask the same question of her maids as she deliberated upon the same problem of 'fair reception'" (xix).

The tragedy has scenes that are sublime genres, and these are reserved for the soliloquies of Barnwell and Barnwell's uncle, all of which pertain to religious and moral utterances. These deal, when spoken by Barnwell, with his guilt; his vision of his doom (II.i), and his moral confusion and desperation (II.xiv). His uncle meditates on death and its mysterious power at a time of anxiety (III.vi, III.vii). Maria's sublime moments come when she confesses her hopeless love for Barnwell before he is to die, and sees herself as a living victim.

THE GENRE OF VICTIMIZATION

Lillo sought to enlarge the domain of tragedy. In generic terms he sought to add to tragedy "Plays, founded on moral Tales in private Life" ("Dedication," vi). None of the genre terms that came to be affixed to *The London Merchant*, such as "bourgeois tragedy," "domestic tragedy," or "sentimental tragedy," were used by Lillo. But if we analyze the genres he includes in his revision of the ballad, we may discern the implications of his altered conception of tragedy.

Millwood's exciting of Barnwell's passions that lead to murder causes Lucy and Blunt to turn against their mistress. They become instruments of virtue, having up to this point been accomplices in Millwood's criminal activities. They have been servants who, in their service to their employer, have had no identity in the drama other than economic. Lucy is given the role of narrating to Blunt the melodramatic scene in which Millwood gets Barnwell to agree to murder his uncle. Lucy is not only the messenger, but she becomes the betrayer of her mistress as well.

Lucy: If we don't do our Endeavours to prevent this Murder, we are as bad as she.
Blunt: I'm afraid it is too late.
Lucy: Perhaps not.—Her Barbarity to *Barnwell* makes me hate her.— We've run too great a Length with her already.—I did not think her or my self so wicked, as I find, upon Reflection, we are.
Blunt: 'Tis true, we have all been too much so.—But there is something so horrid in Murder,—that all other Crimes seem nothing when compared to that.—I wou'd not be involv'd in the Guilt of that for all the World.
Lucy: Nor I, Heaven knows; ... Will you join with me to detect this curs'd Design?
Blunt: With all my Heart.—How else shall I clear my self? He who knows of a Murder intended to be committed, and does not discover it, in the Eye of the Law, and Reason, is a Murderer. (III.iv)

Lucy wishes to inform Thorowgood of Barnwell's intentions, but her intervention is too late to prevent the murder. The sudden shift of importance given to Lucy and Blunt is an example of the dilemma resulting from the incapacity to integrate two contrary generic components: Lillo sought to avoid, on the one hand, a violently charged emotional scene that would be difficult to make credible, and on the other, the use of minor characters to serve as messengers. Lucy did, after all, serve as Millwood's accomplice in persuading Barnwell to continue his support of her mistress.

Lucy's betrayal of her mistress comes from an awareness of her wickedness—"I did not think her or my self so wicked, as I find, upon Reflection, we are." But there exists no basis either for our knowing how wicked Lucy is or why she should be so. Nor do we know what reflections she underwent to effect a transformation. Blunt's view seems clearer: he is governed by self-interest. To know of a murder and not to reveal it is to be considered in the eyes of the law a murderer.

These two characters become the friends of Thorowgood. Lucy becomes religious and Blunt sympathetically describes Barnwell's behavior at the trial. Thorowgood calls the "Proselytes to Virtue" and states, "Pursue your proposed Reformation, and know me hereafter for your Friend" (V.i). Yet although they aim to visit Millwood in jail, the confrontation is not in the play, though Thorowgood's visit to Barnwell is. And in the last scene of the play Lucy and Blunt join Trueman and describe to him the "unalterable woe" of Millwood. The last words of the play spoken by Trueman refer to the reformation of Lucy and Blunt:

Tr. In vain.

With bleeding Hearts, and weeping Eyes we show
A human gen'rous Sense of others Woe;
Unless we mark what drew their Ruin on,
And by avoiding that, prevent our own. (V.xi)

If we seek to understand, to "mark" what drew on, what caused the ruin of Barnwell and Millwood, we are confronted with the same question in regard to the turn to virtue of Lucy and Blunt. What shocks them is Millwood's victimization of Barnwell. But Barnwell is not a passive victim; it is his love that permits his victimization. And if we ask why Millwood seeks to make him a victim, it is that she has been made a victim by men. When she is apprehended, she speaks with hatred of her victimization, a hatred that includes men of all degrees and professions:

Tr: Think not by aggravating the Fault of others to extenuate thy own, of which the Abuse of such uncommon Perfections of Mind and Body is not the least.

Mill: If such I had, well may I curse your barbarous Sex, who robb'd me of 'em, e're I knew their Worth, then left me, too late, to count their Value by their Loss. Another and another Spoiler came, and all my Gain was Poverty and Reproach. My Soul disdain'd, and yet disdains, Dependance and Contempt. Riches, no Matter by what Means obtain'd, I saw secur'd the worst of Men from both; I found it therefore necessary to be rich; and, to that End, I summon'd all my Arts. You call 'em wicked, be it

	so, they were such as my Conversation with your Sex had furnish'd me withal.
Thor:	Sure none but the worst of Men convers'd with thee.
Mill:	Men of all Degrees and all Professions I have known, yet found no Difference, but in their several Capacities; all were alike wicked to the utmost of their Power. In Pride, Contention, Avarice, Cruelty, and Revenge, the Reverend Priesthood were my unering Guides. From the Suburb-Magistrates, who live by ruin'd Reputations, as the unhospitable Natives of *Cornwall* do by Ship-wrecks, I learn'd, that to charge my innocent Neighbours with my Crimes, was to merit their Protection; for to skreen the Guilty, is the less scandalous, when many are suspected, and Detraction, like Darkness and Death, blackens all Objects, and levels all Distinction. Such are your venal Magistrates, who favour none but such as, by their Office, they are sworn to punish: With them not to be guilty, is the worst of Crimes; and large Fees privately paid, is every needful Virtue.
Thor:	Your Practice has sufficiently discover'd your Contempt of Laws, both human and divine; no wonder then that you shou'd hate the Officers of both.
Mill:	I hate you all, I know you, and expect no Mercy; nay, I ask for none; I have done nothing that I am sorry for; I follow'd my Inclinations, and that the best of you does every Day. All Actions are alike natural and indifferent to Man and Beast, who devour, or are devour'd, as they meet with others weaker or stronger than themselves. (IV.xviii)

The process of victimization is the result of men who have corrupted the society and seduce women as part of their corruption. Millwood's revenge is thus directed at the uncorrupted, at the innocent, and it is managed by the manipulation of love. The genre that Millwood is describing is the control and manipulating of others by claiming to love them. This is the practice of corruption by the claim of virtue. Even Barnwell's murder of his uncle begins with masking himself, and when, at the last moment, he changes his intention, he stabs him in what is ironically an automatic act of self-defense. As the uncle dies he forgives his murderer, and when Barnwell reveals himself, he kisses him. True love involves forgiveness, not revenge. This is the condition at which Barnwell arrives: repentance and sacrifice—a refusal to accuse his victimizer.

The London Merchant exposes a number of genres that deal with the consequences of genuine love. Maria's repression of her love for Barnwell leads her and Trueman to alter Barnwell's embezzlement so that Thorowgood does not know his apprentice's theft. Their love makes them accomplices in crime. When she confesses her love for Barnwell in prison, she sees herself as a victim. And Trueman, Barnwell's dear friend, becomes an accomplice as a result of his love for Barnwell despite his promise not to sully the name of merchant. Even Thorowgood, in his patriotic love for the state, helps persuade the Genoese bankers to breach their contract with the Spaniards, an illegal act that he justifies by his love of country. Although he argues for the mutual love the commerce creates, it can be interpreted as another example of corruption or empowerment treated as virtue and love. And in his love for Barnwell, he refuses to hear Barnwell's confession because he believes that it would be "not Mercy, but Cruelty, to hear what must give you such Torment to reveal" (II.iv). But this act of generosity, of the merchant's love, comes in conflict with and is defeated by Barnwell's love and generosity to Millwood.

The tragedy is thus not merely a study of the seduction leading to criminality of a merchant's apprentice, but a study of the way in which true love becomes subject to criminal contamination in a corrupt society. The merchant's credo that is offered as a model of behavior persuades his apprentice and his daughter. But his behavior and theirs circumvent the very law that is supposed to apply to all. But Thorowgood does not punish Millwood's accomplices and it is significant that their transformation comes not from love of virtue, but self-interest. And Thorowgood misinterprets their behavior because he believes it proceeds "from a just Abhorrence of her Crimes, free from Interest, Malice, or Revenge" (V.i).

THE GENERIC CONSEQUENCES OF BALLAD CONVERSION

The conversion of the Barnwell ballad into a tragedy moved the song from the streets to a professional theater. It thus gave the plot and characters an arena in which a more varied and sophisticated audience could observe and participate in the performance. The ballad itself became available to readers and auditors who previously paid it no attention. By using characters and a plot from common life, tragedy extended its range to moral tales previously considered unwritable.

In altering tragedy to include common criminals, Lillo also altered the prefatory genres of tragedy, to provide a theory justifying the change. Tragedy seemed an appropriate genre for experimentation because uses of the ballad in comedy already existed in *The Beggar's Opera*, and Lillo had himself in 1730 composed a ballad opera. The ballad was a performance genre as well as a reading genre so that it was, in its dialogic traits, not completely dissimilar from drama. What the performance of tragedy did was to provide a particular place in which the performance was to occur and scenes in which imaginary events could include real furniture.

The convergence of the ballad to tragedy served to elevate the significance of the moral conflicts of ordinary human beings. Their conflicts were shown to be interconnected with affairs of state. The merchant and his daughter consciously saw their importance as equal to that of aristocrats so that their concern for class elevation paralleled the artistic conversion of ballad to tragedy.

The conventions of tragedy were especially appropriate to the reinterpretation of this ballad because of its characters. The social role of the apprentice was especially important because of the significance of young men as business trainees. Thorowgood stresses youth as an endangered species: "The State of Youth is much to be deplored; and the more so because they see it not; they being then to danger most expos'd, when they are least prepar'd for their Defence" (II.iv). And Millwood served to attack corruption without undermining the state values that the merchant embraced. Thus the merchant could share her attitude toward religion but only by noting that she was an enemy of the state: "Truth is Truth, tho' from an Enemy, and spoke in Malice. You bloody, blind, and superstitious Bigots, how will you answer this?" (IV.xviii).

The interpretation of the conversion as a genre of victimization was not what Lillo's contemporaries saw in the play. For them it was a play about the seduction of innocence and, in this, they accepted Lillo's own interpretation. Any generic designation involves the relation to any audience or readers. In a society in which youthful employment meant seven years of service, it was important to employers that the investment of time and effort should not be squandered.

The merchants of London underwrote performance of the play for their apprentices, and in London alone it had 179 performances between 1731 and 1776. Lillo had insisted in the "Dedication" and in the language of the merchant that its genre was a tragedy based on the seduction of the apprentice. It was a play that stressed the moral significance of avoidance of sexual and criminal involvement. Failure to do so led eventually to punishment and death. The generic identity of the tragedy was thus stipulated by the author. This was one of the points made by Wagstaffe in ridiculing the assumption that critics knew better than authors what kind of genre they were composing. The issue of genre identification was, in the early eighteenth century, linked to origins as the authoritative grounds for explanation. The maker or author was the basis of authority. But Addison and his supporters, when they dealt with anonymous ballads, had to argue for generic characterizations as based upon components of texts. The identification rested on critical tenets that were assumed to be accepted by the best critics, but the components of a ballad could be compared with those of established models. Such comparisons between ballad components and those of epics could be and were often ridiculed, but when an author converted a ballad to an established genre, the extension of the genre was authorized by the intention of the author.

The author's intention is always related, in a generic sense, to the reader or audience that is addressed. As audiences change in their attitudes to theatrical performances, whether in the theater or classroom, the intention that the author initiated ceases to be appropriate. The conversion that Lillo saw as crucial to his extension of tragedy was the demonstration that the lives of common people revealed examples of innocence destroyed, of vice and guilt that was previously confined only to the lives of people in high estate. But my own interpretation of *The London Merchant* finds that the conversion of ballad to tragedy reveals a genre of tragedy that was of only peripheral interest to Lillo. Moreover, the notion of the consequences of tragic viewing that Lillo hoped for and envisioned—that apprentices would be ashamed to engage in destructive vice—was unsupported by subsequent behavior.

The components of genre that I have selected function combinatorially in terms of what I assume to have been unacknowledged and unpursued behavioral patterns. The ineffectiveness of the concept of origins as authoritative, the assumption that the corruption of women by men in a society is best served by avoidance and repression, that colonial trade is a form of mutual love—all of these suggest that Lillo's valuable extension of the realm of tragedy has components that need to be regenerated if the play is to be more than a museum piece. Thus the conversion of the ballad into tragedy is analyzed and interpreted, the process resulting in another genre—criticism (with its varied combinatory components). What were components of a "Dedication" have made the "Dedication" a component. In this respect, genres undergo transformations and this book is a study of the reasons for and explanations of generic transformations. And if it is a study of *trans*formations, it must be a study of formations.

NOTES

1. George Lillo, *The London Merchant: or, The HISTORY OF GEORGE BARNWELL* (London: J. Gray, 1731), iii; hereafter cited in text.
2. Theophilus Cibber, *The Lives of the Poets of Great Britain and Ireland*, 5 vols. (1753; Frankfurt am Main: Outlook Verlag, 2018), 5:229–30.
3. William H. McBurney, ed. *The London Merchant* (Lincoln and London: Univ. of Nebraska Press, 1965), 85; hereafter cited in text.

Generic Combinations and Recombinations: Revising, Editing, Collecting, Anthologizing

LILLO'S ALTERNATIVE ENDING: REVISION AS A GENRE

In the fifth edition of *The London Merchant* Lillo added a revised concluding scene. In the original, the place of the last scene is unspecified though it may be outside the prison, but in the revised version the place is specified as "The place of execution: The gallows and ladders at the farther end of the stage. A crowd of spectators."

Lillo's own explanation of the revision in what he calls "Advertisement"—a statement calling attention to the change—offers a critical and an economic reason for the change.

> The scene added in this fifth edition is, with some variation, in the original copy but by the advice of some friends it was left out in the representation, and is now published by the advice of others. Which are in the right I shall not pretend to determine. There are amongst both gentlemen whose judgment I prefer to my own. As this play succeeded on the stage without it, I should not perhaps have published it but to distinguish this edition from the incorrect, pirated ones, which the town swarms to the great prejudice of the proprietors of the copy as well as to all the fair traders who scorn to encourage such unjust practices.[1]

Authorial revision is a genre in the sense that it distinguishes the revision from preceding versions, especially from the version that is revised.

© The Author(s), under exclusive license to Springer Nature Switzerland AG 2021
R. Cohen, J. L. Rowlett, *Transformations of a Genre*, Palgrave Studies in the Enlightenment, Romanticism and Cultures of Print, https://doi.org/10.1007/978-3-030-89668-3_7

Such revision is significant because it provides an insight into the vulnerable areas of the author's artistic and conceptual system. It can lead to disorders in the system or to supporting more stringently particular components. Lillo's revision has as its major cause his wish to distinguish this edition from the many incorrect and pirated ones that injure the sales of "the proprietors of the copy." The revision itself, however, is predominantly a performance change. The setting of gallows and ladders on the stage creates a melodramatic environment that in the original had been left to the audience's imagination. Thus although the revision was not initiated by any failure in the response to stage performances—for the play was successful—the revision did alter the artistic construction and its effect. There is here a direct relation between book publishing as a genre and its interaction with composition and performances of tragedy as a genre.

The revision itself is an instance of the genre of place since the scene moves from the representation of a cell inside the prison to an unspecified space outside it, to the place of execution complete with gallows, ladders, and spectators. It also brings Millwood and Barnwell onto the stage for the last time, reiterating Barnwell's pity for her and her despair. This scene, not in the ballad, serves the sermonic claim that God's mercy is available to all, no matter how wicked. It is available to victim and victimizer. But if not accepted—and Millwood does not—only despair remains. In one sense, adding the genre of the place of execution reinforces the public humiliation of Barnwell and Millwood, a scene of mass vulgarity altering the "private" spaces in which most of the action takes place. But it also muddles the character of Millwood who at one point declares, "I am not Fool enough to be an Atheist" (IV.xvii), and in the revised scene declares, "I was doomed before the world began to endless pains, and thou to joys eternal" (McBurney, 84). She sees herself as a satanic victim, a view at odds with the explanation of herself as victim of male corruption and societal exploitation and hypocrisy.

Such revision is, as Lillo indicates, a matter of collaboration with others. He indicates in the "Advertisement" that this scene was in the original but was removed at the advice of friends. The revision is "now published by the advice of others." Whether that advice had to do with the economics of book publishing or of artistic construction is not mentioned.

In generic terms there is an interrelation between the genres of aesthetic judgment, of book publication, and authorial revision. The needs of publication lead to the desire for authorial revision which is sanctioned by friends whose judgment one trusts. That friends disagree about the choice of ending for *The London Merchant* merely indicates that the judges of choice can disagree. It will be necessary to consider how the best critics arrive at their judgment if one is to understand the nature of the disagreement. Since aesthetic judgment is a genre, it will be necessary to know how instances of this genre related to each other.

One example of judgmental decision making has to do with the selection of which text to publish when revisions such as Lillo's exist. With regard to *The London Merchant*, Bonamy Dobrée reprints the revision, Brooks and Hartman reprint the original text without the "Dedication," and William McBurney reprints the original and adds the revision from the fifth edition as an "Appendix." What constituted the grounds for textual editing in the eighteenth century?

Editing the Ballad of George Barnwell: Editing as a Genre

The genre of authorial revision can be interpreted as a process of self-editing or a combination of self-editing in collaboration with others. But editing works that one has not written involves principles and practices that in the eighteenth century were only beginning to be formulated. The editing of the ballad of George Barnwell can serve as an example of this generic inquiry.

In 1765 Thomas Percy published "*Reliques of Ancient English Poetry:* consisting of Old Heroic Ballads, Songs, and other Pieces of our earlier Poets, (Chiefly of the Lyric kind.) Together with some few of later Date."[2] There were three volumes and the first contained a dedication "To the Right Honourable Elizabeth Countess of Northumberland: in her own Right Baroness Percy, Lucy, Poynings, Fitz-Payne, Bryan, and Latimer" (v–viii); a "Preface" (ix–xiv); "An Essay on the Ancient English Minstrels" (xv–xxiii); poems; an "Essay on the Origin of the English Stage" (118–128); a "Glossary" (330–344); and a short "Advertisement." The second volume contained poems, an "Essay on the Metre of Pierce Plowman's Visions," and a "Glossary." The third contained poems, an essay "On the ancient Metrical Romances, etc." (226–262), and "The Glossary"; with "Additional Notes and Corrections" to volumes 1, 2, and 3.

The ballad of George Barnwell appeared in volume 3, and it was preceded by the following note:

> The subject of this ballad is sufficiently popular from the modern play which
> is founded upon it. This was written by George Lillo, a jeweller of London,
> and first acted about 1730.—As for the ballad, it was printed at least as early
> as the middle of the last century.
>
> It is here given from three old printed copies, which exhibit a strange
> intermixture of Roman and black letter. It is also collated with another copy
> in the Ashmole collection at Oxford, which is thus intitled, "An excellent
> ballad of GEORGE BARNWELL, an apprentice of London," who ... thrice
> robbed his master and murdered his uncle in Ludlow. The tune is "The
> Merchant."
>
> This tragical narrative seems to relate a real fact; but when it happened I
> have not been able to discover. (vol. 3, 225)

Percy's editorial procedure began with collating three "old printed
copies" and one from the Ashmole collection. But in abridging the title of
the Ashmole Barnwell certain striking omissions and errors occur. The
complete title of the ballad to which Percy refers is "An Excellent Ballad
of *George Barnwell,* An Apprentice of *London,* who was undone by a
Strumpet; who having thrice robbed his Master, and murdered his Uncle
in *Ludlow,* was hanged in Chains in *Polonia,* and by the means of a Letter
sent by his own hand to the Mayor of *London,* she was hang'd at *Ludlow.*
The tune is, *The Rich Merchant Man.*"

The spelling "Barnwell" occurs in some ballads, though not in this one
and it is the spelling in Lillo's play. The omissions in the title indicate that
complete transcription was not a criterion for Percy. Moreover, he was not
averse to speculating that the ballad "seems to relate to a real fact," though
neither he nor any scholar after him has been able to discover such a "fact."

The poem was part of an anthology; as a ballad printed earlier than
Percy's guess—"at least as early as the middle of the last century"—it was
a genre that in the collection served as a component, a "relique," that was
used to illustrate the progress of life and manners from the preceding century to Percy's time: "No active or comprehensive mind can forbear some
attention to the reliques of antiquity: it is prompted by natural curiosity to
survey the progress of life and manners, and to inquire by what gradations
barbarity was civilized, grossness refined, and ignorance instructed"
("Dedication," vi–vii).

The Barnwell ballad was thus an example of a genre that was part of a more comprehensive genre—the miscellany. Its function was thus determined by the function of the collection as a whole as well as by its relation to other poems printed with it. In the "Preface" Percy explained that the miscellany was organized to show the progress of English poetry and language from the earliest ages to the present. Each of the three volumes "contains an independent *series* of poems, arranged for the most part, according to the order of time, and showing the gradual improvements of the English language and poetry from the earliest ages down to the present. Each *volume*, or *series*, is divided into three *books*, to afford so many pauses, or resting places to the Reader, and to assist him in distinguishing between the productions of the earlier, the middle, and the latter times" (x).

Percy assumed a theory of progress with regard to poetry and language, based on oral poetry of minstrels that revealed "a cast of style and measure very different from that of contemporary poets of a higher class" ("An Essay on the Ancient English Minstrels," xxii). When the minstrels disappeared, "a new race of ballad-writers succeeded, an inferior sort of minor poets, who wrote narrative songs meerly for the press" (xxii), began to appear. But poetry of the higher class continued to become more and more refined.

At the end of Queen Elizabeth's reign, written ballads were published in profusion; thus "in the reign of James I, they began to be collected into little Miscellanies under the name of *Garlands*, and at length to be written purposely for such collections" (xxiii). Percy felt the need to justify contributing to this genre since it contained rude "reliques" of antiquity. He did this by claiming that he had been urged to pursue this project by eminent critics despite the fact that it was initiated by the editor's coming upon an ancient folio manuscript "containing near 200 poems, songs, and metrical romances." In addition to this scholarly encouragement, Percy believed that the poems have "for the most part, a pleasing simplicity, and many artless graces, which in the opinion of no mean critics have been thought to compensate for the want of higher beauties, and if they do not dazzle the imagination, are frequently found to interest the heart" (x). He was, in this respect, repeating the argument of Addison.

In order to give the project importance, Percy garnered assistance and support from eminent antiquarians and English and Scottish scholars. He asked and received help from Evan Evans of Wales, David Dalrymple of Scotland, and Thomas Warton, the poetry professor at Oxford. It was Warton who forwarded a copy of the Barwell ballad to Percy.

Percy's editorial procedures involved examining a number of manuscripts—he used four for Barnwell—in order to establish the authenticity of the poem. Authenticity was necessary because it provided reliability about the past; if a historical tradition was to be traced, it was necessary that the texts were neither forgeries nor governed by editorial license. In actuality, authenticity was not based on any particular manuscript or printing but on assumptions of what the ballad would have been if the transcribers and printers had properly known grammar and metrics and if they were preparing the poem for an eighteenth-century reader. This permitted Percy to eliminate what he considered repetitions, or awkwardness, vulgar diction, or "mistakes" in narrative speakers. He also felt free to add words or alter lines he felt would improve poetry.

At the conclusion of Part I the original contains an address to the audience. Barnwell has come to Millwood's house for help when his mater discovers his embezzlement. The original reads:

> But how she used this youth,
> in this his extream need,
> The which did her necessity
> so oft with money feed.
> The second Part behold
> shall tell it forth at large,
> And shall a Strumpets wiley ways,
> with all her tricks discharge.

Percy writes the following in quotation marks:

> "But how she us'd this youth,"
> "In this his care and woe,"
> "And all a strumpet's wiley ways,"
> "The SECOND PART may showe."   (I, 181–184)

Percy omits the relation between the "need" of Barnwell and the "necessity" of Millwood, a relation in criminality that the ballad makes reciprocal. This example is indicative of Percy's effort to follow *The London Merchant* in making Barnwell a victim. Percy's version was published thirty-four years after the play, though he remarked that the play was based on the ballad. The tragedy was not, however, based on the version of the ballad that Percy published.

As a result of his editorial practices, Percy's version contained only 364 lines in quatrain whereas the versions that he consulted contained 392. For example, the original text reads:

> She took me by the hand,
> and with a modest grace:
> Welcome sweet Barnwell then said she
> unto this homely Place.
>
> Welcome ten thousand times,
> more welcome than my brother;
> And better welcome i protest,
> than any One or other.
>
> And seeing i have thee found,
> as good as thy word to be,
> A homely supper e'er we part,
> thou shall here take with me.[3]

Percy's version reads:

> She took me by the hand,
> And with a modest grace,
> Welcome, sweet Barnwell, then quoth she,
> Unto this homely place.
>
> And since I have thee found
> As good as thy word to be;
> A homely supper ere we part,
> Thou shalt take here with me.   (I, 57–64)

Percy's correction of "e'er" or to "ere"—despite the fact that the terms appear with an apostrophe in all early versions of the ballad—seems justified on the grounds of meaning and spelling. But the entire omission of the "welcome" stanza is not a correction but a corruption. Like "e'er" or "e're" it appears in all the early editions of the ballad, yet it is not a matter of a printer's error, but of poetic construction. Percy gives no specific explanation for his omission, which is one of several, but he suggests that the printed versions were often done without artistry, including repetitions that were unnecessary and inappropriate insertions. A reliance on an "authentic" poem permitted him to make revisions that he believed any writer of his own time would take for granted as elementary; ballads that lacked this standard must have been interfered with; they were inauthentic.

But if the term "authentic" is interpreted with these cultural assumptions, they are at odds with the early seventeenth-century cultural assumptions. The ballad ironically contrasts Millwood's "modest grace" with her immodest welcome. Percy retains the repetition of "homely" place and "homely" supper which emphasizes the simple, plain home and meal, but the "welcome" is exaggerated and artificial. Moreover, the reference to her "brother" indicates the manipulative procedure which makes Barnwell an immediate member of the household.

The ballad suggests that the language which indicates simplicity, which designates home as a place of domesticity, is a language of manipulation. Percy assumed that ballads written for publication in the early seventeenth century, although written in "exacter measure" than those transcribed from oral performances of minstrels, "have a low or subordinate correctness, sometimes bordering on the insipid, yet often well adapted to the pathetic" (xxiii). Percy further pointed out in justification of his editing procedures that "the Editor has endeavoured to be as faithful, as the imperfect state of his materials would admit: for these old popular rhimes have, as might be expected, been handed down to us with less care, than any other writings in the world" (xii).

Percy was uneasy about offering as a literary anthology a collection of old ballads. This accounts for his parade of eminent scholars whom he called upon for approval. It was not a genre from which he expected much literary reward. His conclusion to the "Preface" is a modest autobiographical explanation of his effort to prepare the manuscript and a request for the reader's indulgence in what may appear as a waste of time:

> The names of so many men of learning and character the Editor hopes will serve as an amulet to guard him from every unfavourable censure, for having bestowed any attention on a parcel of OLD BALLADS. It was at the request of many of these gentlemen, and of others eminent for their genius, and taste, that this little work was undertaken. To prepare it for the press has been the amusement of now and then a vacant hour amid the leisure and retirement of rural life, and hath only served as a relaxation from graver duties. It has been taken up at different times, and often thrown aside for many months, during an interval of four or five years. This has occasioned some inconsistencies and repetitions, which the candid reader will pardon. As great care has been taken to admit nothing immoral and indecent; the Editor hopes he need not be ashamed of having bestowed some of his idle hours on the ancient literature of our own country, or in rescuing from

oblivion some pieces (tho' but the amusements of our ancestors) which tend to place in a striking light, their taste, genius, sentiments or manners. (xiii–xiv)

Generically *The London Merchant* sought to elevate the ballad by making its plot the basis of an expanded view of tragedy. It rewrote and reinterpreted the ballad. Percy used the ballad in a miscellany which was to illustrate the development of poetic refinement. The claim, therefore, was that reprinting the ballad in its original form could, indeed, serve as an example of early unrefined ballad writing.

By omitting the address to the audience in the direct address of "behold," he removed here and elsewhere the oral character of ballad performance and its presentation of criminal disorder. As a consequence of this procedure Percy created a misleading sense of ballad distribution and performance: By placing the ballad in a "scholarly" collection in three volumes he contributed to the elevation of what had been a part of street culture. It was not achieved, however, without Percy's intervention in the rewriting of the ballad.

Another serious alteration of the ballad was Percy's regularizing of the meter. He printed the ballad in quatrains with the first, second, and fourth lines iambic trimeter and the third iambic tetrameter. The original, however, has this metrical scheme predominantly in Part I. Whatever irregularities occur are made uniform by Percy; the following are some examples:

Original:	As i upon a certain Day,
	was walking through the street,
Percy:	As I, upon a day,
	Was walking through the street

Original:	For to gather some money in,
	that is my masters due,
Percy:	To gather monies in,
	That are my master's due:

Original:	O stay not too long my Love.
	Sweet George have me in mind:
Percy:	O stay not hence too long,
	Sweet George, have me in mind.

This occasional regularizing of the meter in Part I, when continued in Part II, becomes a critical and cultural blunder. Part II alters the meter of the first so that it is predominantly iambic tetrameter. It marks a shift from the seduced innocent of Part I to the experienced criminal who riots in sexuality and criminality in Part II. Whether it is an example of excess or disorder, the implication of irregularity is destroyed by converting the lines to iambic trimeter. Because Percy edited the ballad at a time when *The London Merchant* had become a frequently performed tragedy, his revisions emphasize Barnwell's youth and his feelings of guilt. Examples of this appear at once:

> Original: Here comes Barnwell unto thee,
> sweet Sarah my delight,
> Percy: Young Barnwell comes to thee,
> Sweet Sarah, my delight:

> Original: Our master to command Accounts
> has just occasion found;
> Percy: Our master to accompts,
> Hath just occasion found;

Percy changes "accounts" to "accompts" affecting the older spelling. He alters the language of the original to avoid vulgarity:

> Original: Quoth she thou art a paltry Jack,
> to charge me in such sort,
> Percy: Quoth she, Thou are a knave,
> To charge me in this sort,

When in his cups, George refers to his uncle as a "churl"—"I'le rob the churl and murder him!" (II, 150). Percy revises this to "I'll rob his house, and murder him" (II, 91). So, too, when he murders his uncle, the original ballad has him present his gold to Sara *Milwood* in a "plain" narrative. But Percy omits the particulars of the robbery, conveying the impression of hasty, guilty flight and implying an awareness of its cruelty.
The original reads:

> Most suddenly within a Wood, he struck his Uncle down,
> And beat his brains out of his head, so sore he crackt his crown:
> And fourscore pound in ready coyn, out of his Purse he took,
> And coming unto *London* strait, the country quite forsook.
> To *Sara Milwood* then he came, shewing his store of gold,
> And how he had his Uncle slain, to her he plainly told.   (II, 171–176)

Percy's revision reads:

> Sudden within a wood,
> He struck his uncle down,
> And beat his brains out of his head;
> So sore he crackt his crown.
>
> Then seizing fourscore pound,
> To London straight he hyed,
> And unto Sarah Millwood all
> The cruell fact descryed.   (II, 133–140)

And at the end of the ballad the original refers to Barnwell as a "wilful youth"—"So here's the end of wilful youth, that after Harlots haunt" (II, 195)—whereas Percy removes "wilful": "Lo! here's the end of youth,/ That after harlots haunt" (II, 177–178).

The editorial principles of Percy, when considered generically, reveal that he considered the identity of differently printed original copies as untrustworthy examples of "aesthetic" poems. And they are not trustworthy because he assumes that the poem must have been regular and consistent in its metrical form and narrative speaker. All the instances of metrical change or shift in speaker were thus assumed to be interpolations.

This view was held by Joseph Ritson who was one of Percy's severest critics, attacking the reliability of his historical explanations of English minstrels. Ritson reprinted the Barnwell ballad in his 1790 volume *Ancient Songs and Ballads*, and he included all the passages that Percy omitted. But he supported Percy's rewriting of "irregular" lines on the grounds that first lines written in tetrameter measure were interpolations. He agreed that Percy "restored the measure," although no original existed for such restoration except in the eighteenth-century assumptions of Percy and Ritson:

> Throughout this "Second part" (except in a single instance) the metre of the first line of each stanza is, in the old editions, lengthened by a couple of syllables; which are, occasionally at least, a manifest interpolation. The person, also, is, for the most part, changed from the first to the third, with evident impropriety. Dr. Percy has, very ingeniously, and with the least possible violence, restored the measure, by ejecting the superfluous syllables; and given consistency to the whole, by a restoration of the proper person: And, as it is now highly improbable that any further ancient copy will be

found, and those which exist are manifestly corrupt, it seemed perfectly justifiable to adopt the judicious emendations of this ingenious editor.[4]

Ritson fills in omission in the same way as Percy:

> Original: And eighty pounds in ready Cash,
>   out of his purse he took;
>   And coming up to London Town,
>   Country quite forsook.
>
> Ritson: And fourscore pound, in coin,
>   Out of his purse he took;
>   And coming in to London town,
>   The country quite forsook.   (345–348)

Although possessing copies of the original ballad, Percy did not indicate either his revisions or his reasons for making them. He wrote: "It is here given from three old printed copies, which exhibit a strange intermixture of Roman and black letter. It is also collated with another copy in the Ashmole collection at Oxford, which is thus intitled, 'An excellent ballad of *George Barnwell*, an apprentice of London, who ... thrice robbed his master and murdered his uncle in Ludlow.' The tune is 'The Merchant'" (vol. 3, 225).

The omissions in the title of the ballad refer to Barnwell being undone by a strumpet; thus one clue to Percy's revisions is desire to remove vulgarity from the poem. This desire, based on the principle of decorum, is evident in Percy's removal of low language: he changed "paltry Jack" to "knave" and "Pish, rise, quoth he" to "Tush, rise, I said." This latter revision also indicates another revisionary procedure: the attempt to make the speaker consistent. The original ballad shifts from the first to the third person with apparent randomness. Percy altered these shifts to achieve consistency. But this revisionism must be compared with his procedure in editing *Five Pieces of Runic Poetry Translated from the Icelandic Language* (London: R. & J. Dodsley, 1763). There he criticized Macpherson's editing of the Ossianic poems for not providing examples of the original texts:

> [T]ill the Translator of those poems thinks proper to produce his originals, it is impossible to say whether they do not owe their superiority, if not their whole existence entirely to himself. The Editor of these pieces had no such boundless field for license. Every poem here produced has been already

published accompanied with a Latin or Swedish version; by which every deviation would at once be detected. It behooved him therefore to be as exact as possible. Sometimes indeed, where a sentence was obscure, he hath ventured to drop it, and the asterisks which occur will denote such omissions. Sometimes for the sake of perspicuity it was necessary to alter the arrangement of a period; and sometimes to throw in a few explanatory words: and even once or twice to substitute a more simple expression instead of the complex and enigmatic phrase of the original.

The Editor was in some doubt whether he should subjoin or suppress the originals. But as they lie within little compass, and as the books whence they are extracted are very scarce, he was tempted to add them as vouchers for the authenticity of his version.[5]

"Authenticity" as a Historical Concept

Percy was conscious of the need for authenticity; he distinguished between editorial judgment and editorial license. "Perspicuity" required him to be as "exact as possible" in the translation he published, but judiciousness permitted him to drop a sentence that was obscure, though in this volume he left asterisks to indicate omissions. In the "Preface" to his *Five Pieces of Runic Poetry*, he found it editorially permissible sometimes "to alter the arrangement of a period," "to throw in a few explanatory words: and even once or twice to substitute a more simple expression instead of the complex and enigmatic phrase of the original."

These translations were published three years before the *Reliques*, and these were translations in contrast to originals. But it is necessary to understand the nature of the editorial function as Percy saw it. The Barnwell ballad, when published in quatrains, contained 392 lines, but Percy's version omitted 28 lines. In addition, he made numerous changes in words and in the order of words, changing the first lines in the Second Part from tetrameter to trimeter. The underlying authorization was governed by Percy's view that minstrels provided oral poetry that was "obviously unreliably transcribed" since ballads had to conform to the rule of ballad construction that was, for him, trimeter, trimeter, tetrameter, trimeter. The belief that this ballad and others contained numerous errors in transcription—regardless of the consistence of all earlier copies—indicated how deeply tied to his own prejudices were notions of "authenticity." His contemporary, Joseph Ritson, disagreed with his notion of authenticity by adding the omitted lines in his *Ancient Songs and Ballads*, and in his

"Observations on the Minstrels." He wrote, "instances might be noticed, where the learned collector has preferred his ingenuity to his fidelity, without the least intimation to the reader."[6]

But neither Ritson nor Percy suggested that the "corruptions" ought to be printed with the corrections; they both agreed that "superfluous" syllables ought to be "ejected" and that consistency was what the original possessed. Their view of a broadside ballad was that its model was a sophisticated poem, and, indeed, the analysis of ballads was carried on by Addison and others who subjected them to the received standards of their own age. Historically what we have here is an example of the incapacity of critics to escape the prejudices of their own time: even the disagreements occur within the limits these set. Ritson disagreed with Percy about the nature of British minstrels and about the omission of lines. But he accepted Percy's view of authenticity, his readiness to correct, add, and omit words and lines within the Barnwell ballad. He did, however, by publishing the entire poem, take one step in acknowledging the actual texts that were received.

The idea of "appropriateness" involves omissions or absences as well as continuities. The elimination of some of these mixtures by Percy raises the question of the relation between continuity and absence or omission; what is the meaning of absence for structure? For example, Percy avoided repetition but in doing so he omitted the family reference (brother) and the conniving intimacy which the personal pronouns emphasize: "thee," "thy," "thou," "thou."

> She took me by the hand,
> and with a modest grace:
> Welcome sweet Barnwell then said she
> unto this homely Place.
>
> Welcome ten thousand times,
> more welcome than my brother;
> And better welcome i protest,
> than any One or other.
>
> And seeing i have thee found,
> as good as thy word to be,
> A homely supper e'er we part,
> thou shalt here take with me.

This is Percy's version:

> She took me by the hand,
> And with a modest grace,
> Welcome, sweet Barnwell, then quoth she,
> Unto this homely place.
>
> And since I have thee found
> As good as thy word to be;
> A homely supper ere we part,
> Thou shalt take here with me. (I, 57–64)

Percy eliminates the repetition of "welcome" which, in the original, is used as a deliberate form of exaggeration. As exaggeration, Millwood's welcome not only manipulates the young man but does so by implying that he is dearer to her than a member of her own family. The "homely place" and "homely supper" become, in the original, repetitive instances of ironic manipulation, part of the welcome. In Percy the "modest grace" is constructed with modest language, but in the original the "modest grace" is joined to an *immodest welcome*. Percy omits the exaggerated family relationship, the extravagant gesture of the strumpet after only the second meeting.

There are two other revisions pertinent to repetition that reveal Percy's effort to lesson Barnwell's complicity in the riotous behavior of the ballad. Barnwell's generosity is stressed in the final instance by Percy's alteration of the narrator from the first to the third person. The original reads:

> "Ten pounds, nor ten times ten, shall make my love decay."
> Then from his bag into her lap, he cast ten pounds straight way. (I, 83–84)

Percy's alteration reads:

> Ten pounds, nor ten times ten,
> Shall make my love decay.
> Then from my bag into her lap,
> I cast ten pound straitway. (I, 157–160)

The alteration creates the artistic consistency that Percy sought, but it also personalizes Barnwell's act. It serves to stress the unabashed, generous involvement of the apprentice.

The other example involves a strategic omission. In the second part Barnwell, coming to Millwood for protection after fleeing from his master who is about to review the accounts of his apprentices, appeals to her in the following admission:

> Thou knowest I loved thee so well, thou could'st not ask the thing,
> But that I did incontinent the same unto thee bring. (112–113)

Percy omits this passage but retains the term "incontinent" in the passage describing the punishment of Millwood.

> Whereby she seized was,
> And then to Ludlow sent:
> Where she was judg'd, condemn'd, and hang'd,
> For murder incontinent.   (II, 169–172)

But it was Barnwell who committed the "incontinent" act so that they were, in the original, described as behaving incontinently. Percy omits the passage in which Barnwell admits his incontinent behavior, thus removing an incriminating passage that reveals Barnwell's partnership in crime.

Historically, what takes places in the revision is the elimination of oral qualities, for the repetition and exaggeration are both aesthetic and mnemonic. What is lost is the "homely," the domestic character of the persuasion—a quality that made the ballad part of the street scene. Percy tends, by his omissions, to reduce this instance of Millwood's manipulative behavior. In this respect, the tragedy deliberately makes Millwood a sophisticated woman, an interpretation not found in the original.

The original ballad by its variations of person and by its disjunctions and dialogue provided a sense of the increasing disorder in which Barnwell was involved. Percy's effort to create unity through consistency of speaker and through consistency of stanzaic construction aligned the poem with the lyric, the confessional first-person narration, not with the common poetic or prose narratives of thieves' lives. Historically, therefore, the ballad in its revised form is being reconstructed to conform with heroic ballads rather than with the texts that illustrate the world upside down, the enjoyable participation in sin—and, in general, dangerous and disordered sentiments in early seventeenth-century society.

But it must not be overlooked that the seventeenth-century version was readily available as the first nighters at *The London Merchant* made clear, and it was also available with the chapbook in the 1750s. What takes place, however, is the overriding preference that is given to Percy's revision. I have suggested some reasons connected with class and social change, but others must be connected with Percy's presentation of a body of poems that he sought to establish as the canon of English poetry.

In a historical sense, Percy argued that anonymity did not imply the non-existence of individual authorship but merely its historical loss. He developed a theory of a "minstrel" class to provide this authorship. But such a theory implied, as well, the corruption of the manuscripts and the need of an editor to restore them. At the same time, it was apparent that the ballads dealt with different classes, with wealthy merchants as well as merchant apprentices and criminals. Thus poetry, to be valued as part of a tradition, did not necessarily depend upon a "refined" or "civilized" society. Homer's epics had always been recognized as models of writing. What Percy's *Reliques* did was to demonstrate that England, too, had a new "primitive" poetic tradition.

His editing supported the received views of Pope and his contemporaries, even though it could also be used—and in Wordsworth it came to be used—to set the "natural" in opposition to, rather than in support of, the "civilized" craft of poetry. And this could be done by assuming a sociological view of progress in which "natural" poetry was seen as corrupted by "civilization," or "authentic" poetry corrupted by artificiality or art, or class poetry reducing the possibility of "universal" poetry. Thus rhetoric, diction, and genre came to be analyzed in terms of these embracing oppositions.

Percy's first literary work was a translation from a Portuguese manuscript of a Chinese novel, Han Kion Choaun (1761). He was then thirty-two, a graduate of Christ Church, Oxford, and had been since 1753 in possession of the vicarage of Easton-Maudit, Northamptonshire. His interest in earlier cultures seems to have been tied to an empirical desire to illustrate the universality of poetic qualities and thus may be understood as a form of affirmation of contemporary hypotheses about universal human nature. And during the 1760s, he produced a number of collections: in 1762, *Miscellaneous Pieces relating to the Chinese*; in 1762, *Five Pieces of Runic Poetry*; in 1762, an edition of Surrey's poems; in 1764, a new translation of *The Song of Solomon*; and in 1765, *Reliques of Ancient English Poetry*. The collection as a form was related to the Miscellany and the garland. It served to bring together poems by numerous authors or the various kinds of poems by a single author. Pope had, of course, ridiculed the fascination with collecting in *The Dunciad*, but by then collecting of various kinds was a common practice among members of all classes. "Garlands" of poetry were commonplace and Percy referred to them in his introduction. Poetry garlands thus served to provide variety and the contrasting functions of different genres as well as their interrelations.

Percy's *Reliques* was not the first collection of old ballads. Ambrose Phillips had in 1723 published one; Andrew Cunningham published a Scottish one in *The Evergreen* in 1724. Percy's was, however, far more extensive than earlier collections, and it became one of the major ways of relating popular to polite ballads. Because Percy included contemporary literary ballads with older ones, this generic procedure also became a model for using anthologies to trace the progress of poetry.

Percy argued for a medieval class of poets called "minstrels"—"scolds" in Scandinavian or Icelandic—as composers of oral ballads. He thus insisted on the importance of the individual artist even though the poet's or minstrel's name had ceased to be identified with his work. Thus argument for individual authorship of ballads coincided with the generic self-consciousness of contemporary writers like Pope and Fielding and Sterne. It also served to support the view that poetic composition and transcription involved shared approaches to writing and composing.

Genre as Self-Revelation

Genres provide an insight into authorial composition as a social formation. Writers can be distinguished by the genres in which they write. Addison is a poet, an essayist, a dramatist, a literary theorist, a composer of short stories, a travel writer, and a political commentator. Lillo, on the other hand, wrote only dramas in poetry and prose. Percy was a writer of sermons, an anthologist, a translator, a poet, a literary critic, a wide-ranging letter writer. The choice of genres in which each of these writers is engaged reveals an attitude to the audience and to the social role of different kinds of writing. Multiple genres usually suggest the different audiences in view, from different classes and genders. Addison's and Steele's periodical papers involved not only the effort to educate women but to exchange letters with readers. This was not the function of *Cato*, addressed to a theater audience and readers of the published play. The genres of Percy indicate the impact of collecting (and reading) ballads upon the writing of them. Percy's own ballad was an implicit act of self-advertisement.

Percy's name was originally spelled Pearcey or Piercy. In later life, he "was anxious to deduce his descent from the Percys of Northumberland, with the living representative of whom he was brought into official and social connection."[7] He altered the spelling of his name, and in his ballad,

The Hermit of Warkworth, he composed a work in which Percy's descendent is first lost then found. This desire for social climbing—Percy was the son of a grocer—and class change indicates that he thought it possible to raise his status through literary allusion. But it also demonstrates that at this time social transformation was taking place in the role of the merchant and in the growth of independence for the poet.

The Hermit of Warkworth, published in 1771, provides a clue to Percy's sense of the kind of ballad his time required. On the one hand, it is a narrative of Percy's antecedents and thus a narrative with personal implications. It is the story of Percy and Eleanor, who becomes Percy's bride. It has an inset story (a genre with the genre) of the Hermit Bertram and his accidental killing of his brother and bride-to-be. The two narratives have numerous analogies, not unlike the inset narratives in the fictions of Fielding, and the incidents and places are annotated with documents indicating the reality basis of the story.

The ballad, though divided into three parts, has regular quatrains and deals with knights and nobles who engage in heroic deeds which (in the life of the hermit) become destructive of his family and his future family—his wife-to-be. In this sense the poem presents the symbolic death of one family that permits the symbolic rebirth of another. Could it be that the discovery and preservation of the vanished Percy is the resurrection of the modern Percy through the publication of *Reliques*—of old narratives? Historically, therefore, the genre is used to place Percy's past within the heroic ballad tradition he traced—his poem indeed was republished in Thomas Evans's *Old Ballads, Historical and Narrative, with Some of Modern Date*, in 1777. It becomes, therefore, part of the very tradition he fostered. Contemporary critics who tend to see the mid-eighteenth century as a separate period, or who find that the second half of the eighteenth century constituted a separate period—who base their hypotheses upon particular elements in texts such as sublimity or sensibility or concern with the role of art—fail to see that the interest in romance, ballad, and the gothic novel are part of an effort to accommodate older forms to change without undermining neoclassical tenets. Of course, any such procedure is paradoxical. As a member of a genre, each text serves as a commentary or criticism on preceding members. The changes in components or in the interrelation of components create new filiations with other texts. The resurrection of texts such as sonnets and sonnet sequences after long absences deliberates connections with a poetic past that, in the eighteenth century, was already established in the dramas of Lillo and the Shakespearean adaptations and celebration of Garrick.

Indeed, the connection of literary ballads to folk ballads like "Barnwell" indicated that a tradition was being established between different social levels of members of a genre. The genre of the ballad, of tragedy, of the gothic novel were serving to close the hierarchal gap between the popular and the elite forms of writing. Thus the genre begins to lose several of its features (irregular metrics, varied levels of language, vulgar as well as refined subject matter) that have seemed previously to establish its social distance. A new form such as the novel already takes for granted the possibility and actuality of shift of characters from one class to another—as in *Joseph Andrews* or in *Pamela* or in *Tom Jones*—as do the periodical papers and the shift in the principles of tragedy.

At such a time the editing practices of Percy and Ritson identify "authenticity" with contemporary concepts of "correct" writing. When Percy writes of "authentic" he is concerned with dating, with approximate rule-governed behavior. He is suspicious of unacknowledged sources or behavior. Indeed, at the very same time, Horace Walpole's *The Castle of Otranto* provides a novel variation in which lies and deception form the basis of a tradition. But it also leads to constructive forms in which concealment, architectural and psychological depth, begin to resist the practices of patriarchal and political authoritarianism. The structure of the Gothic novel and the increased education-concern for children and women and for members of the lower classes, complicate the components of received genres and assert the significance of biography and history.

Thus the introduction of earlier ballads to mid-eighteenth-century readers was not a radical procedure but rather a mode of accommodation—though a modification, a historical modification, of the governing concepts. The introduction by Percy of Icelandic literature, of pieces relating to the Chinese of 1762, was part of a more general inquiry stemming from Lockean premises of the role of experience in shaping individual behavior. These inquiries can be seen as test cases for the universality of nature in poetry. Whether it began with Addison's effort to discover epic procedures in "Chevy-Chase," or whether it continued with Thomas Blackwell's *Enquiry into the Life and Writings of Homer*, or Jameson's *Illustrations of Northern Antiquities*, or Collins's *Persian Eclogues*, we have a body of poems and of research seeking, in medieval English texts and in those of earlier societies or non-Western societies, a confirmation of the universality of human nature in poetry. Such confirmations, however, were achieved by discovering in past works the standards and values to be found in the present. This meant that the northern tribes of Iceland, for example, identified as violent and warlike, were held responsible for the destruction of the Roman empire. But their poetry was, so Percy assumed, governed by traditions different from their military behavior. Historically this would seem to imply just the opposite of what the inquiry sought. For it suggested that the poetic tradition could exist outside the military and primitive aggressiveness, that poetry was not affected by this experience but by those experiences that could describe peace and love and non-military values. Types of experience could be generically independent, and one of the consequences of the search for universality was that it led to formulations calling universality into question.

Notes

1. George Lillo, *The London Merchant*, ed. William H. McBurney, 82.
2. Thomas Percy, *Reliques of Ancient English Poetry*, 3 vols. (London: Printed for J. Dodsley, 1765); vol. 3 can be retrieved at HathiTrust Digital Library: https://babel.hathitrust.org/cgi/pt?id=ucl.31175035197105&view=1up &seq=7 (accessed April 1, 2020).
3. *An Excellent Ballad of George Barnwell ...* (London: Printed and sold by L. How; in Petticoat-Lane, 1741–1762?). The Houghton Library edition does not use line numbering. A transcription of the text can be retrieved from the English Broadside Ballad Archive, University of California, Santa Barbara, https://ebba.english.ucsb.edu/ballad/34458/xml (accessed March 27, 2020).
4. Joseph Ritson, *Ancient Songs and Ballads*, 2 vols. (1790; London, 1829), 2: 165.
5. Thomas Percy, "Preface," *Five Pieces of Runic Poetry Translated From the Islandic Language* (London: R. & J. Dodsley, 1763), viii–ix; xiii.
6. Ritson, *Ancient Songs and Ballads*, 1: xxxi.
7. *Dictionary of National Biography* (Classic Reprint), vol. 44, Paston to Percy, ed. Leslie Stephen (1895; London: Forgotten Books, 2019), 44: 437.

Tragedy to Novel: Genre and Value

On the Conflict of Genres in the Novel

In 1798 Richard Phillips published Thomas Skinner Surr's *George Barnwell. A Novel*. In the "Advertisement" prefixed to the novel the author sought to reply to critics at "the selection of so hacknied a subject."[1] He explained that he had seen Mrs. Siddons's performance of Millwood in *The London Merchant* and that it differed from "the vulgar openness of character they [readers] have been accustomed to associate with the original" (1, iv). His reading offered a new interpretation based on the play. In making a novel from the play, Surr wrote: "The Author has deviated in several instances from the story he has adopted; has introduced some new characters, and changed the features of others; yet as the chief incidents are preserved, he thought it more candid to retain the original title, than to invent a new one" (1, v).

The authorial remarks about preserving the "chief incidents" of the Barnwell narrative while urging a new interpretation of Millwood indicate some important aspects of a generic interpretation. The most obvious is that Surr conceived of his novel as repeating the chief incidents in the plot of a tragedy. Now the novel and the tragedy are different genres, but what makes these two formally different genres comparable is that they share characters and key incidents of the plot: Barnwell is apprenticed to a merchant and is seduced by a prostitute who leads him into criminal theft

R. Cohen, J. L. Rowlett, *Transformations of a Genre*, Palgrave Studies in the Enlightenment, Romanticism and Cultures of Print, https://doi.org/10.1007/978-3-030-89668-3_8

from his master and finally to the murder of his rich uncle. Then Barnwell and Millwood are apprehended. The genre of tragedy and the novel are characterized by some different formal characteristics. With regard to tragedy these characteristics are marked by textual features or by performance of these features. Surr's production of his novel illustrates how what are considered "literary" genres serve critical functions. If performance of *The London Merchant* served to depict Millwood as a vulgar and common prostitute, Mrs. Siddons's performance provided a resistance and alternative to this conception. By placing the Barnwell plot within a narrative genre, Surr provided the rationale for the particular interpretation this novel served as a representation of behavior in which repression and secrecy rather than openness characterized Millwood's behavior.

This literary production indicates one of the interrelations that different genres have to each other. Comprehensive genres such as tragedy and the novel include other genres as components. Comparison of members of different genres can contain similar genres which make comparisons appropriate. This similarities-and-differences phenomenon can complement each other or indicate the particular temporal or spatial differences that identify their social, political, religious, and other differences. The tragedy takes place in the time of Queen Elizabeth whereas the novel's time is its present. Moreover, Mr. Emery to whom Barnwell is apprenticed is a merchant whose social status is not in question and who is befriended by Sir James and members of the aristocracy. He is described as a later generation than his uncle's merchant friend, Mr. Freeman, who arranges for his younger partner, Mr. Emery, to employ Barnwell.

The novel like the tragedy is a member of a genre, but these two genres have quite different histories. From *Oedipus Rex* to *Macbeth* to *The London Merchant* tragedies undergo changes within the genre, both in the reading text and in the material aspects of performance. The genre retains its dialogic structure, its murder plot, its distinction between readers and audience. However much each of these changes they remain part of what can be considered rule-governed aspects of the genre. Certain other aspects remain but undergo substantial change, such as the status of the protagonists, which, in *The London Merchant*, alters the class status. So, too, the relation of the plot to affairs of state is substantially changed in eighteenth-century "domestic" tragedies.

Genre is a basis for charting the changes within a genre while retaining some components (not necessarily the same) over time. Moreover, as a genre adds or subtracts certain components, it provides an insight into the cultural practices of a society. Surr's novel was composed almost a hundred years after the initiation of the novel as a genre, but it still retains the multiple narrators and genres which formed its comprehensiveness. Still, it is more closely related to members of the genre that immediately preceded it than to those of Defoe, Richardson, and Fielding.

Surr was aware of the disdain in which the Barnwell story was held as well as the fact that children's stories continued to form the basis for sophisticated genres. In his "Prefatory Dialogue," he writes a prologue in verse that is a dialogue between the author and his "Friend." It is an effort to forestall criticism that the subject is dull, "low-bred," and "vulgar." The friend predicts how men and women of fashion will greet the novel:

> "Barnwell!" cries Emma, "pshaw, the name's enough
> To fright all fashion from such *hum drum* stuff!
> Stol'n, I imagine, from that vulgar play,
> That forms the pastime of my *Lord Mayor's Day*
> How monstrous low-bred must the creature be,
> Who writes such trash—don't offer it to me!
> Give me some novel of a different kind,
> Where castles, ghosts, and demons are combin'd,
> To rouse one from the stupor of the spleen,
> With *sights* that never have, nor can be seen."   (1, ix)

The irony of the dialogue is directed against the fashionable world that rejects the work of young authors who base their work on old stories and ballads but praises established authors who do the same. And there are the concluding couplets with their apparent humility for the author's moral probity:

> One secret voice, at least, shall sooth my heart;
> (Nor will I tremble at the Critic's dart;)
> Conscience shall sweetly whisper this applause,—
> "Thou hast not injur'd Virtue's sacred cause."   (1, x)

When the dialogue is read in conjunction with the genre of the "advertisement," it becomes apparent that the author's interpretation is an explication of the town's foremost actress in the part. A more effective ally in supporting his novel would be difficult to find. And in the fourth edition (1802) the novel was dedicated to Mrs. Siddons with her approval. The manner in which one genre undermines the satire of another by exemplifying the very support it satirizes serves as an introduction to the process of generic doubling that forms the plot of the novel.

A CONTESTATION OF GENRES

The Barnwell plot on which the 1798 novel was based was a historical tragedy set in the time of Queen Elizabeth. But the character of the merchant whose importance was upgraded with that of the aristocracy was an anachronistic depiction. The depiction of the financial and moral condition of merchant, his daughter, and his apprentice was not a phenomenon of the early sixteenth century. Moreover, the representation of Barnwell and Millwood as protagonists of tragedy had no generic model in the early sixteenth century.

There are, however, certain actions of the plot that are continuous: the seduction of the innocent apprentice, Millwood's manipulation of him so that he becomes first a disobedient apprentice, then a thief, and finally a murderer. This plot is not represented in the same language in the ballad, the chapbook, the tragedy, and the novel. And this underscores the realization that the term *genre* functions like collective nouns—people, men, women, class, race, gender. It abstracts characteristics from the particulars to which it refers so that is renders any inference about a particular instance inadequate. What is more, any generic member can belong to more than one genre as the plot as genre can belong to a ballad, to a short narrative, to a tragedy, to a novel. The text as production needs to be identified in terms of the addition or subtraction of particulars that include the analysis of formal traits such as language, rhyme, characters (numbers, gender, class, race, etc.), place, time, and any other formalizable characteristics.

The novel is the genre that characteristically includes other genres. Not only was it combinatory in its origins, but between the time of Defoe and that of Surr, it had added components that came to be seen as a genre in its own right—a derivative category called the "gothic novel." Surr refers to components of this genre when Emma, his imagined reader, declares in his dialogue, "'Give me some novel of a different kind,/Where castles, ghosts, and demons are combin'd/To rouse one from the stupor of the spleen,/With *sights* that never have, nor can be seen'" (1, ix). His own novel has a cleric who believes in such fictions only to have his beliefs shown to be mistaken. The point is that genres exhibit members that attack as well as follow particular components, themes, beliefs that other members possess. It is not merely that they have been recognized as attacking or undermining members of the same genre in satire or parody or limericks or jokes, but, as deconstructive critics have argued, within particular texts there can exist undermining contradiction.

There are two kinds of argument that I am making: the first is that genres develop from other genres. The second is that when a genre member is produced, the genres from which it is produced can become components in the new texts. Thus the claims that the novel's origin derives from news accounts, travel accounts, romance components, conduct books, biographical and autobiographical accounts can be seen as the characteristic procedure of generic production. But what is lacking in such accounts is an inquiry into how such accounts relate to other textual and innovative genres at the same time. Why do certain genres disappear at this time while others are revived and thrive?

Thomas Skinner Surr's novel can help to answer some of these questions, but in order to do so it is necessary to explain how I see my own text and task in this enterprise. I have argued that texts are combinatory but that different genres are combinatory in different ways. The production of a ballad, a chapbook, a tragedy, an anthology, a novel, a memoir all may share components, but what they share and how they share them is not sufficient to describe what kinds we take them to be. The nature of the sharing is only a part of what constitutes a text or generic member. Each individual text is constituted of components that can relate to different genres. This book thus represents what it describes; it offers an argument that redefines the nature of the literary and does so by attending to historical arguments and those of contemporary theory. Its genre is critical theory and practice, though it is also affiliated with genres like poetry, history, periodical papers, autobiography, and so forth. The basis for this is the distinction between filiation and affiliation. Filiation refers to the genre or genres with which one classifies a text. The basis for classification depends on the genealogy one wishes to identify as the basis for examination. It is thus possible to establish a genealogy for the Barnwell plot and analyze it generically just as it is possible to identify the ballad or tragedy as genres and analyze each in terms of its rule-governed characteristics or its constituents. It has been conventional to think of genre in terms that are exclusively rule-governed constituents or formal constituents. But any constituent, such as heroic couplet or character or plot or idea, can become a genre if it has a history. Thus genres can be combinatory without implying unity or denying generic contention.

As for affiliation, this is a characteristic of any text. Insofar as genre is a collection of textual components that have an existence independent of any entity in which they occur—so that genealogically they become entities themselves—they are filiated, not affiliated. Affiliation is found in quotations, even in genres that can be placed in larger genres, such as poems in novels or proverbs in essays. Affiliations suggest connections. They constitute clues to the associations that can be found between texts.

AFFILIATION AS NETWORK

George Barnwell. A Novel was published in two volumes, the first of which had twenty-four chapters and the second twenty-one. Its publisher was Richard Phillips, who was Surr's brother-in-law and who was at this time the publisher of radical books. Each chapter of the novel had an epigraph and these provided clues to the texts with which Surr indicated discourse affiliations. The writers from whose works he most frequently chose the epigraphs were Shakespeare, Pope, and Bowles. Each had five. Addison, Thomas, and Cowper each had three. Then there are two from Milton, Dryden, Akenside, Hume; and single references to Cicero, Spence, Johnson, Goldsmith, Chesterfield, Mason, Shenstone, Rowe, Dyer, D'Israeli, and Godwin's *Memoirs*. The affiliations extend not merely from the writings of the early seventeenth century, the two eminent seventeenth-century writers, and selected eighteenth-century writers, but include some of his contemporaries. Forms of affiliations can include allusions, quotations, even texts from other genres such as poems, proverbs, interpolated narratives.

Some genre scholars have assumed that such affiliations are instances of destabilization of a genre. But they assume that individual texts belong to a single genre, and if a text has such affiliations, it calls the genre into question. But such assumptions fail to recognize the combinatory nature of texts and the inevitable combinatory character of groups of texts that form genres. One of the earliest contemporary statements about the destabilization of genres was made by the anthropologist Clifford Geertz in his essay entitled "Blurred Genres."[2] His argument was based on the assumption that up to this time genres were always unified, recognizably coherent texts. It was a misconception that writers about literary genres could have corrected—by pointing to inclusions in Fielding's novels of interpolated stories or discussions of literary criticism, or by identifying the combinatory components in *Tristram Shandy*. What Geertz identified was a change in the components that had previously been included in texts that were scientific or historical. What was being shifted were the cultural fragments of texts; the components of subjectivity were being included in what had previously been the objectivity components, and the gender components were being introduced into texts not previously gendered. The process was not destabilization of genre but the alteration of what was considered the range of textual change within a genre. Even the assumption that fragmentation was being introduced as a new genre or that pastiche has been innovated has turned out to be the resurrection of genres, not their innovation. The innovatory genres have derived from the technological developments of film and television and the consequences of computer-generated genres.

The example of a shift in the reader response to *The London Merchant* can be seen in the contemporary reference to Milwood (the spelling of which Surr changes) as the most moving character in contrast to her treatment as a vulgar prostitute in the eighteenth century. Surr's novel, in introducing the generational conflict, also introduces a second plot: the story of Mental. The double plot serves to historicize the Barnwell narrative and to construct a generic history. The novel becomes a biographical study of Barnwell beginning with the opening death scene of his father. It includes the autobiographical history of Mental and the false autobiographical narrative of Milwood. There are also minor narratives of the family life of Mrs. Griffiths, of Maria, and the narrative of the Emery family. These narratives are often commented upon by the anonymous narrator whose moral judgments are directed at the reader to help distinguish lies from truth.

The development of the novel to which these narratives point is its relation to marriage and to family fortunes. The Barnwell narrative is a middle-class narrative in which the youth is apprenticed to a successful middle-class merchant with hopes of future wealth and improved status. But in Surr's novel, Barnwell, at sixteen, is with his sister and another at the deathbed of his father, rector of Hanworth. When his father dies, the bereaved family goes to live with Sir James. It is a departure from Paradise. The departure from the rectory with its memories of the father and his father's promise that George would follow in his religious footsteps open a different life. Sir James "had spent the greater part of his life in a counting house, and on the Royal Exchange" (1, 14–15). And though he loved his new family, he lacked the sensibilities of his new family, and he persuades them of the practical wisdom for George to be trained in the profession of merchant. This situation is the first instance of George entering into an apprenticeship that he does not desire.

George Barnwell. A Novel represents a significant shift in the commercial initiation of George and in the interpretation of the merchant to whom he is apprenticed. *The London Merchant* can be read as a historical study of the political rise of the merchant class. It is placed in the Elizabethan period and becomes the basis for merchants preserving the state from war with Spain. The merchant, who in the ballad is an anonymous figure, is reconceived in Lillo's play as equal in authority and significance to the members of an aristocracy, especially since these are anxious to ally themselves to the wealth as well as to the daughter of the merchant.

In Surr's novel, we have two generations of merchants—the older generation who belong with Lillo's Thorowgood are Barnwell's uncle and substitute father, Sir James Barnwell, and his friend, Mr. Freeman. These represent the dependable merchants, men of high moral value who have made their fortunes honorably. But the succeeding generation of merchants is depicted in the key figure of Mr. Emery to whom George Barnwell is apprenticed. Mr. Emery is a partner of Mr. Freeman, but he has become a man of fashion: "Instead of the merchant of the old school George expected to meet, Mr. Emery was a man of the most elegant deportment, dressed in the extreme of fashion" (1, 101). And Mr. Emery's involvement with government ministers was not in preserving society's highest moral values, but in supporting risky ventures.

Even George's role in the firm has changed from what clerks were in his uncle's time:

> He was established in Mr. Emery's house in the capacity rather of a private secretary than a clerk. Instead of being confined from an early hour in the morning till late at night, in posting ledgers and copying invoices, as Sir James had taught him to expect, and as was the case with all merchants' clerks when Sir James was in trade, George found that the sons, or nephews, or cousins of merchants, who threw a capital into the firm, underwent no such drudgery, which is consigned to boys who had learnt to write fine hands at charity schools. (1, 105)

The shift in time that the novel describes is matched by the significance of the shift in place. George not only leaves the paradisal rectory to live at the home of his uncle, but he leaves that to live in the London home of the Emerys. And in his affair with Milwood, he moves from place to place in London. The idea here of the novel is thus marked by dislocation, by the sense of instability and even mystery that it shares with the romance and the gothic novel.

It is at the home of Sir James that George meets Mr. Mental, who lives in the seat adjoining which is the remains of a monastery. Both Mr. Mental and his abode constitute a mystery for the residents of the neighborhood. "Now Mr. Mental was neither whig nor tory, nor a high, nor a low church-man, yet were his principles more at variance with Sir James than a Jacobite presbyter's, the latter only differed with the knight as to the person of a king and the modes of religion. Mr. Mental was supposed to be equally averse to all kings, and to all religion" (1, 25). Mr. Mental becomes inter-ested in George whose views on national religion he comes to respect. When he learns that George is to go to London to become a clerk even though he does not like the profession, Mr. Mental narrates to him the story of his life. The mystery surrounding Mr. Mental's role initially involves concealment, masking, and strange music. These affiliations with the gothic genre provide a basis for distinguishing between superstition and rational religion. His narrative involves an apprenticeship to a grocer whose notion of virtue is dictated by Calvinistic bigotry. The story of his marriage and its destruction involves affiliation with poetic readings and writing.

A Generic Interpretation

The novel begins with Barnwell's loss, and in moving from his valued home, it is followed by displacement. The plot of the Barnwell narrative, no matter in what genre it is placed, deals with Barnwell's loss of virtue. But in the novel, the loss extends beyond Barnwell's individual loss to the loss of the role of the merchant in society. Whereas the tragedy sought to create a significant social role for the merchant, in the novel this role has lost its integrity as a profession. It has, in the life of Mr. Emery, become fashionably involved with untrustworthy ministers of state and followers of corrupt, fashionable manners and behavior. The novel, which is in part based on the tragedy, refers to the time when the merchants of the past generation were honorable figures in society and thus deals with the his-torical change that has taken place in the profession. It does this, however, by the narrative procedure of the novel: it provides a series of linked nar-ratives, most of which are invented to deal with responses to the novel as a genre. Thus the narratives deride gothic novels, deal with the relation between dream and reality, and attack the application of Calvinistic belief in contrast to that of rational religion.

It may be helpful to note the relation of *Barnwell*, published in 1798, with that of the *Lyrical Ballads* of the same date. The novel went into six editions by 1834, excluding Sarah Wilkinson's abridgement of the novel and the publication of the chapbooks that seem based on it in the early nineteenth century. The *Lyrical Ballads* was a poetic experiment in ballad writing and in the use of poetic language and subjects. Surr's novel is experimental in the sense that Surr based it on the performance of Millwood by Mrs. Siddons, which altered the interpretation of Millwood. In considering the rewriting of a well-known narrative with the rewriting of ballads that included children as subjects and Coleridge's ancient mariner, it may be provocative to note that Thomas Skinner Surr was born in 1770, the same year as Wordsworth, and that he lived almost as long as Wordsworth, who died in 1850 whereas Surr died in 1847. Wordsworth's subject of loss and remembrance, the sense of lost innocence that recurs, the sense of guilt and the desire for, but incapacity to bring back, a paradisal past. These themes are shared by Surr and Wordsworth at the turn of the century, however different may be their undertaking and expression of them.

The novelist develops two stories—that of Mr. Harry Mental and that of George Barnwell, and insofar as Barnwell is told the story to prevent him from making the mistake of choosing the wrong profession, the point is that circumstances prevent him from following the career he hoped to pursue when his father was alive. If the aim of the ballad was to teach others to learn by Barnwell's experience, one might say that by the end of the eighteenth century, it was apparent that this advice was pointless; that the experience of others was never possible because the experience could not be duplicated. Just as imitation was abandoned as an artistic critical principle, so the advice that one should learn from another's mistakes was not a usable principle, even though it was possible that some individuals might indeed learn from the mistakes of others.

Surr's novel does not begin as the previous versions of the plot do, with the meeting of Barnwell and Millwood. The very fact that the work identifies itself as a novel—and the "Prefatory Dialogue" indicates that it is about everyday life rather than a gothic story of "castle, ghosts, and demons" (1, ix)—places it within a tradition that has come to be recognized as a conventional genre. That the first extended story it tells is a narrative by Henry Mental that deals with the loss of his university education, his marriage and the accidental loss of his adulterous wife by murder, and the loss and unsuccessful search for his daughter, all foreshadow events that Barnwell will in some measure find himself involved. The novel as genre combines numerous narratives that are a basis for social commentary. Thus Mental's story is used to attack religious support for belief in ghosts and raises instead questions about the relation between dreams and reality, the interfusion of the real and the imagined, a sensibility ascribed to young women.

When Barnwell enters the service of Mr. Emery he has passed his seventeenth year. He is younger than the Barnwell of *The London Merchant* who is, according to Millwood's guess, about eighteen when they met for the first time. The novel as social document contains discussion of dress, manners, and dining. It also deals with the changes in the attitude toward trade. Mr. Freeman, the model of the merchant in the earlier eighteenth century, expresses his view of the business: "'Merchandise, in my younger days, consisted in imports and exports; … and I can't say I much like the new sort of merchandise, where the freight is invisible, and the bills of exchange are abundant. Not but, in my time, if the state stood in need of assistance, the merchants of London could advance their cash at fair interest, but they never made the distress of their country the means of their profit, or degraded the character of an English merchant into that of a money lender!'" (1, 126).

The London Merchant and the previous prose "History" were based on the Barnwell ballad, but Surr's novel was the beginning of a tradition that was based on Lillo's tragedy. Surr's dedication makes this distinction clear: "The project of writing a novel founded upon the story of George Barnwell, which the tragedy of Lillo has made familiar to every English reader, seemed to require some apology." And in the "Prefatory Dialogue" he remarks on his subject that had a well-known novelist undertaken the task he would be welcomed, but not a beginner like himself:

> Had such a Novelist pursued *your* thought,
> And from an *old play* to some *new novel* wrought,
> 'Twere well: —but unfledg'd *Authorlings* like you,
> Must lowly aims thro' beaten paths pursue.   (1, viii)

The notion of the novel that Surr provided was based on the novelistic procedures developed in the eighteenth century. His story of Barnwell was told by multiple narrators of which the anonymous narrator served primarily to connect the contributions of other narrators. These involved first-person narratives by Mr. Mental, by Milwood, by Mrs. Willis,

Nehemiah Blackmore, Mr. Norris, and Mr. Rigby, and he included letters written by his mother and sister and uncle, Sir James, to bring their views into the story. There remains in Surr's narrative the conception of the novel as a combinatory genre, best revealed by the incorporation of numerous points of view expressed autobiographically, all of which are joined together to give coherence to the narrative.

One of the purposes served by this narrative procedure is to indicate temporal social changes by generational change. Thus the story of Mental and Sir James and his friend, Mr. Freeman, refers to generations that precede Barnwell and Milwood. The novel thus permits a discussion of the change in the role of the merchant from the honorable behavior at midcentury to the reprehensible attempt to link the merchant with the fashionable society and reckless involvement with behavior of reckless ministers. Thus the code of Thorowgood in *The London Merchant*, the desire to establish the merchants as a supporter of society at the time of Queen Elizabeth, is, in Surr's novel, a status achieved by Mr. Emery.

The London Merchant was a historical play that anachronistically treated that society as though it was identical with that of the early eighteenth century. But the historicity of the novel *Barwell* is an important aspect of the change that takes place in the character of Barnwell. Since Barnwell is identified as someone who seeks to fit himself to the environment of which he is a part, the change is made possible by adapting himself to the manner of the Emerys even though he has the greatest reservations about them. But more significant than this adaptability is his ignorance of love and of the difference between true and false expressions of love. In this narrative Milwood's claim of familiarity with his father and his youth is a narrative that he doubts but cannot substantiate because of a promise to keep Milwood's affection a secret. Although Barnwell is drawn to Milwood by sexuality, he offers her marriage, an offer that was made in the "History," referring to his future—after he completed his apprenticeship. But in Surr's novel the offer of marriage is finally rejected by the admission that she is already married. Barnwell thus sees himself as an adulterer.

When Mental and Barnwell walk to the dueling field in which Mental was to meet Captain Middleton, the man he mistakenly assumes has caused his death, Mental addresses his companion, starting his apologia for his life. Although a skeptic, he states: "the expectation of *some hereafter*, seems to me, upon mature consideration of all opinions, and a scrupulous investigation of my own thoughts, to be the *only innate idea* of Man,—a universal principle implanted by the common Parent, and influencing, under various forms, the tenants of each quarter of the globe" (2, 93).

This limited sense of religious conviction leads the man of "enlightened mind" to hesitate to identify one particular place as the "Divine Revelation of Futurity." Such a person does not seek to reconcile the "Justice of Omnipotence" with his own littleness. Rather, he regards the limits imposed by prejudice and education, and "he acts, he speaks, he thinks— deeds, words, and thoughts, truly his own" (2, 94). But such originality must not be imposed upon mankind suddenly; it calls "for the *slow* and *gradual* removal of the veil of prejudices" (2, 94). Any too sudden revelation "must necessarily produce effects, the very opposite to those intended by the benevolence of true philosophers" (2, 94).

Mental then confesses that he has been responsible for having published "strong truths" which "unsettled many minds from that foundation on which they had rested, ere any new and more solid base was formed for their support, and has confirmed me strongly in the opinion, that *Reformation* is much better adapted to the purposes of philanthropy than the best planned *Revolution*" (2, 94). Mental then turns to Barnwell and urges him to regard his comments as a caution that should "most carefully regulate the propagation of your sentiments, and even the effusions of your fancy" (2, 95). The narrator refers to these comments as a "sermon," but the sermon as a model for behavior is in opposition to the actualities of Mental's behavior since he is about to engage in a duel based on information that is incorrect. Even when he seeks to act with caution, as in the effort to identify Milwood as his daughter by spending a night in her home, she poisons him even though she identifies him as her father. The caution he advocates cannot prove effective if others are not constrained by it.

In expressing the enlightenment principle of "deeds, words, and thoughts truly one's own," of the originality of mind, he points to the need to practice this procedure gradually. But in a society where corruption and deceit reign, there is no assurance that others share the principles that Mental now subscribes to. In a situation such as the one Barnwell now finds himself, the urging of caution comes too late. It is ironic that Mental warns against "too sudden a glare of light" when through Milwood's insistence on silence Barnwell lives within the darkness of her lies and manipulations.

As Mental seeks his daughter in the prisons of London, he has an opportunity to observe the situation in the prisons. He refers to John

Howard, the prison reformer. The novel as a form deliberately refers to contemporary figures in order to establish the contemporary relevance of the narrative. In contrast to the historical references to Queen Elizabeth and the Spanish armada, Surr deliberately makes contemporary reference to ministers of the government, but especially to the performance of Mrs. Siddons as Milwood and to the reference of David Garrick's performances.

In the search for the seducer of his daughter, whom Mental mistakenly believes is dead, he decided to change his course of action and to observe "those whose lot I might ameliorate" (2, 61). He chooses "the path of that superior man among mankind, whose life was spent in doing good— the *Great HOWARD!*" (2, 61–62). There follows a description of the prisons of London, especially the Fleet, with its apartments for the wealthy prisoners and the cells of the improvident. The narrative of Mr. Norris leads Mental to the knowledge of Captain Middleton as the seducer of his daughter.

Milwood does not appear in *George Barnwell* until chapter 20 of volume 1, and her presence begins with a letter to Barnwell requesting his visit while he is in London. He makes the visit and she provides him with an autobiographical narrative expressing her long felt love for him, a narrative that relates this part of the novel to the narrative in *The London Merchant* when Millwood visits Barnwell explaining that she is being pursued by her guardian. Both these narratives are lies, and one difference between the Millwood of Lillo's play and that of Surr's novel is the storytelling. The Milwood of the novel is a far more inventive narrator than Lillo's protagonist; she is also a woman far more intent on secrecy because she is a known prostitute and because she invents narratives that can readily be questioned, though they never are by Barnwell.

Her insistence on secrecy is matched by the merchant Mr. Emery's secret investments and financial dealings that are withheld from his partner and supporter, Mr. Freeman. He falsifies his records in his reports to Mr. Freeman that lead to the downfall of the firm and his imprisonment. Thus the role of the merchant espoused by Thorowgood in *The London Merchant* and that exemplified by the generation of Sir James and Mr. Freeman are seen as connected with monsters and unworthy aristocrats. Thus the relations of the tragedy to the state and the attack on the state by Millwood are not continued in the novel. Milwood has no interest in affairs of state or in revenge on men as a generalized group. Unlike Lillo's

Millwood, Surr's has an affair with the Italian Zelotti with whom she is in love and on whom she calls when murder is in prospect.

The novel takes place at the end of the century and the character Mental pursues the seducer of his wife to America and finds himself involved with having to decide whether to support Britain or the colony with which he sympathizes. The decision to support his country, though he disagrees with its policies, indicates that the political aspects of the novel are subordinated to the personal rather than the personal being an expression of the political as in *The London Merchant*.

The secrecy that Milwood insists on is indicative of her desire to protect personal from public knowledge. The public role that Millwood insists on in the ballad and the tragedy is based on establishing a respected and known role. Living in a particular place and establishing herself prevents her from being generally known as a prostitute. But the Milwood of the novel is generally known as a prostitute; she needs secrecy to avoid having anyone recognize her. She moves from place to place, changes her name, expresses her past in lies—all of which assume that her exposed public recognition would result in identifying her for what she is—a liar and a prostitute.

Surr's novel is thus a bid for openness in human relations, especially the young and innocent country children. Barnwell is from the country—he has been brought up in Hanworth, and upon the death of his father goes with his mother and sister, Eliza, to live in the country estate of his uncle, Sir James Boswell, and after a short time is apprenticed to Mr. Emery who lives with his family at Portland Place in London. The secret investments of Mr. Emery and his moral neglect of his family lead to bankruptcy and familial disintegration. In this respect Surr's novel merges the procedures of the popular chapbook with that of the sophisticated novel. Although Surr's "Prefatory Dialogue" ridicules the gothic secrets, mysteries, ghost, and palaces, it does offer ancient monasteries, cloaks, and other disguises, and the readiness to murder. Mental's cloak and dagger are only one of his disguises, and his murder is a result of another of his disguises so that his daughter—Milwood—does not know that the man she poisons is her father. Such knowledge might not have altered her behavior, but it does show the inadequate conception of concealed behavior in a serious novel.

In using the novel to depict the corrupt side of London society, Surr introduces Emery's wife and daughters, who have as friends titled figures ready to take advantage of their hospitality and wealth—only as long as these exist. In addition to these aristocrats are stereotypes who figure incidentally but reveal the limits of Surr as novelist: the figure of the fop, Mr. Rigby, the military rake, Captain Middleton, the anti-Semitic stereotype of the Jewish moneylender, Mr. Negotiate, Zelotti, the Italian conniver and poisoner, Mr. Nehemiah Blackmore, the unscrupulous and untrustworthy solicitor, and Mrs. Willis, the landlady who cannot tell a straightforward story.

However limited the expansion of the Barnwell plot is, the novel does continue a tradition throughout the eighteenth century that can be found in Ned Ward's *The Spy*, in *Pamela*, in *Tristram Shandy*, and in the novels of Charlotte Smith, namely, the use of poetry that appears as interventions in the prose. In *George Barnwell*, the poetry is heard in Eliza's dream that foreshadows Mental's story of his murder of his wife. As a lyric sung with accompaniment of a harp, it suggests the relation between dream and actuality. There is the ballad that Barnwell hears as he seeks to establish the identity of the figure who moves among the ruins of the monastery. The singer accompanying herself on the harp sings the melancholy ballad in which a voice warns, "'I'll not rest till Henry dies!'" (1, 59). This is a ballad that is sung by Henry Mental, the same Henry Mental that is poisoned by his daughter, Elinor Milwood. When Barnwell is established in Emery's house he finds at first that he has considerable time on his hands. He spends it in reading and, after reading Gregory's life of Chatterton, he writes a sonnet about the need for Britain to aid British artists in need of help and support. This is Barnwell before he meets Milwood.

These songs are connected with the motives of loss and they draw attention to the role of the father in this interpretation. The novel opens with the death of Barnwell's father and the loss not merely of his guidance but of the home in which he has lived. And Elinor Milwood is the child of Mental and the wife he accidentally kills. He then refuses to see his child and arranges for her education. Her upbringing is thus without a father, and she finally escapes from the suppression of her guardian. Although this is the first attempt to explain the behavior of Milwood, it does so by pointing to her loss and the dependence on money that she needs for her survival.

The notion of loss was identified in the original ballad with the loss of sexual innocence, and in the tragedy the loss extends to his friends and his uncle. But in the novel, it is identified with the loss of Barnwell's innocence, and it is also identified with the loss of his father, with Milwood's loss of her father, with the Emerys's loss of their father in prison and with Barnwell's loss of his mother and Mr. Freeman's loss of his daughter,

Maria. What this sense of loss implies at the end of the eighteenth century with the American Revolution and the French revolutions marking the loss of a colony for Britain and the loss of a traditional way of life for France may explain in part the shift of one kind of society to another. Surr's novel deals with the replacement of one generation of honest merchants by another, one which abandons the moral role for reckless speculation and the neglect of familial responsibility. The familial devastation at the end of the novel begins with Milwood's poisoning of her father, Emery's imprisonment for debt and his wife and daughters dependent on Eliza, with Maria's death, Barnwell's murder of his uncle, Milwood's death in prison, Zelotti's suicide in prison, and the death of Barnwell's mother. The survivor who inherits the wealth of Sir James is the young Eliza, Barnwell's sister, and she becomes the ward of Mr. Freeman. Not yet come of age, Eliza exhibits the mercy and generosity that marked paragons of the earlier generation. Living as she does in the estate of Sir James, she represents a return to a moral past that has its roots in national religion.

The conclusion of the novel, unlike that of the ballad and the tragedy, ends with Eliza, who, having "imbibed some early lessons of sound and pure philosophy, the advantages of which now shone conspicuous" (2, 178), exercises these lessons with generosity to the mother and daughter of Mr. Emery and with thoughtfulness and kindness to Mr. Freeman, her temporary guardian: "In such delightful employ, we leave Eliza, whose discriminating generosity afforded her many heart-felt pleasures, and the exercise of which was her constant resource, whenever memory pointed to the consequences of *concealed errors* in the melancholy fate of her brother" (2, 178).

Although it is with the remaining member of Barnwell's family that the novel concludes, it is apparent that more than the Barnwell plot is at issue. In the "Advertisement" of the first edition that I quoted in opening this chapter, Surr pointed to the retention of the plot—"the chief incidents"— while adding new characters and dropping out others such as Trueman and Lucy and Blunt. In adding the narrative of Mr. Mental, who refused to supervise or even to see his child although providing for her education and a guardian, Surr provided a basis for Milwood's lack of moral scruples. When Mental finally begins a search for her, he is a man haunted by guilt of his accidental murder of his wife and the neglect of his daughter.

In telling Barnwell his story, Mental exhibits the need to alleviate his personal suffering by sharing it with another, even though the other is a boy of sixteen. Barnwell's subsequent meeting with Milwood and his sexual involvement with her are governed by the prohibition to talk about her to anyone. In the last paragraph of the novel, the "concealed errors" of Barnwell's behavior are what seems the moral of the tale. Concealment from Mr. Freeman is what governs Emery's merchant behavior and leads to his downfall.

The deliberate suppression of Barnwell's voice is Milwood's protective measure. When Barnwell offers her marriage, she refuses at first to give him an explanation, but finally tells him the falsehood that she is married. Milwood's falsehoods are identifiable by those who have known her or by people with a knowledge of the world. The difference between lies, dreams, and imaginary fictions are matters of verifiability or honesty. The injunction of secrecy when it is practiced in the ballad was to protect oneself—Barnwell—from detection by the merchant and the constables after his embezzlement. In *The London Merchant*, when Barnwell meets Thorowgood after he spent the night away, he is "o'ercome" by the merchant's kindness in dealing with his absence, and offers to tell the merchant the reasons for his behavior, but the merchant refuses to listen on the grounds that it would be too painful for Barnwell to confess. But secrecy in *George Barnwell*, as insisted upon by Milwood, is a procedure necessary for her to sustain her lies. And though Barnwell once tells Mental of his relation to Milwood, she absolutely forbids him to do so again. In one sense she is the very opposite of her father who loved argument.

There is no Thorowgood in Surr's novel in the sense that such a character is announcing the moral role of a merchant and informing his apprentices of the importance of the merchant to the state and to the model of family life. Surr uses Sir James and Mr. Freeman as examples of honest merchants who, when young, looked after their accounts reliably. But Mr. Freeman is too trusting in letting his partner run the business end, trusting to his honesty and care in investments. When Mr. Freeman brings his young daughter Maria to spend time with the family of his partner, he assumes that she will be carefully introduced to London society by Mrs. Emery and her two daughters. While in their care, she falls in love with Barnwell, who treats her as a sister rather than as a loved young woman. As she begins to find out about his affair with Milwood, she begins to pine away and eventually dies of unrequited love. Unlike Maria in *The London Merchant* who finally reveals to Barnwell her love for him when he is awaiting execution in prison, and faints at the prospect of his execution, the Maria of the novel will have nothing to do with Barnwell once she learns of his liaison.

This reconception of Maria offers an insight into Surr's conception of human behavior. Human behavior changes gradually in consequence of the environment in which people find themselves and in some cases, this change becomes obsessive as it does with Barnwell and Maria. With regard to the generality of mankind, Mental remarks progress to be gradual rather than revolutionary. But the problem arises when the individual cannot tell the difference between statements and behavior that are deliberately false and those that are true. The case of Lucy and Blunt, servants and complicit in the actions of Millwood, suddenly balks at the inciting Barnwell to murder. Lillo has Thorowgood exclaim that they have—with no self-interest—turned against their mistress' incitement to murder. This is not quite true in view of Blunt's awareness that they will be considered co-conspirators if they do not separate themselves from their mistress. Lillo's point is that average miscreants have moral limits that are not governed by self-interest but by moral absolutes. Sudden change is thus possible in *The London Merchant* whereas in *George Barnwell* such behavior does not form part of the world he creates. His creation is governed by association of ideas, so that there is in Surr a marked difference in Barnwell's response to his life at Hanworth under the guidance of his father, and his life in London with the family of Mr. Emery that lives in the corrupted fashions of London life. Insofar as he is able to engage in dialogue with the representatives of the Emery environment, he remains able to at least express his reservation about the moral life lived. But when he is forbidden by Milwood to speak to anyone about his liaison, he becomes totally dependent upon her version of human behavior.

In this respect the omission of Lucy and Blunt from the novel points up the difference between performance and storytelling. In the tragedy, Lucy narrates to Blunt what she has heard, but in the novel the explanation of Barnwell's consent to murder is the result of believing that this is the only solution to preventing the death of his beloved (2, 88). The jail scene with its religious redemption of Barnwell is an extended farewell to his earthly life in the Thorowgood household. But in the novel, Barnwell in jail refuses to see anyone other than the cleric. The novel closes not with Barnwell's warning to avoid lewd women, but with the kindness and thoughtfulness of his sister Eliza who, younger than her brother, has lived her life away from London and has remained innocent and kind in the paradisal atmosphere of Sir James's estate.

In 1804 Sarah Wilkinson published an abridgement of Surr's novel. Wilkinson was a prolific publisher of chapbooks; her short version of the novel is informative in granting at least one specific example of how omissions from a serious novel were made into a reading for a chapbook audience. The most obvious procedure was the elimination of chapters and the epigraphs preceding each chapter. This procedure reduced the range of affiliation or reference that Surr sought to attribute to his narrative. The epigraphs indicated the extension of the themes that the novel touched that were beyond those to be found in the tragedy, and these included prose as well as poetic passages. Not only did the abridgement limit this range of reference, it also eliminated all the poetic passages. What the novel made possible the chapbook removed to leave the bare plot. In this relation between the comprehensive text as novel and the reduced text as chapbook, we have different audiences as well as different prices of published works.

If we conceive of this novel as reduced to a short story—forty-five chapters reduced to thirty-six pages—we can speculate upon the bridgeable as distinguished from the assumed essence of the novel for an audience that seeks a digest of fiction rather than the full undigested text. What Wilkinson eliminates are components that make Surr's narrative a novel, that establishes it as a work that moves beyond the plot. Surr's novel continues the tradition of inset stories told by different narrators. Mental's story is the most extensive narrative, but there is the fictitious narrative—a lie—that Milwood tells Barnwell, there is Morris's narrative about how he came to be imprisoned, and there is an omniscient narrator who tells the story of the Emery family and the fashionable political and social environment in which they live until their downfall.

The novel not only includes multiple narrators but diverse kinds of writing. Mental as a young man composes poetry and the Elinor he marries is a novelist. The novel has a "Prefatory Dialogue" in heroic couplets in which his friend warns him of the ridicule his book will receive for its reworking of the Barnwell story by quoting from a beauty's life:

> "How monstrous low-bred must the creature be,
> Who writes such trash—don't offer it to me!
> Give me some novel of a different kind,
> Where castles, ghosts, and demons are combin'd
> To rouse one from the stupor of the spleen,
> With *sights* that never have, nor can be seen."

The abridgement is entitled "The Pathetic and Interesting History of George Barnwell," and on the title page is an injunction: "founded on facts." And the beginning of the story is headed "The History of George Barnwell; carefully abridged from Mr. Surr's celebrated novel" by Sarah Wilkinson. The "facts" that govern the abridgement seem to refer to events in the narrative so that whatever is included can be found in the original narrative. But what is omitted is what provides a sense of the contemporary London life contrasted with the paradisal life of the country, the openness that the country provides in contrast to the concealment that Milwood insists upon.

Surr's novel differs from Lillo's play not merely in the historical corruption that characterizes the merchant's behavior; it treats the family to which Barnwell is apprenticed, and Maria is received as a guest, as dominated by false fashionable behavior. And it is a family in which the father has little if any time to provide a moral center. By eliminating most of the narratives that are not directly related to Mental or to Barnwell's passion for Milwood, it removes the values that Surr seeks to achieve with reference to contemporary society. In his conclusion, which does not exist in the abridgement, it is the teenaged Eliza, who, as a ward of Mr. Freeman, plans for a future that will return to the religious values of kindness and sympathy that true religion offers.

This fictional return to a pastoral past that exists outside of London and in the behavior of a teenager happens at the end of the eighteenth century. Surr's novel and *Lyrical Ballads* were published in 1798, and despite their different generic genealogies, there are narrative intersections that derive from the shared cultural situation. In reference to the immense population growth, the colonial wars, especially with the American colonies, the revolutionary movement in France, a variety of alterations in all texts were taking place. One of the most obvious had to do with the need for public expression. Whether this was Coleridge's ancient mariner who stopped one in three passersby who needed to hear his story, or Wordsworth's child who treats the dead sibling as living presence, there is a need to express the presence of the past. *George Barnwell. A Novel* has one of its important aims to reveal the consequences of concealed expression of one's behavior and feelings. Milwood prohibits Barnwell from revealing his liaison, and this suppression of his freedom to share his thoughts and feelings about Milwood with his friends and family is responsible for his inability to control his decisions.

Milwood's insistence on Barnwell's secrecy is a device to prevent him from exposing her behavior to the opinion of his friends and family who have his interests at heart. Her motives would thus be exposed to examination. But in a larger sense, suppression of freedom of speech prevents inquiry, prevents the relief that sharing brings, prevents a consideration of one's self by confrontation with others. The need for secrecy is accomplished in Surr's novel with Milwood's frequent change of location. She keeps moving from one residence to another in order to avoid detection, and this behavior represents the lack of stability that her life represents.

This instability is another version of the instability of the merchant Emery whose speculative ventures lead to his downfall. The secrecy that Milwood imposes upon Barnwell differs from the silence and secrecy that Barnwell imposes on himself in *The London Merchant*. In the tragedy, secrecy is a consequence of Barnwell's awareness of his moral and sexual guilt. In Thorowgood's terms, Barnwell's behavior is an act against the code that links merchants' behavior to the state. I have discussed the impact of tragedy upon the plot, and it is appropriate to discuss the procedures of the novel as these alter the plot.

From the initiation of the novel of everyday life in the early eighteenth century, one procedure was to make it multi-voiced. Whether there was one narrator who constructed a fictitious autobiography as in *Remembrance of Things Past*, or several different narrators as in Fielding's *Joseph Andrews* or *Tom Jones*, the novel included many kinds of genres such as letters, journal, poems, memoirs, epigraphs, literary criticism, dreams, dialogues, and histories. In fact the novel itself was often identified as a "history" just as the chapbook or short narrative could be both a particular history of a fictitious character and a narrative that included poems as well as a history, or a history that included poems. It was possible for a novel to be both a novel that included histories and a "history" that included fictional stories.

The relation of parts to wholes and wholes—like letters or short stories—that became parts of a larger whole was especially characteristic of the novel. One reason for this was that the novel did not develop isolated from other genres but developed together with the periodical paper, the magazine, the miscellany, the fictitious autobiography. Since these genres were interrelated but distinct, the basis of their interrelation has tended to be observed as a consequence of the so-called rise of the novel.

What *George Barnwell. A Novel* demonstrates is that at the end of the century the need for expression by multiple narrators of their feelings and experiences had become the subject of their fictions. It is not merely that

Barnwell's suppression of his affair has to be governed by his love for Milwood, but that her narratives are lies governed by self-interest. Unlike the Millwood of the tragedy who is the enemy of the state and all men, the Milwood of the novel, while proclaiming her hatred of men, is in love with the Italian villain, Zelotti. In the tragedy, the reference to revenge becomes Millwood's defense and is the climax of her manipulation, but in the novel revenge is a trivial feature of her behavior. What dominates is her desire to accumulate wealth to make her life comfortable regardless of the manner by which such wealth is attained.

In the tragedy and the novel, there is Maria, the daughter of Thorowgood, and Maria, the daughter of the Thorowgood clone, Mr. Freeman, who repress the expression of their love for Barnwell. In both, the repression results in depression which leads Mr. Freeman's daughter to her death. Although in each case manners are the basis of such feminine behavior, and thus an example of the construction of feminine sensibility, this behavior is not recognized by Barnwell. In the play, for example, before his death he hopes that he will not be responsible for still another innocent death.

The driving force in the plot from the ballad to the novel is the seduction of Barnwell—his sexual initiation. This event unleashes forces in Barnwell that cannot be controlled by his reason or his obligations. His commitment to family, to employer, to the state are all put aside as he immerses himself in the sexual energy that is released. The youth's dependence upon his seducer makes him both a victim and victimizer. When his friend Trueman visits him in prison and seeks to comfort him by saying that if only Barnwell had spoken to him about his situation, Barnwell responds that he would have killed *him* if Millwood had told him to. The energy that is unleashed as a result of his sexual engagement makes him in the ballad a replica of his seducer; when she accuses him to the mayor and constable, Barnwell in revenge accuses her of complicity in all his crimes.

But in the novel, Barnwell enters the criminal life with misgivings and guilt. His relation to Milwood first gives him the sense of seducer so that he is prepared to sacrifice his moral principles to aid her since he is responsible—he believes—for her victimization. But the role of victimizer is reversed when he finds himself unable to resist her urging to kill his uncle. The love he feels for Milwood reduces whatever moral strength he still possesses. And at the trial, which is not shown in the play, he refuses to accuse Milwood or reveal her complicity in his actions. The love that he believed at first to enable him as victimizer has resulted in time to deprive him of his will. He becomes the craven instrument of his beloved.

In Surr's novel, Barnwell justifies his love of a prostitute by saying to her father, Mental, "Oh, were Milwood virtuous *now*, not all the screams and howlings of a wondering world should fright me from her arms!" (2, 103). His attachment to her now gives him the moral courage to defy the conventional views of society.

Early in the second volume Milwood admits that she is married and cannot possibly accept Barnwell's offer of marriage (2, 4). He sees himself as an adulterer. And as he wishes to leave her three masked men enter. They carry Milwood away and gag and bound Barnwell (2, 34). This is the event that occurred in the prose narrative at the end of the seventeenth century. Then it was an event that was presented in fabliau; here it is an example of Milwood as victim, together with Barnwell. It is not clear how Milwood arranged this, but it belongs to the fictitious story of her marriage and her vengeful husband. The narrative of Milwood as victim of domestic violence is only another instance of the lies with which she has entwined Barnwell.

Milwood's insistence on keeping her relation to Barnwell a secret is central to the novel. She is a known prostitute and reference to their relationship would jeopardize Barnwell's belief in his love for her. In the earlier versions secrecy is Barnwell's choice since if revealed it would indicate his disobedience and his criminality. In Surr's novel, the Emery daughters gain knowledge of Barnwell's illicit relationship and treat it as a subject of secret misbehavior.

Maria's knowledge of Barnwell's displacement of love leads to her illness and eventually to her death. But Barnwell's vow not to share his experience with Milwood with anyone prohibits him from exercising his openness of character. He has to repress ready exchange of thoughts and feelings to his friends, and after the first conversation about Milwood with Mental, he does not reveal his involvement to anyone.

Although Surr's novel borrows the murder of Barnwell's uncle from *The London Merchant*, the additional narratives alter the implications of the tragedy. Milwood not only incites Barnwell to murder his uncle, but she is a murderer herself, poisoning her father. What is a defiant act of revenge in the play is transformed into an avaricious act. In this respect the gothic apparatus introduced into the novel has affiliations with the chapbook of the previous century in which Milwood cuts the throat of

Barnwell's uncle. That Millwood was a gang leader whereas this Milwood is in league with a refined Italian prisoner, Zelotti.

The novel introduces a second plot, the father's search for his daughter that finally leads to parricide as Milwood's seduction of Barnwell leads him to parricide as well. The merchant in the tragedy announces a moral role for the Elizabethan merchant whereas the novel, situated in present time, reveals how the political connection has become immoral and unwisely speculative. In the novel, the moral merchant is presented as belonging to an earlier generation in the person of Sir James Barnwell and Mr. Freeman, men whose role has been supplanted by Mr. Emery, the fashionable and unreliable figure who has little interest in controlling his wife and daughter. But Barnwell is given a family—a mother, sister, and uncle—that offers moral guidance which is not followed.

In this respect the novel resembles the tragedy by making Barnwell drunk and deranged as he attempts to murder his uncle. In neither case is Barnwell's sexual passion discussed and in both he is comforted after his apprehension by a divine who teaches him that "There is another and a better world."

But there is a difference between the assurance of divine mercy in the tragedy and the novel's refusal to provide answers for the power of sexual passion or its source. The narrator remarks upon "love" as Milwood leads Barnwell to consider the murder of his uncle:

What is that potent, most mysterious influence, to which is given the name of Love? Say, ye, who aim at defining all the influences and operations of our nature, who presume to have discovered causes for all the actions of men,— how it is, that a being, endowed with more than the common powers of reason, whose heart has been fenced with the lessons of virtue, should, by the influence of this most powerful passion, be impelled to the commission of deeds, at which, when that influence ceases to operate, his heart recoils with horror, and his reason surveys with astonishment? (2, 145)

The tragedy indicated that love could subject Maria and Trueman to criminal vulnerability, but that such vulnerability could be seen as forgivable. This is what led to Lucy and Blunt's pardon. But the novel depicts Milwood as falsifying her feelings of love. Her deceit is not recognized by Barnwell whom she prevents from revealing their relationship to others. Secrecy and concealment become the means by which sexual passion remains unlegitimized. Barnwell's desire to marry Milwood is ultimately rejected by her false admission of marriage to another. Secrecy is thus to be understood as a masquerade, but it is related to the masking of Mr. Mental who uses it to shield his feelings. Masquerading thus belongs to father and daughter, and it brings to the novel the social issue of liberty and suppression.

The very last sentence of the novel notes that it is about "*concealed errors*," about the consequences that stem from prohibitions that prevent expression. The outspoken model of behavior at the end of the novel is Eliza, the teenage sister of Barnwell. She it is who redefines love: "Doubt not that God is Love, and when necessity demands no more *some* evil, then from the source of love, shall flow *UNMINGLED GOOD!*" (2, 172). As the inheritor of her uncle's wealth—her mother, brother, and uncle are all dead, and Mr. Emery is imprisoned—she becomes the benevolent ward of Mr. Freeman, whose daughter Maria is dead. The merchant's family is dependent on her generosity. As an unchallenged youth, her trials have yet to come, for necessity still seems to demand evil.

NOTES

1. T. S. Surr, *Barnwell: A Novel*, 2 vols. (Dublin: Printed for P. Wogan, H. Colbert, W. Porter, J. Moore, and N. Kelly, 1798), 1, iv. [I have used the Gale ECCO Print Edition. Editor.]
2. Clifford Geertz, "Blurred Genres: The Refiguration of Social Thought," 19–35.

Intervention 2: Problems of Generic Transformation

It is particularly relevant, I think, to inquire in a book on genre why critics consider genre a viable explanatory tool. After all, the alternatives to genre dominate contemporary criticism whether in the practice of interpreting a work without dependence on generic theory or in the analysis of *écriture* as a substitute for genre or in the preference for modes of discourse. Michel Foucault, in explaining his abandonment of genre, attributes the concept to categories that have lost their validity for us:

> Can one accept, as such, the distinction between the major types of discourse, or that between such forms or genres as science, literature, philosophy, religion, history, fiction, etc., and which tend to create certain great historical individualities? We are not even sure of ourselves when we use these distinctions in our own world of discourse, let alone when we are analysing groups of statements which, when first formulated, were distributed, divided, and characterized in a quite different way.[1]

In this quotation, the use of "literature," "fiction," and "science" as "genres" indicates the aberrant uses to which the terms have been put. Without pursuing the critical fortunes of genre theories, I can point to some general reasons for rethinking genre theory. The first is that contemporary genre theory is rooted in problems of continuity and discontinuity especially significant for a period such as our own. Any theory of genre ought to explain why and how genres originate and the reasons for their

R. Cohen, J. L. Rowlett, *Transformations of a Genre*, Palgrave Studies in the Enlightenment, Romanticism and Cultures of Print, https://doi.org/10.1007/978-3-030-89668-3_9

variations, interrelations, and discontinuance. Second, a contemporary genre theory ought to assume that a text is a hierarchical network, a system that is linked with other texts in a larger system to form a generic hierarchy. Thus some forms, like tragedy, or epic, or satire, or lyric, are dominant at one time and recessive or subordinate at others. A genre theory provides us with a comprehensive system to study all texts as a family of forms. It is thus possible to select from these all such texts as have been identified as literary. Again, a genre theory can provide us with analyzable features that interconnect and interrelate genres while permitting each text in which they appear to retain its generic identity. For example, some genres, like proverbs or the epigram or the maxim, are not only independent but tend to form parts of other forms. Bakhtin, for instance, declares that the novel is the genre that is especially distinguished by multiple voices and the multiple dimensionality of languages: "Diversity of voices and heteroglossia enter the novel and organize themselves within it into a structured artistic system. This constitutes the distinguishing feature of the novel as a genre."[2] And, finally, a genre system is valuable to us because it brings to our attention a body of texts the variety of which has only too frequently been ignored in literary study.

Genre systems have had various functions in a history beginning with Aristotle's explanation of the structure, aim, and effect of tragedy as a dominant form of artistic education in a community. There have been, since Aristotle, numerous genre theories with somewhat different aims for classifying texts, relating them, and analyzing aspects of their structure. And each of these theories advocates or supports certain values of literary study for the audiences they address.

Maria Corti, for example, points out that up to the present, theories of genre have generally belonged to one of two categories: "those of an abstract, atemporal, deductive nature and those of a historic, diachronic, inductive nature."[3] She has serious objections to both categories and offers her own historical-inductive approach, complemented and corroborated by structuralist methods. Her approach "poses the problem of the transformation of literary genres and of their functions" and "relates genres to the universe of senders and addressees," procedures that have as their social aim a contribution "to our understanding of literary communication and of the relations between literature and society."[4]

The very term "genre" contains, in the various meanings given to it, some of the problems of genre. Is genre a text or a discourse, a product or a process, or both? Is it a member of a class or is it a class? Within a class, what changes does it undergo without losing its membership? Can a genre be a member of more than one class? Under what conditions does one genre become transformed into another? What is the relation between a literary genre and society? The term has its source in the Latin *genus*, which refers to "kind" or "sort" or "species" or "class." Its root terms are *genere, gignere*—to beget and (in the passive) to be born. In this latter sense it can refer both to a class and to an individual. And it is of course derived from the same root as "gender."

I have stated that there were important reasons for rethinking genre theory in our time, but perhaps the most interesting is our own sense of the widespread exemplification of generic change and our realization that a genre theory is analogous to social and scientific theories which seek to explain changes in matter, man, and society. In ancient and modern written texts, we note the pervasiveness of kinds and their transformation. Biblical Genesis narrates the earliest generic transformations by describing the origin of the heavens and the Earth and of man and woman.

> In the beginning God created the heaven and
> the earth.
> And the earth was without form, and void;
> and darkness was upon the face of the
> deep ....
> And God said, "Let there be light," and there
> was light.
> And God saw the light, that it was good: and
> God divided the light from the darkness.   (Gen. 1:1–4)

God created light from darkness, man from the dust of the ground: "And the Lord God formed man of the dust of the ground, and breathed into his nostrils the breath of life; and man became a living soul" (Gen. 2:7). The transformation of Earth into a living soul is an elemental transformation; but it is transformation because it implies a continuity, for man returns to the dust from which he came. Dust to dust: for something to be transformed it must retain some features, aspects, or elements that permit us to recognize that we have, indeed, a transformation, not a completely new object. Something in the form needs to be transferred in order for something to be transformed. In some way, a transformation must be reconstituted so that its form change is not totally disconnected from that which has been changed. Robert Nisbet puts it this way: "Change is a succession of differences in time in a persisting identity." And he goes on to say that "only when the succession of differences in time may be seen to relate to some object, entity or being the identity of which persists through all the successive differences, can change be said to have occurred."[5] The crucial term here is "identity."

Consider the problem of identity and form change in mythological stories. Zeus, Hera, and other Greek gods and goddesses are constantly changing shape. Such form change, whatever its aim, is governed by a consciousness of the god's power and the god's knowledge that whether he becomes a bird or a beast, he can return to his original form. In other words, the language, soul, or spirit retains an identity. We can see this clearly in Apuleius's story (written in the second century) of Lucius, who is transformed into an ass though he continues to think in the language of a human being: "though I was no longer Lucius, and to all appearances a complete ass, a mere beast of burden, I still retained my mental faculties."[6] Or consider the famous twentieth-century story which begins, "As Gregor Samsa awoke one morning from uneasy dreams he found himself transformed in his bed into a giant insect."[7] Gregor's shape changed but he continued to think in human language and to be concerned about his human affairs. Such transformations, such continuity and discontinuity, create moral, conceptual, and self-identity problems. In a theory of genres the principle of identity is more complex. The critic constructs such identity knowing full well that each instance of a genre is in some way different from all previous instances. They must accept the openness of a class, and it is not always clear that a work belongs only to one genre. The very multidimensionality of language makes texts candidates for more than one genre. It is as though every text is endowed with an ambiguous identity whether by author, critic, or both.

Oral and written discourses proceed by linguistic transformations regardless of whether the speaker or writer accepts or denies a theory of genre. The reason for this is that language characteristically converts nonlinguistic behavior into language. Language is, at least in this respect, transformational, and any attempt to narrate another's discourse by retelling, revising, or reconstructing it necessarily involves a process of construction. Within language we can see that figures of speech like metaphor and personification are transformational figures. In metaphor, two different kinds—for example, a woman and a rose, a river and poetry—are joined by relating certain common features and implying a continuity within discontinuity. Metaphor, therefore, operates by demonstrating that what may appear to be two distinct and unrelated identities can be understood as a transformation. Personification, too, can be understood as revealing a universe in which nonhuman objects and beings possess the gestures, features, languages of human beings and are thus characterized by transformations. I do not equate metaphor or personification with genre, but I wish to indicate that genre theory is part of a larger explanatory enterprise concerned with understanding identity and change. And this enterprise applies not merely to literary forms but to the world of matter as well. Matter undergoes change, and the language that describes it is ambiguously generic: a seed *becomes* a seedling, a caterpillar *becomes* a butterfly. A theory of genre, therefore, attempts to characterize the processes of continuity and discontinuity, and its language is inevitably ambiguous.

Any instance of a genre is analyzable as pointing backward to its diachronic ancestry, forward to its alteration of this inheritance. Any text, therefore, in a theory of genre can be understood as being at a point of intersection between past and present, in which it is revising, supporting, supplementing, and undermining the class in which it is placed. This is what I mean when I said that every text is a process and a product. The language of genre is metaphoric, and genre theories pursue different aspects of the generative metaphor. But we should not forget that such pursuits of theoretical explanation form a genre of their own with their own distortion mechanisms. Inquiries into the classifications of writing, into the structure of these classifications—their interrelations with norms and values—make the various generic theories continuous while they also alter our notion of what a literary theory is.

To put it paradoxically, a theory of genre seeks to explain the continuity that governs discontinuity and the discontinuity that governs continuity. A theory of "genre," whether it refers to tragedy or epic or epigram, is a construct of criticism; it is a theory of our own making. If we grant the value of a genre theory, which theory should we embrace? Do we wish a theory which takes for granted that its subject matter is the forms in which authors write, or shall we proceed by extrapolating from the writings an ideal story or form such as "narrative" or "romance"?

I am aware that "narrative" and "romance" can be interpreted as empirical generic forms. Gérard Genette wavers between considering "narrative" as an abstraction to be found in numerous genres—that is, as a "mode" of writing—and "narrative" as a synonym for novel. So, too, "romance" can be a particular literary form, the "romance," or a mode of writing that is a feature of comedy, tragedy, novel, poem, and other genres or subgenres. It is the confusion of mode with genre that I wish to examine, a confusion that conflates the abstract with the empirical.

Narrative has become one of the more salable and assailable theories of genre. No one familiar with contemporary theory is unaware of the valuable distinctions pertinent to the structure of narrative. There is *story*, "a sequence of actions or events, conceived as independent of their manifestation in discourse," and *discourse*, "the discursive presentation or narration of events."[8] There are points of view, author, implied author, reader, implied reader, rhetorical distinctions such as prolepsis, analepsis, and so forth. By concentrating on distinctions between story and discourse, critics have been able to introduce important distinctions in explaining the devices and procedures of narrative structure. Yet narrative critics disagree even about these elementary distinctions. And if we regard narrative as a genre theory, there are two major dilemmas that it faces: the first is that, since a drama, a painting, or a novel can have a narrative, the theory provides no procedure for distinguishing and evaluating the nonnarrative elements from the narrative. The second is that writers do not produce narratives; they write stories, poems, novels, dramas, but not narratives. The narrative is an extrapolation from a drama, as in Jonathan Culler's discussion of Sophocles's *Oedipus Rex*: "The analysis of narrative would identify the sequence of events that constitutes the action of the story."[9]

But in this play there are several other narratives; for example, the second messenger describes in detail the death of Jocasta. What we have here is another narrative that cannot be distinguished from the first by reference to discourse. For the discourse of the first narrative is that of the *critic*, not of the dramatist. The theoretical entanglements that this creates result from the separation of genre theory from the kinds of writing that actually exist. The drama as a symbolic, ritualized performance may function differently at different times, but its role as a genre cannot be deciphered without some historical understanding. A genre like the drama or epic has a social function which audience or listeners grant, and it cannot be analyzed in disregard of these. Accordingly, in this study, as I explained in Chap. 1, I use "narrative" as the name of a part, or feature, of a genre and make distinctions of continuity and change by attending to the language and social function of specific texts. In my own statements, I extrapolate the series of actions that persist. These statements are an abstraction offered in the words of the critic-historian. They are intended to make distinctions apparent, not to identify actual continuities.

We can see the difficulties that will arise if we study "romance" as a genre in the manner in which critics have discussed "narrative." When Northrop Frye refers to "romance," he refers to Schiller's two terms—"naive" and "sentimental." Naive romance is "a kind of story that is found in collections of folk tales and *märchen*, like Grimm's Fairy Tales"; sentimental romance is a "more extended and literary development of the formulas of naive romance."[10] He wants the reader to see "romance" in early and modern times as primarily "prose narrative" of a certain type. But this is not the view of narrative structure. Romance, he points out, has recurrent structures such as two types of narrative linkage, and heroes and villains who "exist primarily to symbolize a contrast between two worlds, one above the level of ordinary experience, the other below it."[11] His concept of structure is subtle and provocative, but it is committed to the view that its features, however drawn from different times, are divisible into the basic structure.

But such a theory does not seek to answer why such different actual genres arise as tragedy, comedy, history, pastoral, pastoral-comical, historical pastoral, tragical historical—indeed why the whole Polonian classification should arise. Such a theory is not interested in explaining why literary conventions arise or decline, why genres are constituted as they are, when they are. If, however, we consider such questions appropriate, then the process of naming the genre to which a work belongs steers us to a view of artistic structure, its literary and philosophical ramifications.

Henry Fielding calls *Joseph Andrews* "a comic romance," which he defines as a "comic epic poem in prose; differing from comedy as the serious epic from tragedy: its action being more extended and comprehensive; containing a much larger circle of incidents, and introducing a greater variety of characters."[12] This definition, relying on epic, comedy, and romance, indicates that for the author the work possessed features from all three genres that were combined in imitation of *Don Quixote*. The text therefore was, for the author, a combination of structures from several different genres.

If *Joseph Andrews* is a romance, it also includes authorial commentaries that are not romantic structural features. It includes interpolated narratives in which the heroes become listeners and minor characters become narrators. It includes a fragmentary narrative as well as a long digression on the *Iliad*. It is, in fact, an example of the multidimensionality and multitemporality of a text, since many of the procedures are borrowed from Cervantes and others contain allusions to biblical and later texts.

I have been noting the author's generic identification of *Joseph Andrews*, but you are all aware that such identification is also made by critics in transaction with the text. The author's identification is surely pertinent, but it is not final, especially in the cases of a genre name such as the "novel," which was not in currency in Fielding's time. It is evident that in a transaction genre critics might locate the novel in the subgroups of romance; it might be considered within the novelistic genres that mix fact with fiction. But it would not be considered an epistolary novel or a comic epic poem in prose which is a genre without members.

But, more important, its generic identification would be determined by the works to which it is related, for example, as a parody of *Pamela* or as a work with a romance conclusion in which the true identities of hero and heroine are discovered, and they live happily ever after, or, indeed, a romance ending that provides a fantasy that steers the reader away from the attack on the vanity and hypocrisy of most of the characters in the novel.

Whatever the generic identification of *Joseph Andrews*, it is a text that is part of a continuing generic process. As such, its structure will inevitably be somewhat changed from prior instances of the genre, supplementing, supporting, questioning, parodying it. It is to this process of genre change that I now wish to turn.

Thus far I have suggested the reasons for a genre theory, the nature of genre theory in relation to change in matter, man, and society, the manner in which a text might be constituted for genre theory, and some of the dilemmas that involve narrative and romance theories. I use as a test case a story that exists as a poem, a prose fiction, a drama, and a novel.

"The Ballad of George Barnwel" is a poem about a merchant's apprentice who fell in love with a prostitute, was seduced by her, and was persuaded to rob his master and murder his uncle. The prostitute was tried and hanged, and Barnwel escaped to Poland where he too was hanged, but for a murder he claimed he did not commit. This story with some revisions was made into a prose fiction that was published in 1700. It formed the basis for George Lillo's *The London Merchant*, produced in 1731, and it was revised as a ballad by Bishop Percy in 1765 and became part of a novel called *Barnwell* by Thomas Skinner Surr in 1798.

My aim here is to examine the ballad, the play, and the revision and to bring to the fore some of the problems pertinent to genre transformation and to distinguish these from other genre changes. To begin, the ballad falls within a genre that is sung, and this ballad was set to the same music as Thomas Deloney's "The Rich Merchant Man." Its subject matter, while dealing with a merchant's apprentice, contrasted with the noble merchant of the earlier ballad. The poem is narrated in the first person by Barnwel but is concluded by a third-person narrator. Within the poem there are several inexplicable narrator shifts. The poem begins with an address to "all youths of fair England" and concludes with a warning to beware of harlots.

The poem presents a picture of debauched innocence and of the gross pleasures of the flesh and their consequences. The characters are of low descent, the diction often vulgar, but among the more interesting aspects of the ballad is its computational imagery, reflecting the merchandising and accounting characteristic of the apprentice's task.

When the ballad was converted into a tragedy, a number of changes took place that throw light on genre as a shaping of artistic force. The eighteenth-century tragedy was still considered a dominant form, and it was still reserved for conflicts among princes, kings, and their followers. To convert a vulgar ballad into a tragedy demanded that the characters be elevated and that the problems become affairs of state. What takes place in *The London Merchant* is the elevation of the merchant—not a character in the ballad—to the status of a gentleman who deals in political matters and sees his role as a moral model. The subject matter of the play becomes the typical subject matter of heroic drama: a conflict between love and duty, Barnwell's love for the prostitute and his duty toward his master. And Barnwell, who is no more than a youth, compares himself, as a betrayer of trust, to no less than Satan, "the grand Apostate, when first he lost his Purity; like me disconsolate he wander'd, and while yet in Heaven, bore all his future Hell about him."[13]

If we examine an elementary change in which a passage narrated by Barnwel in the ballad is spoken by the prostitute in the drama, we can see that there is an ideological shift. The ballad refers to a "dainty gallant dame," indicating the readiness of the speaker to succumb to temptation. By shifting the speech to the woman, it is she who forces the meeting and designs the seduction. In the ballad, Barnwel states:

> As I upon a day,
> Was walking through the street
> About my master's business,
> A wanton did I meet.

A gallant dainty dame,
And sumptuous in attire;
With smiling look she greeted me,
And did my name require.[14]

In the drama, the prostitute declares:

having long had a Design on him; and meeting him Yesterday, I made full Stop, and gazing wishfully on his Face, ask'd him his Name: He blush'd, and bowing very low, answer'd, *George Barnwell.* I beg'd his Pardon for the Freedom I had taken, and told him, that he was the Person I had long wish'd to see, and to whom I had an Affair of Importance to communicate, at a proper Time and Place. He nam'd a Tavern; I talk'd of Honour and Reputation, and invited him to my House: He swallow'd the Bait, promis'd to come, and this is the Time I expect him.[15]

The dramatic form provides a different structure of character from that of the ballad. Millwood addresses a servant who she believes shares her values and, in the tradition of the drama, informs the audience of her motives and manipulation of Barnwell. The ballad provides no such information but resorts frequently to repetition, especially in the rhyme, as one would expect in an oral performance. The tragedy requires a conflict that introduces two families, two sets of values, two households. It provides a local habitation and a fictitious past to justify its significance.

The two genres have different conceptions of the nature of character. The tragedy, however, unlike the ballad, is concerned with redemption and punishment. Female viciousness brings atheism along with it, but Barnwell is redeemed by biblical instruction and goes patiently to his death.

These additions bring in the merchant and his daughter and a trustworthy apprentice to counter Barnwell, as well as bringing servants into the prostitute's household who first support her values and cater to her needs but turn against her when she urges Barnwell to become a murderer. But the point of the additions, contrasts, and character transformations is to establish moral principles to underlie the conflict and to show the extent to which principles can be bent without being broken.

The tragedy is conceptually different from the ballad. The latter is governed by mutual guilt; the former lays out the difference between venial and fatal crimes. The tragedy focuses on class changes and the moral responsibility that accompanies such changes; the ballad outlines the consequences of sensual indulgence. We have here two different sets of values rather than a transformation of one set into another.

My use of this hypothesis of genre change is meant to support two points. The first is that if we fail to attend to the actual written form, the ballad or tragedy, we overlook the control that the genre exercises on narrative material. The music of the ballad, for example, acts as generic bonding with other ballads; other features of the poem, such as imagery, diction, and character become subordinated when the story is transposed into a quite different genre. My second point is that generic control requires an awareness of historical connections for adequate understanding.

If *The London Merchant* is an example of a transposition of some ballad features into a tragedy, what would a transformation be? I have tried to suggest that transformation involves continuity and that examples of it might be revisions or alterations that result in modifying a genre or in providing it with a different concept. The term "transformation" is used by critics to refer to two quite different categories. It refers to the variations a genre undergoes that do not involve a conceptual change and to genre modifications that do. This seems a simple enough distinction, but if a text is itself a system and part of other systems, how do we distinguish concept changes from surface variations? If Tzvetan Todorov is right in urging that new genres are formed from old, how can we determine which variation merely supports, which defends, or which supplements a concept and which overturns it?

Is *The London Merchant* a transformation of a narrative found in "The Ballad of George Barnwel"? Of course it is, but I doubt the usefulness of considering narrative a genre. As a structural feature of a ballad, it is transformed, but the ballad itself does not become a tragedy. Some of its features such as characters can be included in the drama; particular sentences can be identified. But most of the generic features of the ballad, its poetry, its song, its narration are not transformed and do not lead to the tragedy.

If we adhere to some kind of historical-inductive theory, we still need adequate explanatory principles, but we will not assume that a ballad can be transformed into a drama. It can, as in the ballad opera, become a component, a feature of a dramatic form, it can be absorbed into a more comprehensive structure so that some novels contain ballads, but we need to distinguish this process from a gradual movement within a form. The simplest example of a transformation is the ballad revision of 1765. In it the poulter's measure is turned into four-line quatrains, the diction smoothed, the narrator made consistent, the repetitions reduced. Thus, the original lines

> Quo' she, "Thou art a paltry Jack, to charge me in this sort,
> Being a Woman of credit good, and known of good report;"   (II, 115–116)

become

> Quoth she, Thou art a knave,
> To charge me in this sort,
> Being a woman of credit fair,
> And known of good report.[16]   (II, 25–28)

Bishop Percy, who made the revision, retained the second half of the lines in this passage and made his revisions in the first half, displacing the vulgar "paltry Jack" with the colloquial "knave" and removing the repetition of "good." These are, however, part of a systematic attempt to refine the vulgarity, ungrammaticalness, and discontinuity of the original. There is an attempt to remove the ballad from its common origins and to locate it in the realm of contemporary balladry. We can thus see, if we examine the many aspects of his transformation, that they include omissions, diction shifts, repetition removals, stanzaic alteration, and narrator manipulation.

These add up to conceptual change, even though much of the original ballad is retained. The shift in concept might be put this way: the original structure accepted versification and metrics that permitted vulgarity, discontinuity, unevenness. The revision sought to refine the language and the rhyme scheme and remove irregularities and repetitions. It transformed the ballad into an eighteenth-century artistic achievement. This is the transformation that Pope wrought when he "versified" Donne's satires. It is a process governed by a concept of refinement addressed to a literate audience rather than the populace at large.

But the study of revision seems an easy and not very usable example. The more difficult project is to undertake an explanation of a transformation in which one genre seems to lead into another. Here the explanatory principle is to trace the steps in the transformation with sufficient care so that no gap is too broad for leaping. One of the most eminent examples of this effort is M. H. Abrams's explanation of the transformation of the georgic-descriptive poem into what he calls the "greater Romantic lyric." He declares "that the most characteristic Romantic lyric [poems like Coleridge's 'Frost at Midnight,' Wordsworth's 'Tintern Abbey,' Shelley's 'Ode to the West Wind,' and Keats's 'Ode to a Nightingale'] developed directly out of one of the most stable and widely employed of all the neo-classic kinds."[17] He selects features from John Denham's *Coopers Hill* and from Gray's "Ode on a Distant Prospect of Eton College" and finds these to be variations of the neoclassic norm; finally he turns to William Bowles's sonnets and finds there the conceptual transformation he has been seeking. Its structure includes above all "a determinate speaker, whom we are invited to identify with the author himself, whose responses to the local scene are a spontaneous overflow of feeling and displace the landscape as the center of poetic interest."[18]

Despite the care with which Abrams moves from features in a georgic-descriptive poem to a sonnet that lyricizes them, there remain questions about the relations between the two forms. There is no doubt that features can change their function and that functional change may be associated with conceptual change. But is it likely that this is the case here? Poets from Dryden to Johnson eschewed the sonnet as genre. They did so because its structure seemed inhospitable to their antithetical poetic structures, to the heroic couplet as a norm, to the segmental sense that the couplet provided. From Denham onward the couplet became for neoclassic writers a favored poetic verse, one that Dryden and later Pope recognized as consolidating the social and moral values they were intent on promoting. The sonnet, constructed on cyclical or other principles, did not lend itself to these values or, at the very least, the poets thought it did not.

The theoretical issue is whether a return to a form rarely used by one's predecessors constitutes a revolutionary change, that is, a conceptual change, or whether such a form, when eventually used, is made to function within eighteenth-century concepts—whether these imply a Lockean empiricism, a Hartleyan associationism, a segmented, additive poetic world. In other words, its external change conceals an internal acceptance. The techniques of resistance with acceptance can include renewed older forms that function as do the contemporary ones, additions that exaggerate the principles they are supplementing, the introduction of a new diction that does not undo but does subdue the force of the received concepts.

In an article entitled "The Structure of Romantic Nature Imagery" (1954), published before Abrams's article (1965), William Wimsatt analyzed Bowles's sonnet "To the River Itchin" (1789) and compared it with Coleridge's imitation "To the River Otter" (1796). He found that the Bowles sonnet provided a flat announcement of Hartleyan association, whereas Coleridge's sonnet showed him to be "concerned with the more complex ontological grounds of association (the various levels of sameness, of correspondence and analogy), where mental activity transcends mere 'associative response.'"[19] Wimsatt recognized a continuity between Bowles's sonnets and Coleridge's; the difference lay in a shift of intensity which affected and enacted the structure of nature imagery. The criterion for conceptual change was, for him, intensity or depth, a romantic "dramatization of the spiritual through the use of the faint, the shifting, the least tangible and most mysterious parts of nature—a poetic counterpart of the several theories of spirit as subtile matter current in the eighteenth century, Newton's 'electric and elastic' active principle, Hartley's 'infinitesimal elementary body.'"[20]

What Wimsatt sought to do was to trace within the same form a transformation of values. The sonnet possesses a rather rigid external form, and he sought to show a change in its construction of metaphor, in its move from the tangible aspects of nature to the intangible. Concepts in poetry— ways of knowing and thinking—can be found in any of its structural features. Wimsatt found them in the imagery, but they can be found in the versification, in the meter, in the form itself. We need to understand that genre transformation can be traced through these structural elements. The subject matter itself is no necessary indication of the concepts that a work is enacting.

What seems valuable in Wimsatt's presentation is the recognition of the multidimensionality of Bowles's sonnet so that its imagery of nature is future-related and its associationism is past-related. Wimsatt does not raise the question of the sonnet as a genre, nor does he inquire whether it functions symbolically to resist or supplant the values of the georgic poem. He does argue, I believe correctly, that features of nature imagery reveal epistemological and moral hypotheses.

What signals conceptual change other than intensity of imagery, shifts in versification or diction? One important indicator is parody of a norm or form, as in Keats's first stanza of "Ode on Melancholy" followed by stanzas that offer a contrary norm. We can see this in Coleridge's parody of the sonnet and his own practice as an alternative. Another indicator is a poet's use of a verse form that is later rejected because it represents values he no longer shares. This is the case with Wordsworth, who begins with the couplets of "An Evening Walk" and "Descriptive Sketches" and turns from them to the lyrical, autobiographical poem. Or we can observe the shift in function of a form as in Blake's use of a hymn form in "London," which in the violence of the diction and the synesthetic imagery undermines the form and converts it from a peaceful support of social and religious values to a violent attack on them.

It has not been my aim in this intervention to solve the problems of generic transformation but to show their complexity and to offer some possible solutions. I have stated that we construct the problems of genre, and I have tried to explain why we wish to do so. The problems of genre and generic transformations are not insoluble. Their solutions will help us resolve other issues such as those of periodization and the relation of generic change to social and scientific change. But our success lies in so formulating our problems that they are soluble and that the solutions do lead us to enhanced understanding of our subject and our society.

NOTES

1. Michel Foucault, *The Archaeology of Knowledge*, trans. A. M. Sheridan Smith (1969; New York: Pantheon Books, 1972), 22.
2. Mikhail Bakhtin, "Discourse in the Novel," *The Dialogic Imagination: Four Essays*, trans. Caryl Emerson and Michael Holquist, ed. Michael Holquist (Austin: Univ. of Texas Press, 1981), 300.
3. Maria Corti, *An Introduction to Literary Semiotics*, trans. Margherita Bogat and Allen Mandelbaum (Bloomington: Indiana Univ. Press, 1978), 115.
4. Corti, *An Introduction*, 117.
5. Robert A. Nisbet, "Introduction: The Problem of Social Change," *Social Change* (New York: Harper and Row, 1972), 1, 2.
6. Apuleius, *The Golden Ass*, trans. Robert Graves (New York: Farrar, 1951), 72.
7. Franz Kafka, *The Metamorphosis*, trans. Stanley Korngold (New York: Bantam, 1981), 3.
8. Jonathan Culler, "Story and Discourse in the Analysis of Narrative," *The Pursuit of Signs: Semiotics, Literature, Deconstruction* (Ithaca, NY: Cornell Univ. Press, 1981), 169–70.
9. Culler, "Story and Discourse," 172.

10. Northrop Frye, *The Secular Scripture: A Study of the Structure of Romance* (Cambridge, MA: Harvard Univ. Press, 1976), 3.
11. Frye, *The Secular Scripture*, 53.
12. Henry Fielding, *Joseph Andrews*, ed. Martin Battestin (Middletown, CT: Wesleyan Univ. Press, 1967), 4.
13. George Lillo, *The London Merchant: or, The HISTORY OF GEORGE BARNWELL* (London: J. Gray, 1731), II.i.
14. Thomas Percy, "George Barnwell," *Reliques of Ancient English Poetry*, 3 vols. (London: Printed for J. Dodsley, 1765), 3:226.
15. Lillo, *The London Merchant*, I.iii.
16. Percy, "George Barnwell," 3:234. (Line numbering begins again in the second part.)
17. M. H. Abrams, "Structure and Style in the Greater Romantic Lyric," *From Sensibility to Romanticism*, ed. Frederick W. Hilles and Harold Bloom (Oxford: Oxford Univ. Press, 1965), 535.
18. Abrams, "Structure and Style," 540.
19. William K. Wimsatt, Jr., "The Structure of Romantic Nature Imagery," *The Age of Johnson*, ed. Frederick W. Hilles (New Haven, CT: Yale Univ. Press, 1949), 295.
20. Wimsatt, "The Structure," 299.

Undermining a Genre: Parody, Value Reversal, Counter-Genre

"*Memoirs, or* Memorials, *a term now much in use for histories composed by persons who had some share, or concerns in the transactions they related, or who were eye-witnesses of them; answering to what Latins call* commentaria. *See* Commentary *and* History."
"*Memoirs is also used for a journal of the acts, and proceedings of a society; or a collection of the matters debated, transacted, etc. therein. Such are the memoirs of the royal academy of sciences, etc. See journal, academy, etc.*"

—E. Chambers, *Cyclopedia*, 4th ed., 1741

By 1810 the story of George Barnwell had been in print in one form or another for 200 years. Although it started as a street ballad in London, it became a tragedy that played throughout Britain. Queen Caroline had asked for the manuscript of the play and *The London Merchant* had become one of the most popular plays in Britain throughout the eighteenth century. Surr's novel updated the plot so that it was a post-revolutionary story. The plot had become part of British culture; from the street to the home to the stage, it was performed, abridged, read, sung, and parodied. If in 1798 it was no longer admired by fashionable ladies, as Surr suggested, it was nevertheless a story about cultural as well as sexual

© The Author(s), under exclusive license to Springer Nature
Switzerland AG 2021
R. Cohen, J. L. Rowlett, *Transformations of a Genre*, Palgrave
Studies in the Enlightenment, Romanticism and Cultures of Print,
https://doi.org/10.1007/978-3-030-89668-3_10

corruption that had moral import for contemporary life at the same time that it had begun to be ridiculed as a conduct narrative for apprentices.

In an attempt to reassert the significance of the plot for young people, there appeared in 1810 a volume entitled "*Memoirs of George Barnwell*; the unhappy subject of Lillo's celebrated tragedy. Derived from the most authentic source, and intended for the Perusal and Instruction of the *Rising Generation*. By a Descendent of the Barnwell Family."[1] Since these memoirs are written anonymously, there is no way to trace the genealogy of the author who claims to be a descendant of the Barnwell family. The claim rests on newly revealed documents—so called—in the possession of his family, documents dictated to the ordinary when Barnwell was in prison detailing the particulars of his past life, especially the autobiographical account of his murder of his uncle and his subsequent trial. These are identified as "authentic" sources, meaning that they were dictated and written by George Barnwell while in prison.

> His time was occupied in prayer, in opening the state of his mind, and all his guilty conduct, to the ordinary, who was extremely attentive to him, and in writing down the particulars of his past life, for the benefit of young men, who should feel themselves tempted to leave the paths of integrity and virtue. It was from a copy of this narrative, a few of which were printed and dispersed by Mr. Strickland, after the melancholy event, that the author of this sketch was enabled to draw these minute circumstances in the preceding pages, which, were their authenticity not unimpeachable, would give to it the appearance of fable. (106)

There was indeed a genre of penitential narratives in the early eighteenth century. The criminal told their stories to the ordinary who, with his own embellishment, published the prison accounts. There was reason to believe that such accounts were not without fictional additions, or, like the stories of Jonathan Wild and Jack Sheppard, the prison narratives could be converted into fictions. The anonymous author of the *Memoirs* insists that he possesses an autobiographical account of Barnwell's murder of his uncle: "We have received a description of the unfortunate youth's feelings at this period, from the same source whence we have derived the preceding minute detail of antecedent circumstances, and as the statement was drawn up by him, while pent up in his dungeon, we cannot do better than to give it, exactly in his own words, since the reader will form a more correct opinion of the state of his mind" (85).

The first-person account belongs with the use of other generic documents inserted into the text as evidence: one such is the letter—also anonymous— informing Barnwell of Millwood's home as a "bawdy house," a house of prostitution. Another is the "transcript" of Barnwell's trial which is intended to support the reality claims of the narrative. Still another is the author's reference to some previous accounts of the Barnwell narrative and his correction of their "facts." "This sad tale has given birth to a very interesting tragedy from the pen of Lillo, and a novel by Mr. Surr, as well as some trifling productions, all of which have, as will be seen, deviated from the real facts, with an intention to render the productions more suitable to the taste of their readers" (134). The author, however, now provides the authentic "facts."

This statement near the conclusion of the *Memoirs* draws attention to the primary justification of this narrative; namely, that its truth can serve as a warning to vulnerable youths. Truth is especially important in this narrative because the author declares that

> a LIE is the fertile parent of every crime, and he who has once falsified his conscience, has laid the foundation for every species of guilt. ... The odium of lying is more easily incurred than shaken off, and every young man, before he subjects himself to an imputation of such a disgraceful nature, will do well to weigh in his mind, the present advantages which may be derived from it, against the pain which is inseparable from it, the effect it may produce of rendering vice familiar, and the shame which must inevitably attend its discovery. (24–25)

The creation of an actual human being from the fictional character is a significant event in the history of the Barnwell narrative. It indicates that the persistence of the Barnwell plot had so entered British culture that one could assume that readers would accept the reality of the fiction. The argument of art as imitation of life had led to influences about the import of actual experience in comparison with that of fictive experience. The anonymous author restates the by now conventional claim that a narrative of actual life, of "authentic" experience, possesses more interest than any fictions "notwithstanding fiction, in the hands of talent, may be made the vehicle of much instruction, example affords a more profitable medium, inasmuch as scenes of real life must teem with an interest which could scarcely ever be excited by the most able and refined effusions of the imagination. The latter may forcibly affect the feelings, and provoke the passions to enthusiasm, but it is the province of the former alone, to speak to the heart" (5). This distinction between feelings and passions as the

physiology of sensibility and the heart as the center of moral responsibility
was one of the ways of justifying the distinction between art and life. It
accounted for the importance of manners, memoirs, biographies, autobiographies, letters, journals, diaries as significant examples of life histories.
The claims of Daniel Defoe in merely serving as an editor for *Moll Flanders*
(1722) and *Roxana: The Fortunate Mistress* (1724), or John Cleland's
Fanny Hill: Memoirs of a Woman of Pleasure (1750) and his later *The
Memoirs of Maria Brown* (1766) are fictitious memoirs with no effort to
defend "authenticity."

What distinguished the anonymous author of the *Memoirs of George
Barnwell* is the conscious insistence on authorship, on the writing of the
memoir as composed or narrated by George Barnwell. Making Barnwell
into an actual human being with a life history answers to the importance
of authorial identity at the beginning of the nineteenth century. To make
George Barnwell's story into a criminal biography resembling those of the
early eighteenth century, or to present Barnwell as movement from virtue
to vice, involves a rewriting of the various versions of him as sacrificial
victim and as failed model.

The narrator justifies his claim to authenticity of his narrative by referring to a document dictated and in part written by Barnwell, though no
such document was ever written. Yet the narrator insists that a lie "is the
fertile parent of every crime, and he who has once falsified his conscience,
has laid the foundation for every species of guilt" (24). It is difficult not to
treat the *Memoirs* as a hoax such as Chatterton's putative medieval compositions. But the *Memoirs*, if not authentic biography, is surely a conduct
book intended for the instruction of youth. The author addresses himself
"to the rising generation of Great Britain, and more particularly to the
youth of the metropolis" (3) as he begins his volume with a statement
about the improvement of the youthful mind: "The improvement of the
youthful mind is an object which the wisest men of all ages have not considered as totally unworthy their attention. Even the capacious mind of
the immortal Dr. Johnson, cast in nature's amplest mould, willingly
descended from the proudest elevation of genius, to teach the rising generation the way to happiness" (5).

Every incident in Barnwell's affair with Millwood is used as an example
of the descent into vice that eventually leads to one's destruction:

> As the object of the subsequent pages is to trace the gradual progress of a
> youth, from this first lapse into error, through all the labyrinth of vicious
> depravity; and to mark his deviation from the path of rectitude, step by step,

until he had obtained a proficiency in crime which rendered his further existence incompatible with the safety and interests of society, it would be irrelevant to our subject to wander from the dark side of the picture, and to
paint attractions, where it is our duty and intention to erect a beacon, to
warn off the thoughtless youth from the rocks and shoals of criminal indul-
gences and illicit pleasures. (6–7)

As a conduct book it provides warnings for youth to avoid behavior that
deviates from the moral and social behavior sanctioned by middle-class
society. Such behavior requires a proper guide who can "communicate
correct ideas of persons and things to their pupils" (8). Failure to provide
such a guide leads to moral laxity and vice, and Sarah Millwood is an
example of this. Her parents do not provide the proper moral guidance.
She was the daughter of a respected merchant in Bristol "who, with a view
to the further aggrandizement of himself and family, spared no expense in
endowing her with all the fashionable accomplishments of the age" (17).
But while being taught the expected graces, she was spoiled by her teachers and parents: "her principles were undermined and corrupted by the
flatteries of those who surrounded her, and the subtile poison contained
in the immoral publications to which she had daily access" (17). The result
was that at the age of eighteen she eloped with her father's hairdresser and
went with him to London unmarried. He opened a barber shop and in
order to augment their income she made her home into a house of prostitution. Her paramour died in a brawl, and Sarah was left to follow her
profession. And it was at this time that she encountered Barnwell.

All of this information was new to the Barnwell story and it was supposedly drawn from the ordinary's account.

> Yet instances have occurred, and that not infrequently, where the best edu-
> cations have not proved a sufficient buckler against the temptations of riper
> periods. It has been seen that minds carefully imbued with the purest moral
> and religious principles have gradually lost those images, and received the
> taint of vice, until after being hurried through a maze of depravity, their
> termination has been diametrically opposite to what ought to have resulted
> from their earlier habits and associations. Since depravity has become fash-
> ionable, and vice, in the estimation of the world, has been divested of its
> criminality, these examples, as might have been expected, have become less
> rare; and the unrestrained indulgence of the appetites has been considered
> as characteristic of a youth of spirit, and as a necessary qualification for his
> introduction into the polished circles of society. (9)

The failures of moral behavior and associations to ensure the continuance of such actions in adulthood are attributed to the same reasons that ensured its earlier success: the customs of the "world" in which the youth moves. But the depraved world which Barnwell enters is Millwood. There is no knowledge of the prostitution in which she is engaged so that the simplicity of the narration does not—as in Surr's novel—reveal the depravity of "the polished circles of society." Rather, it is the sexuality of Millwood's body that "gradually" displaces the control exercised by his moral education. Barnwell's sexuality is more powerful than the habit and training of restraint. The author is aware that there are "numbers of those who have fallen into ignominy or obscurity" (8) as a result of poor monitors or guides, but there are others who have fallen despite good guides and good education.

What takes place in *Memoirs* is that the effects upon reality can be achieved by a narrative of the imagination. One of the general assumptions held by Dr. Johnson was that imaginary writings did influence the behavior of young readers, and in his well-known *Rambler* essay, his views summarized a widely shared position:

> The purpose of these writings is surely not only to show mankind, but to provide that they may be seen hereafter with less hazard; to teach the means of avoiding the snares which are laid by Treachery for Innocence, without infusing any wish for that superiority with which the betrayer flatters his vanity; to give the power of counteracting fraud, without the temptation to practice it; to initiate youth by mock encounters in the art of necessary defence, and to increase prudence without impairing virtue.[2]

The point is that for Johnson this view was accompanied with the injunction that a consequence of the behavioral effect of imaginary writing was that it should exclude unpunished wicked or immoral actions even though such did exist in society. The point of identifying the "memoirs" as a sketch "of a biographical nature" (6) was that it permitted inclusion of behavior that would not be as readily accepted if it were merely a story of a youthful criminal. This is especially true of Millwood who goes unpunished in this version.

As I have indicated, the Barnwell story was, by this time, a recognized part of British common culture, and in the same volume as the *Memoirs* there was published a narrative (by the same anonymous author) entitled *Parallel between Sir Richard Whittington and George Barnwell* (137–142). Because Dick Whittington was a historical character, the comparison served to support the claim that Barnwell was equally historical.

But in addition to the biographical strategy, the comparison served to support the importance of behaving within the standards of accepted society: "By comparison, the mind is the more readily enabled to detect the faults and appreciate the merits of individuals, according to the standard of just discrimination; and those minutiae of character which might otherwise pass unnoticed, are brought into the scale, and assist to guide the opinion" (137). From the meanest obscurity and poverty, Whittington rose to wealth, honor, and fame by the "duties of industry and integrity" (137). George Barnwell, on the other hand, "from a situation much superior to that which Whittington originally filled, shaped a downward course, and gradually fell from respectability to ruin" (138). The instances of rise and fall are gradual. The progress and regress are seen as conformity to or deformity of social aims and values; and Barnwell's behavior is attributed first to inclination and then to disregard of his obligations to his master: "He first ceased to be industrious from inclination; then he lost sight of his master's interest; from this step he fell into dishonesty; and thence inured himself to crimes of the most black description, until he wound up the climax of his guilt by *murder*" (139). But although the explanation based on the comparison stresses the acceptance or rejection of the social norm, the *Memoirs* suggest an important divergence for these progressive and regressive explanations. "Inclination" is incompatible with the acceptance or rejection of social norms. What the narrator implies is that these are different "societies" within a "society," and as one moves from one society to another the moral and social norms change.

The narrator attributes the vice of Barnwell to a general contamination of society, without realizing that deception of principles rather than confrontation is the problem. It is a problem exemplified by claiming that fiction is reality:

> The evil consequences of such a system may be more easily conceived than described: the destruction of the barriers which reason and experience had erected, must, of necessity, be followed by an inundation of false principles, which, unless timely checked, must produce general contamination: and it most seriously behoves [sic] every true friend of mankind, by continually opposing the torrent with the most striking precepts and examples, to place a bound to its destructive influence. (9–10)

Barnwell was twenty when he came to London, having spent the three previous years living with his uncle, after whom he was named, in Camberwell in Surrey. His own family was wealthy and lived in the Vale of

Evesham in the county of Worcester, but little information is available about them and why he came to live with his wealthy uncle.

There is no claimed ordinary's account of this, so that it is necessary to explore the reasons for the inclusion of this and other instances in the narrative. One reason for this is the subordination of the received plot to the added events that show the inadequate training of children by parents—in this instance, the setting up as a model contemporary social behavior rather than the traditional moral education offered by adherence to religious principles. The attempt to make Sarah a commodity that would prove salable to a wealthy young man (the family selects one) results in the lack of a sense of moral responsibility. It is a lack that leads their daughter to elope and to enjoy the sexual behavior that leads to crime. Even though the author does not "wander from the dark side of the picture," what is implied is the pleasure that Sarah takes in sexuality.

Another reason for the introduction of educative information is the development of narratives of education and the fictive form known as the *bildungsroman*. The key work for this was Rousseau's *Emile*, as well as the role of mentors, guides, and parents in the education of children.

But probably the most significant factor has to do with the conception of form chosen to narrate the story of George Barnwell. The *Memoirs*, although associated with the autobiography and biography, was a collection of instances or events that were chronological but not successive. Considerable time elapses in this narrative—three years—from the time that Barnwell meets Millwood to the time of his hanging. Under the auspices and patronage of his uncle, George entered the counting house of Mr. Strickland, "a very considerable woolen-draper, in Cheapside," who aimed to retire after George had learned the trade and could take over his business.

Since George had always lived in rural surroundings and had no experience of the city, London represented a severe challenge:

> With all his virtues and endowments he was as yet inexperienced in the study of mankind; his amiableness was at best but a negative goodness, since it had never been brought to the ordeal of temptation, and, consequently, the genuine nature of its constitution remained unproved. But the moment of trial was now at hand; and, removed from the immediate presence of his accustomed mentor, he was left, to stand alone, in the midst of a vicious community. (13)

The *Memoirs* shared with Surr's novel the view of London as a city of vice. In the *Memoirs* there is not only an increase in the warnings to youths to avoid prostitutes; but in order to show the consequences of not doing so, there is an increase in sexual descriptions. The previous fictive meetings of Barnwell with Millwood had been accomplished in the street or by a letter promising information, but in the *Memoirs* it is accomplished by Millwood's feigned falling and hurting her ankle and requesting that Barnwell help her to her "residence," actually the residence of a friend, also a prostitute. "Eager to improve the moment, Millwood threw herself upon a sopha, and raising her leg from the ground, apologized for her apparent indelicacy, and solicited the youth to examine if the ancle [sic] appeared swollen. The request, coupled with the appearance of the most delicately turned foot which can be imagined, produced an emotion in our hero to which he had been hitherto a stranger" (21).

On the first visit to Millwood that same night, Barnwell is seduced. The author then remarks: "The youthful reader will do well to pause here awhile, and remark how closely connected are the links in the chain of folly and vice" (24). Barnwell's progressive descent into vice is contrasted with the purity and virtue of Maria, Mr. Strickland's daughter and two other young workers—Thorowgood and Trueman—whose probity had been proved. The names of Maria, Thorowgood, and Trueman were drawn from *The London Merchant*, though in the tragedy Thorowgood was the father of Maria and Trueman was an apprentice together with George. In the *Memoirs*, George and his coworker are not apprenticed and the *Memoirs* are supposed to serve as an actual correction of these details.

The Maria of the *Memoirs* is, like her antecedents in the play and novel, in love with Barnwell, but her love is acknowledged and her relationship to him is virtuous. Maria's love for Barnwell is not made public either in *The London Merchant* or in Surr's novel. After Barnwell returns from the bed of Millwood, he behaves vulgarly:

> His affection for this lovely girl, had hitherto been pure, but it was now alloyed by crime; and those passions which had been excited by the embraces of a wanton woman, urged him, at this moment, to take unbecoming liberties with spotless innocence. The angel of virtue interfered, and rescued her, in the moment of danger, and, after some transient upbraidings, the offence was forgiven, and the youth was again received into the favour and undiminished affection of Maria. (26)

The sexual advances that Barnwell makes imply a pleasure that he received from Millwood and his desire to obtain the same from Maria. Nothing is written about such pleasures except that the "angel of virtue" interfered. It is the aim of the narrator not to encourage lasciviousness by suggesting that pleasure can be derived from sexual initiation and indulgence. In this respect, one can trace the shift in the sexual pleasure and cheerfulness Barnwell feels in the original ballad to its suppression in the *Memoirs*. In the ballad, once Barnwell decided to live with Millwood, he writes:

> So Wine and Wine i called in,
> and cheer upon good cheer,
> And nothing in the World i thought
> for Sarah's love too dear.
>
> Whilst i was in her company,
> in Joy and merriment,
> And all too little i did think,
> that i upon her spent.[3]

The pleasure of dissipation suffuses the original ballad and the seventeenth-century prose version, but the tragedy, the novel, and the *Memoirs* suppress the pleasure that the crimes make possible. Whereas the earlier ballad and chapbook had affiliations with other ballads and criminal biographies as autobiographies, the *Memoirs* had affiliations with sermons and moralizing fictions. The sermon that occurs rarely in the novel becomes in the *Memoirs* a frequent feature moving this novel away from the fictive construction and toward the advice found in conduct books.

The pleasure that Millwood receives in her encounters with George are always mixed with monetary rewards. The *Memoirs* is primarily concerned with the thought and feelings of Barnwell; the character of Millwood is identified as governed by sexual and avaricious desires and needs. Although she is identified as the "daughter of a respectable merchant in Bristol," she is not given a family name. She takes the name of Millwood from the hairdresser with whom she runs off to London. There the hairdresser opens a barbershop and as their gains were scanty, Millwood "bethought herself of other means of procuring wealth, and after silencing a few scruples which arose in her breast, began to barter her charms for hire" (19). When her paramour is killed in a brawl, she converts "the house into a brothel, and determined to gain her subsistence, by making her residence the receptacle of lewdness and infamy" (19).

Unlike the anger, resentment, and desire for revenge felt by the Millwood of the tragedy that resulted from her seduction, or the lack of parental supervision and love that leads the Milwood of the novel to a series of sexual encounters, the Millwood of the *Memoirs* receives a fashionable education that corrupts her: "Her voice was tuned to the most refined melody; her feet were taught to describe with peculiar grace the fantastic figures of the mazy dance; while her principles were undermined and corrupted by the flatteries of those who surrounded her, and the subtile poison contained in the immoral publications to which she had daily access" (17).

This fashionable education is provided by her merchant family. The corrupted education is provided by a merchant and this procedure can be understood as a continuation of the fashionable education Mr. Emery provides for his daughter in Surr's novel. Millwood's desire for finery is understandable since she comes from a pampered upbringing. So, too, is her merchant-like procedure in bartering sex for money.

But the *Memoirs*, like *The London Merchant*, is supposedly a historical document: "It was on Friday, the 18th of October 1706, when Barnwell was placed at the bar, to take his trial for the wilful murder of his uncle, before Lord Chief Baron Bury, and Mr. Justice Powel" (112). But the situation the narrator describes gives no indication of a historical situation even though he claims that "Lillo, the author of the play, was contemporary with the unfortunate object of our Memoir, and was a Jeweller of an estimable character as a tradesman and a man" (134). The reference to real figures in fictional works was not unusual in the early eighteenth century, as the line accountant Sir Robert Clayton in *Roxana* exemplifies; today it is commonplace to find real characters in novels and cartoon films. Recall Marianne Moore's definition of poetry as live toads in imaginary gardens.

In *The London Merchant*, *George Barnwell*, and the *Memoirs*, the killing of Barnwell's uncle is the climax of his moral corruption. But in each, the killing marks the end of his submission to Millwood. In *The London Merchant*, his killing occurs when he is besotted with wine, but even then his killing is an instinctive reaction of self-defense. In the novel, he is masked and the killing is a culmination of the disguise and repression of speech that dominates Barnwell's relation to Millwood as well as Mr. Mental's relation to his daughter Millwood, who kills her father. In the *Memoirs*, the act of murder is seen as mythological, as an act resembling that of Cain, as an act in which Millwood not only made Barnwell insensible with wine but sought to give him a new moral sense. When Barnwell embezzles money a second time, Millwood urges him to persevere in a line of conduct "which she depicted as certainly tending to make him honourable and wealthy, the envy of mankind, the pride of the female sex, and the object of universal imitation" (60).

Success no matter how achieved becomes the basis for admiration in society; Barnwell's abandonment of his merchant's honor is supplanted by his capacity to appear to others unchanged. Lying becomes unrecognizable from the truth. His language and behavior appear the same though they now function for different purposes than the original. And his language begins to confound vice with (mere) error: "to call knavery and want of integrity, a failing; and to hear of the execution of the vilest malefactors with something more than compassion" (61).

The Barnwell and Millwood of the *Memoirs* are examples of the ambiguity of the claim that, in writing, truth is of greater interest than fiction. The very claim is a fiction. The kinds of writing differ, but not because of the truth claims. They differ, as in the case of the trial of Barnwell, by changing the method of narration. The trial is written like a court report; each figure in the trial is identified and the address or evidence is summarized or quoted. Characters are introduced in the *Memoirs* who have not been mentioned earlier but who, like Thomas Price and Constable George Whittington, can give evidence pertinent to the murder. The aim is to add to the impression of historical accuracy. Sarah Millwood is called and she admits knowing Barnwell and getting money from him, but claims no knowledge of the murder. The justices of the court tell her that "if there was a sort of wickedness which placed its perpetrator above the reach of the law, it was that which characterised her conduct, and that she was secure" (118). This is the major plot change in the *Memoirs*. Millwood remained unpunished despite her complicity. Barnwell does not accuse her in the trial, but in his address before his hanging he predicts her punishment: "I go a little before her, to meet an offended judge; but she will soon be cited to the same tribunal, where I hope she will find more favour than she extended towards me" (131–32).

Another procedure that the author of the *Memoirs* uses to erase the distinction in his text between fiction and historical reality is to refer to the works of Lillo and Surr as having deviated from "real facts." As noted previously, the author writes: "This sad tale has given birth to a very interesting tragedy from the pen of Lillo, and a novel by Mr. Surr, as well as some trifling productions, all of which have, as will be seen, deviated from the real facts, with an intention to render the productions more suitable to the taste of their readers" (134). And still another procedure is to append a discussion of the fictitious Barnwell as a contrast to the historical Sir Richard Whittington with regard to the faults and merits of each individual.

By including Barnwell's self-description as part of the *Memoirs*, it provides the reader with a divided character. If in Surr's novel we have two narratives in which one aims to serve as a guide to the other, but both are defeated by contingent circumstances, then the *Memoirs* is the narrative of a young man whose love for Millwood permits him to be remade into thief and murderer only to discover that he could not live up to her version of what it meant to behave "like a man": "now that he seemed turning coward, and there was danger in harbouring him, she did not care how soon she was rid of his company" (99). Barnwell, tormented by Millwood's rejection, carries the curse of Cain as he departs as a wanderer to escape detection. Betrayed by Millwood for the reward, he is brought back for trial in a state of irrationality, but is brought to his senses by a helpful clergyman.

If we compare the *Memoirs* with the chapbook, published probably in 1811, all the references to reality versus fiction have been removed. The narrative is introduced by an epigraph about the sight of vice that, becoming familiar, is finally embraced.

Vice is a monster of so vile a mien,
That, to be hated, needs but be seen;
But seen too oft, become familiar with her face,
We first endure,—then pity,—then embrace.

The chapbook is entitled "The Life and History of George Barnwell" and is told in the third person by an anonymous narrator.[4] The *Memoirs* begins with a discussion of truth and fiction; and although both texts are intended for the instruction of youth, the chapbook is "intended as a beacon to deter the youthful reader from the indulgence of criminal desires and vicious pleasures" (5). The *Memoirs* begins the passage, from which the quotation in the chapbook is taken, with the following lines: "Of all the most approved methods of communicating wisdom, none can possibly be more fraught with entertainment than sketches of a biographical nature" (6). The *Memoirs* is concerned with the biographical and autobiographical aspects of the narrative as depictions of what actually occurred, whereas the "History" makes no reality claims for its narration. As a genre the chapbook is more closely related to the chapbooks of *The London Merchant* and to *George Barnwell. A Novel* than to the texts from which they are taken. Since the tragedy, the novel, and the *Memoirs* were popular works and went through numerous editions, as did each of the chapbooks, the categories of polite and popular to distinguish these two groups are insufficiently appropriate to characterize the distinction between the two groups. The distinction should probably apply to the single genre of the chapbooks and the varied genres of the other texts which cannot identify the audiences of the groups, especially since the audience of the playhouse may include readers of the chapbooks.

Although the aim of the primary text and the chapbook may be the same, it is apparent that the reading of the two kinds results in quite different responses when read in the years of publication or in time quite distant. One procedure for making such distinctions applies to the method of distribution—lending libraries, chapmen, subscriptions, bookshops. Another might be how the texts are produced, the size and expense involved, the inclusion or omission of illustrations. There would need to be some consideration of what is included in and excluded from chapbooks that are derived from primary texts.

The comparison of the *Memoirs* with "The Life and History of George Barnwell" reveals that the chapbook deliberately omits any references to the generic character of the original text; not only is it identified as a "life" and "history" rather than a memoir, but in dealing with the trial it avoids any reference to the characters taken from earlier works; indeed, all the characters belong to the same fictional world: "As our limits will not allow us to enter into a detail of the evidence, we can only give the depositions of the infamous Milwood [sic], and the worthy Mr. Strickland; the parallel will, however, show how completely our hero was the dupe of his own over-heated passions; and how fatally he was deceived in supposing she would make any sacrifice to save him from destruction" (28).

The "history" is correct in identifying the original as a depiction of Barnwell "as the dupe of his own over-heated passions." The *Memoirs* differ from *The London Merchant* and *George Barnwell* in its disregard of the society in which the story occurs. In the tragedy, the behavior of Millwood and Barnwell is related to the obligations of merchants to the state and the corruption of the state as a male-dominated society that corrupts women. In Surr's novel, Mr. Emery, the merchant, and his family are corrupted by the fashionable life of London and by unreliable, aristocratic representations of the state. But in the *Memoirs* these play no part in the seduction of Barnwell. Just as the generic distinction between truth, or actuality, and fiction turns out to be a fiction, so, too, Barnwell's belief in Millwood's love amounts to a self-deception. The *Memoirs* as a literary kind has its analogue in the plot; both are examples of individual misconstructions.

In a cultural sense we have in the *Memoirs* a release of sexual passions that were latent in the model life that Barnwell was leading. But this release leads to a bondage that changes his character. In needing Millwood's love and in believing in it, he becomes an embezzler and a murderer. But theft and murder are seen by Millwood as heroic behavior provided one is not caught. She encourages him to murder his uncle in the following words: "'Intrepidity and resolution are marks of a superior mind; they distinguish it from the common herd, and illumine it with a brilliant lustre. I would never urge you to commit a *crime*, since that which necessity impels us to, cannot be criminal. Your concealment cannot be effectual without you have money to render it secure, and you have but one method left of supplying your wants. Shake off cowardice, and be a man'" (78).

To be a man was to be fearless, determined, and ready to take what one wished without regret. The transvaluation of values, this notion of the heroic, is difficult for Barnwell to accept. He needs liquor and love to undertake the task of murder. He proceeds to meet his uncle in dreadful agitation. In his own words, Barnwell describes how he saw a sparrow fly into the thickest of a bush followed by a hawk that pursued it: "the little fugitive surrendered itself to the destroyer, and as the bird flew off with its prey, the feathers of the sufferer fluttered around me" (88). This natural event, indicative of the murderous procedure, gives him pause but does not prevent the deed. But in another sense, Millwood is the hawk and Barnwell the sparrow.

The image suggests the incapacity of Barnwell to be the heroic force that Millwood admires. In believing that Millwood reciprocates the love he feels for her, he assumes an equality between them in this regard. But in failing to live up to her values, the transformation he undergoes is a process of feminization. Indeed, Barnwell's loss of virginity, not of honor, is the beginning of his downfall. He is used by Millwood only as long as he can provide her with funds. Barnwell returns half-mad from the murder, but it is not long before a search for him begins and a reward is offered.

Millwood alarms him with threats to bring him to justice, and realizing for the first time "a right conception of the nature of her attachment to him" (98), he decides to leave London. He now sees himself in the tradition of the fateful wanderer: "'I have incurred the curse of Cain, and heaven has set the murderer's mark upon me'" (100). Even in his guilt, he sees not an embezzler or, in murder, a vicious and ungrateful nephew, but a biblical villain.

In the years between the staging of *The London Merchant* (1731) and the publication of the *Memoirs* (1810) political and social changes had altered the population, manners, and commercial status of London. And with these there came significant changes in the legal systems. The court scene in the *Memoirs* conveys detailed procedures that do not appear in previous instances of the Barnwell plot. In the ballad Millwood is apprehended, indicted, judged, and hanged based on Barnwell's letter, but Barnwell escapes. In *The London Merchant*, she is tried and hanged on the evidence of her servants Lucy and Blunt, but Barnwell does not give evidence against her. In the *Memoirs*, her servants do not provide evidence of her instigation of the criminal behavior of Barnwell, and Barnwell himself declares: "'She led me astray, but I have refrained from accusing or reproaching her; the fault was mine in lending too credulous an ear to here seductive arguments'" (126).

The *Memoirs* differ from all previous narratives of Barnwell in leaving Millwood unpunished. The situation can be understood as the final example of the shift in values which this version of the Barnwell story represents. Millwood, who instigated the relationship and incited Barnwell by feigned affection to commit his unlawful acts, achieves the heroic status she sought in Barnwell. The moral to be drawn is to learn to evaluate the statements or acts of others more carefully, or perhaps to bring into the open the sexual passions latent in oneself.

NOTES

1. Anonymous ["A Descendent of the Barnwell Family"], *Memoirs of George Barnwell; the unhappy subject of Lillo's celebrated tragedy* (London: Harlow, 1810).
2. Samuel Johnson, *The Rambler*, in *Essays from the* Rambler, Adventurer, *and* Idler, ed. W. J. Bate (New Haven, CT: Yale Univ. Press, 1968), 13.
3. This version from the Houghton Library, EBBA 34458.
4. Anonymous, "The Life and History of George Barnwell ..." (London: Dean and Munday, 1811?), 1–34.

From False History to Historical Novel

Edward Lytton Blanchard's novel *The Life of George Barnwell; or, The London Apprentice of the Last Century* was first published in London in 1830 and again in 1841 and carried in its title the indication that it was a historical novel. What the historical novel as a form meant to Blanchard cannot be gleaned from his letters, but the novel itself suggests how he treated the time immediately before Queen Anne's death and soon after the accession of George I. The novel contains a number of examples of history as a geographical description. For example, the second chapter opens as follows (George is asleep in the "flying waggon" going from Lichfield to London):

> Whilst our hero is thus forgetting his cares in sleep, let us turn the reader's attention for a moment to the state of travelling in England at that time. It must be recollected that no other communication existed, at the period we write of, from one end of England to the other, than by waggon. The merchant to gather in his accounts; the lover to unite himself with his mistress; the soldier to join his regiment; and the mariner to reach his vessel; found no other mode of travelling open to them than by throwing themselves upon the tender mercies of a country waggoner, whose clumsy machine was equally well-adapted for the carriage of goods and the conveyance of their owners. ... "Flying waggons," as they were termed, set out from Liverpool, then a comparatively obscure town compared with its present state of afflu-

R. Cohen, J. L. Rowlett, *Transformations of a Genre*, Palgrave Studies in the Enlightenment, Romanticism and Cultures of Print, https://doi.org/10.1007/978-3-030-89668-3_11

ence, with the expectation of never reaching London under ten or eleven days after their departure, at the soonest—an assertion that may perhaps create a smile, when the present "coach travelling to Liverpool in four-and-twenty hours" is taken into consideration.[1]

The contrast between the narrator's London and that of George Barnwell serves Blanchard's view of the inroads made in the natural environment in the name of progress.

When Alice escapes from Sir Robert Otway's home, she gains a hill which provides a prospect of Old London. At one point she sees a scene of "quiet Arcadian repose":

> Cottages embosomed in the vale below, wreathed around with ivy or ever-green, that seemed the very abode of rural happiness; homesteads thatched with straw, in true country fashion; and farm-yards where the feathered inmates spoke well for the condition of the proprietors: these were the chief objects of attraction. Above rose clumps of trees, that imparted beauty and variety to the landscape, and formed a natural link with the thickly-wooded country beyond; whilst in the foreground, pasture lands, and the snow-white blossoms of the almond-tree, then in bloom, diversified the scene, and charmed the eye of the spectator.
>
> But let not the reader delude himself into the belief that this is the pros-pect he will have now, when, taking advantage of some invitingly sunny morning, he provides himself with a hearty breakfast and an oaken staff, and journeys forth, to explore the beauties of the ground we are describing. If he does, we give him warrant beforehand he will be most grievously disap-pointed. The Hill indeed remains there still, but the prospect is gone—swal-lowed up in a vortex of bricks and mortar. London now stretches its gigantic arms to the very foot of the mound, shutting out the contemplation of green trees and meandering rivulets, and presenting us instead with a clumsy combination of brick-built tenements, the leases of which, as a board in the vicinity informs us, give the buyer possession for a century abating the last year. The trees have long been cut down and uprooted, to make way for gentlemen's villas and stuccoed mansions; and a railroad company have undermined a portion of the Hill, for the purpose, one would imagine, of experimentalising upon the probable tendency of earth to fall inwards. The cheerful sounds of the farm-yard are superseded by the shrill whistle and uneasy bellowings of the steam-engine; and where gardens once redolent of blossoms and fragrance existed, a public house has been lately built, with skittle-grounds and concert-room complete, and boards displayed in front, alluding to something having reference to the New Police Act, and the

twenty-fifth of George the Second. Such is the effect of time! A few years more, and a green leaf may be exhibited in London as a rarity, and a tree itself be thought worthy of a niche in the British Museum. (73)

Blanchard conceives of the industrialization of England as destructive of the natural environment though he conceives of human nature as pretty much the same in more than a century and a quarter (128–130 years). At the conclusion of his novel, for example, he declares, "In all ages, and in all countries, there have been, and will be, those who will realize too closely the career of Milwood; and, unfortunately, too often do we behold in the ruined prospects of some youth lured by pleasure from the paths of virtue, the semblance of Barnwell" (251–52).

But what of the relation between actor and environment? Blanchard develops a relation between men and nature that is marked by the pathetic fallacy, even though the destruction of the landscape does not seem to be carried out by vicious builders or industrialists. Still, if these are the overt views of history, there are other views that are developed in Blanchard's conception of the novel. *The Life of George Barnwell* was his first novel, and he seems to have written it in an attempt to improve his fortunes.[2] "The Preface" declares that "both Author and Publisher have in this aimed at producing a volume calculated to amuse and interest all classes and all ages, at home and abroad, in the fields or at the fire-side."

If we compare the historical function of the first scene in *The London Merchant*, which places the tragedy in the Elizabethan period, we can note that the eighteenth-century play connects the past with the earlier period. Blanchard's version of a historical novel is to place it in terms of his own time in the nineteenth century as a comparative instance. His view of history, therefore, is to consider the eighteenth century in terms of the nineteenth; for Lillo, the eighteenth century is conceived in terms of the late sixteenth century. But that aspect of the past which Lillo selects is the role of the merchant, and this selection functions to raise a class (the merchants) in economic and moral terms. The Elizabethan past does not function either in the language of the characters or in the moral values that the characters profess or in the structure of tragedy. In fact, the dedication to the tragedy contains Lillo's version of tragedy that was an eighteenth-century innovation, not an Elizabethan one. History, therefore, functioned for Lillo as emblematic—as an attempt to establish a class by referring to its role in affairs of state rather than as a situation that controlled the very concepts governing language and behavior. For, of course, the prose of the tragedy was no Elizabethan procedure.

The changed concept of history that we find in Blanchard serves no emblematic function; rather, it derives from the view of an objective past that can be recaptured by referring to facts and data substantiated by records outside the novel. The novel is "historical" in the sense that it reveals the geographical artifacts and the recorded events of the past. Thus Betterton, Addison, Steele, and others are mentioned as connected with the theatrical environment of Milwood as actress. But there are several other senses in which Blanchard's novel is "historical" even though the author may not have been conscious of these.

The separation of "objective" facts from imagined characters and incidents leads Blanchard to conceive of behavior in individual terms. This is a conception that Carlyle developed in detail in his own view of history. When Blanchard characterizes George Barnwell, he refers to his physiognomy as characterized by "want of firmness": "a physiognomist might have detected those lines in the upper portion of the face, said, by those skilled in Lavater's art, to mark the owner's want of firmness" (1). It is unnecessary for me to note the anachronistic reference to Lavater, but the point is that Barnwell is born with this lack.

Once the character wants firmness, he can be manipulated by those who have it. Thus, although Milwood is firm in her determination to exploit men, she has undergone a change from virtue to vice. This change was, in her case, the result of vanity and dress, and these were the sources of her seduction and desire for revenge. So, too, the astrologer Edmund Fuller is seen by Trueman to have markedly changed in appearance: "'One thing more and I have done,' cried Trueman; 'when I last saw you, I beheld a venerable and age-worn man whom Time had appeared to have used most rigorously; I now see a person whose advancement in years is scarcely to be observed. How am I to reconcile this contrast?' 'By knowing more of human nature and human exigencies;' answered the seer, and continued with a smile, 'this innocent masquerading has often been practised for more dishonest purposes than those for which I adopted it. Disguise I found necessary, and I availed myself of its aid'" (134).

The sudden changes that Blanchard's characters undergo—Mark Haydon the rake and drunkard, when facing death, confesses his role in the robbery and murder of Mrs. Royster, and thus frees Alice from imprisonment. The sudden change in Milwood after she is freed from the charges brought against her seems to disregard the normal behavior of others; she loses her looks, her friends, her energy. And it seems that she does this, in part at least, as a result of her behavior to Barnwell: "But whether her energies failed her, or that her spirit was really broken, her success was not, as formerly, commensurate with her endeavours. Since her recent incarceration, her health had suffered much, and her beauty with it had undergone sad mutations. Those by whom she had been formerly welcomed, now shunned her. One by one her acquaintances dropped off, and with them vanished her resources" (245).

Constancy, on the other hand, is what characterizes the unchanging characters: Alice, Luke, Julie, Sir Robert Otway, Trueman, Clara, and Thorogood. "Constancy" is the sexual term and "consistency" the social term for continuity of unchanging behavior. If we conceive of the Barnwell narrative from the ballad to Blanchard in terms of guilt and punishment, we can see that in the ballad, Barnwell's escape from England is ultimately punished in Poland, and in the chapbook many of Millwood's gang escape unscathed from their exploitation of Barnwell. Even in the tragedy the maid and butler, collaborators in Millwood's misdeeds up to the instigation of murder, are relieved from payment for their misdeeds because of their change of heart. The legal institutions seem to play no part in the narrative other than in the apprehension of the murderer and his accomplice. But as we move into the nineteenth century, the novels recognize that there is a difference between instigation and accomplishment, between work and act, and Millwood is distinguished from Barnwell by his deed.

But there is another reason for the changing concept of Millwood. The 1790s were a time of reassessment of the role of women, and Mary Wollstonecraft's *A Vindication of the Rights of Woman* is but one of numerous tracts of the time. Surr's novel was based on a changed interpretation of Millwood, and the novel explains the estrangement of Milwood from her father and the sense of abandonment that is a consequence. Blanchard is unable to explain with any conviction the rationale of Milwood's vicious behavior to Barnwell. And the argument that one vicious man made her vengeful toward all men is a rather strange, if not unbelievable and stupid, response.

The narrator explains the role of woman in the early eighteenth century:

Then, woman had not gained her proper station in society—that society which now awards her an eminent position. Education was denied her; and the young beaux and fops of the period began to look upon the whole sex as if intended by Heaven only to supply their wants, or minister to their pleasures. It is necessary for the reader to consider these circumstances, in order the better to understand what has preceded the present chapter, and to enter into the spirit of what follows. (178)

Blanchard was not interested in exploring why the "beaux and fops" assumed this attitude, in contrast to Trueman, for example, whose subservience to the wiles of Clara is a model of class and female worship. So, too, the manipulation of the "beaux and fops" as well as the innocents by Milwood indicates that the generalization does not even accord with the events described in the novel. Indeed, Blanchard's novel attributes to Milwood a sense of guilt and remorse that did not exist in any previous interpretation. The original ballad depicts a mercenary whose aim is "to have good Cheer in gallant sort/And deck us fine and brave." And when Barnwell can no longer supply the money for dress and debauchery, she flings him out of doors and betrays him to the constable. Millwood is of the devil's camp in the seventeenth century and in the chapbook, it is she who, with George, slays the uncle.

The London Merchant gives her a new role by providing a rationale for her behavior. She has been used by men who have betrayed her and she wishes to avenge herself on all men and the institutions of church and state that they control. Her anti-formal religious views permit her no remorse or hope for eternal forgiveness. This is a major change in the concept of Millwood, and I have in Chap. 6 listed some of the reasons for this change. Lillo's belief in the validity of law for all and in the value of the institutions when governed fairly and equitably for all makes Millwood's argument against individual corruption and institutional misuse sound, while rejecting her solution of destroying these institutions. Her role as woman fits the roles of Moll Flanders, who manipulates all institutions for her own purposes but ultimately becomes a solid member of society, and of Pamela, who acknowledges the misbehaviors of her beau but merely wishes to change him rather than the institution that bred him.

The Milwood who is found at the end of the century in T. S. Surr's novel belongs to a different set of institutions. She is a woman who comes from a broken family; her mother has been involved in adultery and killed; her father leaves her to be educated without his interest or guidance. As a displaced daughter, she becomes vulnerable to false fashion, to the depredations of the military who function as a group outside society, and governed by male rules and roles. Her seduction of Barnwell involves a phantasy of childhood desire for him. Her seduction and her instigation of Barnwell to murder his uncle are part of a parricidal revenge. She poisons her father as Barnwell his uncle. In Surr's novel, Barnwell is part of the corrupt fashionable world that governs the merchant Emery, and he is involved as well with embezzlement. Milwood incites Barnwell to murder in order to save her, not to provide riches: "she recollected, that there is a crisis in mental operations, and knew, that if she suffered the crisis of desperation to arrive, without accomplishing her end, it would never return. She well knew the state of languor that would succeed it, and, with a boldness of determination, resolved upon the risk. When she had resolved, she took his hands, she kissed them, bathed them with tears, and called him by the dearest title of Saviour" (2:150).

After slaying his uncle and accidentally overhearing Milwood as the poisoner of her father, Barnwell contemplates suicide: "now the torments of his situation drove him almost to self murder; and now the dread of what another world might prove, deterred him from the crime" (2:160). When Barnwell and Milwood are apprehended, Milwood goes mad: "Her despair now rose to fury; her expressions were horribly blasphemous, and assistance was necessary to keep her in her bed. Her exertions were fatal. In the paroxysm of her despair she burst a blood vessel, the blood gushed rapidly from her mouth, and, notwithstanding every possible assistance was instantly procured, before the sun arose, despairing she expired!" (2:166).

The violence and madness of Milwood in her last hours find her succumbing to the dangerous prevalence of the secular imagination and the refusal to acknowledge the life of a heavenly Father because of her rejection by an earthly one. Blanchard's Milwood is both a French woman and an actress. In her autobiography she sees her childhood as producing "vanity and love of approbation": "I was from a child fond of showy and costly attire, and in this did my mother encourage me, little thinking that she was cherishing such a serpent in my bosom. This inordinate love of dress increased from day to day; and by the time I had thought fit to arrogate to myself the title of a woman, it had reached its full extent. Here was laid the foundation of my pride" (234–35). Her seduction by a young French officer, Ernest Clairmont, and his abandonment of her in Paris formed the basis for her desire for vengeance on all men. Blanchard's

Milwood is the only one who is unpunished and who goes free. It is Barnwell who attempts suicide in prison. Yet Blanchard's view of poetic justice leads him to provide a suicidal death by drowning for Milwood. His version of a character torn by her desire for revenge, and shame for her revenge on an innocent youth, is characteristic of the polarity between good and evil, moral and immoral, that characterizes his novel. It seems a consequence of his belief in the individual's choice and shape of his own destiny and the consequent despair that results from irresolution.

What Blanchard does is to disengage the narrative from its English origins, place Milwood in a role-playing profession, and displace the narrative from present time. This temporal displacement serves Blanchard in several ways. It permitted him to avoid the parody and comedy into which the Barnwell narrative had fallen in his time by pointing to a time long past and suggesting that human nature has not been changed by industrial changes: "Let not the reader so delude himself—the world still teems with occurrences such as we have described—motives as vile still lead to the same results, and, in fact, human nature is still the same, and the race of Milwoods is not yet extinct" (87).

The temporal stage permitted Blanchard to describe in detail figures and places of the early eighteenth century to an audience that was not readily familiar with this history: "The descriptions interspersed, throughout, of public entertainments and public characters, may be relied upon for their accuracy; and he trusts will be found, at the same time, far from uninteresting" (252). But other and weightier reasons governed Blanchard's choice of a "historical" novel. In the opening number of *Chamber's London Journal*, the journal he edited, he declared the importance of historical exploration as an aim—and this on June 5, 1841, the year in which he published *The Life of George Barnwell*:

> To unfold, therefore, the ponderous tomes of history, and to read its sybil leaves in the fresh language of our day, unencumbered by the wordy heaviness with which its facts and circumstances have been clothed, is a portion of our duty—to illustrate the stirring events of the olden time, with the commentaries of travellers and the rhapsodies of poets, is another—and to point this moral from the whole, that the past is a lesson of emphatic usefulness, and capable of apt and earnest application to the state of society in our own time, is an equally important branch of the task we have undertaken to perform. To teach men to think, and to give them matter for reflection—aided and accompanied by lighter literature, which pourtrays life and man-

ners as now existing—which disrobes fashion of its silken gloss, and tears the veil of hypocrisy and superstition from the countenance of society—which instructs the inquirer in the sources of domestic comfort, and plants an attracting influence by his family fire, from whence may spring the joys of active life and the sedater raptures of a comfortable old age—these, and corresponding duties, are all necessary portions of the education we are desirous to confer.[3]

In addition to his own views of history and of change, Blanchard's interest in the historical novel formed part of the norm of 1840s novelists in that he extended the range of characters and of geographical locales. Kathleen Tillotson points out that the "widening of the novel's social range carried with it the widening of its geographical range. ... And the cultivation of both low and middle-class life as material necessitated more variety of setting."[4] The description of Milwood's place of birth, of Lichfield and London in the early eighteenth century, supports this view as do the characters from the fringes of society—the London gang of Jack Meggott—through the merchant class to that of Sir Robert Otway, not excluding the theatrical environment and the revels of the law students. Blanchard was intent in characterizing the language of the fringes of society and he takes note of the language of the gaming tables as follows:

> The various hangers-on at the gaming-tables of the day, who obtained an excellent and comfortable livelihood by victimizing some "Lamb" or *Pigeon* as the phrase now goes, out of his hard-earned gold, were, generally speaking, composed of the very sweepings of society. The whole tribe of sharpers, known by the generic appellation of "Rooks," and subdivided into jills, huffs, hectors, setters, pads, biters, divers, lifters, filers, budgers, droppers, and cross-tilers, were men who were equally ready to rob a man of his money, or deprive him of his existence; to pick a hole in his purse, or pink a hole in his body. Versed in all the nefarious arts of palming, cogging, topping, and slurring, they added thereto an intimate acquaintance with the workings of the human heart. (122)

The temporal dimension of the historical novel compelled Blanchard to be conscious of the shifts that had taken place from the early eighteenth century to the 1840s. When Trueman on his trip to Scotland visits the ruins of Thornton Abbey, he reflects "on the vanity of human grandeur and the unerring progress of the spoiler Time":

"Alas!" thought he, "how many hours and years have passed since human forms have gathered round that table, or since its surface has been illumed by lamp or taper. ... The cross and crozier have yielded to the mattock and the spade; whilst the once costly tesselated pavement is now overspread with a slimy green mould; and the proud towers have sank, like their builders, to the ground, and delved for themselves a grave in the yielding surface of the earth beneath. And this is the end of man's proud ambition! This is the goal to which all his wishes tend; and this the realization of his most ardent hopes! How sad a monument of human vanity; how melancholy an illustration of human frailty." (131)

Although these reflections belong to a religious tradition and are not necessarily a consequence of the historical novel, the point is that the self-conscious concern with historical change is a necessary part of the structure of the historical novel. And in comparison with these reflections upon the past are the concerns with synchronic time, that is, the time in which the novel takes place. Blanchard wishes to record a number of diverse events that take place at the same time. This contrasts with the narrator's comments upon the relation of present time to past and with narratives such as Milwood's autobiographical statements about her childhood— time antecedent to the present, or "The Schoolmaster's Story" of his love for a merchant's daughter (92, chap. 12) and her death in the Great Plague. In establishing a group of narratives in simultaneous time, Blanchard has to resort to numerous devices indicating time shifts and the interruption of a narrative. He can conclude a chapter with a sentence indicating future narration—"Of the cause of the interruption, and the consequences attending it, we shall speak more fully in a future chapter" (111, chap. 13). Again, "and gladly turning from so revolting a scene, we pursue our narrative in another chapter" (121, chap. 15). He can begin a chapter by announcing a continuation of the interruption: "We left Alice, at the conclusion of a former chapter, in a situation of no little perplexity. It will be remembered that" (137, chap. 18). Or he can juggle the various narratives in the following manner: "Before we can return to Barnwell, it will be necessary for the advancement of our story, and in order the better to preserve the continuity of the narrative, to see Trueman a little farther on his journey towards Edinburgh" (144, chap. 19). And no sooner is this narrative continued than it is interrupted by an "anecdotist" (Samson Skelton) who Trueman meets at a country inn and who recounts: "The

Story of the Fairy Cross, A Legend of Northumberland" (144–45, chap. 19).

The narrative disjunctions are an attempt to characterize simultaneous time in different series of narrative events some of which interlock at different moments. But the events refer to different classes—from that of London gangs to that of London aristocracy. This view of narrative time— a way of telling the stories—contrasts with historical time which compares the early eighteenth century with present time. This narrative disjunction, this deliberate avoidance of straightforward linear narrative or of disjunction within a single narrative, implies continuity by discontinuity. As Blanchard writes, "when their characters are withdrawn for a time from the eye of the reader, they are still supposed to be actively engaged in their various occupations, although no actual mention of them is made" (153, chap. 20).

There is also in Blanchard the inset story which involves a time warp. "The Story of the Fairy Cross" is a St. Agnes Eve fairy tale in which the father, a Norman Baron home from the Crusades, pursues his daughter Madeline and her peasant lover whom she wishes to marry against the Baron's wishes. The pursuit on St. Agnes Eve leads him into the clutches of fairies and elves, and he is returned to his land after a century in the air. The function of time in the narrative is to establish discontinuity between the Baron and his present relatives who hold his land. This supernatural intervention should be compared with the changes that develop from the early eighteenth to the mid-nineteenth century in the novel and to the astrologer's predictions which seem to be based on a special form of prophetic knowledge coupled with actual historical knowledge of events.

It is important before leaving the subject of time to examine the role of interpolated stories from Fielding to Surr to Blanchard. Consider the death of the father. The first scene in T. S. Surr's novel deals with the deathbed depiction of George's father and his uncle who comes to act as a surrogate father. It leads to a scene in which George feels himself cheated and rejected, and he finds himself unable to pursue his desire to enter the ministry. His mother urges him to become a merchant-apprentice. The original ballad, of course, merely mentions that "My father's rich." But the father plays no role in the poem. The 1700 chapbook begins with a mention of Barnwell's parents and their hopes for him. But *The London Merchant* does not refer to Barnwell's parents nor do they appear in the scenes in prison. The chapbook, *Youth's Warning-Piece; or, The Tragical History of George Barnwell*, based on the tragedy, refers for the first time to the death of George's father: "George Barnwell, the unfortunate young man who is the subject of this mournful tragedy, was the son of Mr. William Barnwell, a very eminent and wealthy Goldsmith in Lombard-street." And the narrator goes on:

> George's father dying whilst he was very young, he was left to the care of an uncle, who lived in a village near London. This gentleman had a great affection for George, and having no child of his own, treated him in all respects as a son; giving him a very liberal education, and when he was old enough, put him apprentice to Mr. Thoroughgood [sic], a merchant, with whom he lived three or four years, behaving himself in such a manner, as endeared him to the whole family. (4–5; undated, but after 1731)

The deathbed scene, therefore, is the first occasion of the death of the father as a significant figure in the testimony of Barnwell.

If we consider that such scenes play an important part in the art of the period, we can see that the opening scene of Blanchard's novel includes George swearing constancy to Alice on his father's grave: "On my father's tomb do I swear that I am wholly and only thine; and as he, who rests beneath, while living breathed nought but truth, so, when dead, may his avenging spirit punish my falsehood with his vengeance, if I prove false to thee!" (3).

Now consider symbolic time. There are two incidents that use time symbolically. The first is the scene in which Edmund Otway leads his brother to the room in which Sir Robert suffocated Julie twenty years earlier: "In this room that, twenty years ago this very day, a murder was committed that to this hour burns my brain as I recall it to my recollection. ... Well may you shudder at the recollection of that night—the fatal 10th of July, 1700—a night stamped on my heart with an indelible brand, singeing my brain as if 'twas torn with red hot pincers. ... On this very night, twenty years ago, you entered this room comparatively an innocent man, you left it—a murderer" (171; 172–73). It is in this very house that the metaphors of burning, of singeing become the literalization of the event. As Sir Robert burns the evidence of his marriage to Julie, the room ignites and he is enveloped in flames, an accidental yet symbolic death in which he is unsinged by thoughts of his evil deeds but singed and burned by an actual fire. Thus death takes its fiery vengeance on a man who sought to erase time.

The other death is that of the symbol of mother love. For as Barnwell is hanged, his mother, Rachel, drops dead in the group of onlookers: "a surgeon that attempted to open an artery, found that the blood—so great

had been the shock—had stagnated in her veins. It seemed as if the principle of life that had been imparted from the parent to the child, so as to
cause the existence of the one to depend upon the other. They had both
died at the same moment" (244).

The novel concludes with the marriage of Clara and Trueman and with
a picture of the idealized life they led: "To Clara, his youngest daughter,
who in figure and features as well as in name was the very counterpart of
her mother, he would often relate the story of his life" (251). For Trueman
and Clara duty and constancy had been rewarded, but in the structure of
the novel such optimistic conclusions falsify the narrative. For Alice's constancy leaves her with a broken heart: "Alice had died of a *broken heart*—
no unusual disorder, though it is one that makes no appearance in the
registers of mortality. Her heart was cankered with blighted hope; her
health undermined by the inward brooding on her sorrows" (209).

Constancy and change—these are the polarities with which the novel's
structure deals. Yet constancy is, in the novel, no guarantee of happiness—
as witness not only Alice's death but that of Luke Martyn who loved her
in vain: "Poor Luke Martyn! His case is no solitary one. Hearts have
throbbed, pulses have beat in unison with the vain passion that has actu-
ated the breast; but too often do these vibrate for nothing. We build up
images of snow, and weep when they melt!" (229). George's mother,
Alice's father, Julie Desanges, all these characters who are constant are
inevitably condemned to sorrow or death, and this is so because the world
that the narrator offers in this historical novel is dominated by the changes
that the environment and that people undergo. Constancy is a value only
if the situation in which constancy exists changes so that constancy can
adapt itself to different situations. But this is to put adaptation as an active
principle whereas in the case of Trueman, for example, his role is changed
by becoming a nobleman and inheriting the estates of his father, Sir Robert
Otway. In this novel, the son displaces the father in winning the approval
of the merchant for his daughter.

George Barnwell's first meeting with Milwood is accidental in contrast
to the planned meeting of the ballad and tragedy. And although he is
attracted to Milwood, he does not immediately abandon his vow to Alice.
But in time he comes to feel that the vow of constancy was made without
awareness of the urban environment, and that his attraction to Milwood is
something beyond his power: "'Eleanor!' he at last exclaimed, 'you exercise a strange power over me, so strange that I doubt sometimes whether
you derive it from heaven or elsewhere'" (125). The world that Blanchard

creates involves name changes as well as role changes: Milwood was a vir-tuous young woman until seduced; her French name was Helene St. Victoria; as an actress she became Eleanor Merton; and as an Englishwoman she was Eleanor Milwood. Blanchard even alters the received spelling of Milwood's name. This novel is the first occasion in which Milwood is identified as an actress, and the reason is that she is a role-player, and act-ing is marked by roles that are played. The purpose of roles is to perfect oneself in dealing with men, so that in a more general sense it involves adaptability to a changing world in order to control it for one's own purposes.

Yet Milwood is unable to control her youthful love for Ernest Clairmont, nor is she able to control her downfall even though she is acquitted of all crimes and set free. The world that Blanchard describes is not the world of law that Lillo postulates with its upright merchant and his code. Nor is it Surr's fashionable world which leads to economic and social breakdown. It is a world in which the separate classes are no longer kept apart and Mark Haydon, a learned and middle-class youth, becomes a member of a London gang.

> Descended from one of the first families in Lincolnshire, he had at an early period of his life come up to town. The money with which he had been most liberally supplied by his father, was now found to be inadequate to defray the nightly expenses of his follies and debaucheries. Afraid to ask for more, and receive it with the reproaches of his father, he forged upon him to an enor-mous amount. The crime carried with it its own punishment. The intelli-gence of his son's dishonesty contributed to hasten the old man's death, and Mark Haydon became, soon after, the inmate of a madhouse. On his recov-ery he plunged still deeper into dissipation to drown the remembrance of his conduct; and thieves, burglars, and women of questionable character, henceforward became his nightly companions. (16)

When Mark Haydon on his deathbed reveals who killed Tabitha Royster, such a change of character is not accounted for, just as the initial indul-gence in debauchery is not accounted for.

The name changes apply, also, to Sir Robert Otway—he is "Arlington" to Alice; just as his brother is an astrologer—Edmund Fuller—as well as Edmund Otway. Trueman, it turns out, is an Otway just as the gangster Jack Meggott appears at first as a "self-styled Quaker" (6–7). And there are, of course, "the Grand Masque of the law students in Gray's Inn"

(198, 199–201). These shifts show different characters moving between high and low conditions and reveal Blanchard's effort at writing a comprehensive novel with intermingling classes. Thus his historical novel functions to falsify eighteenth-century history despite Blanchard's effort to establish intertextual connections between his own period and that of Pope. Luke Martyn's poem, written after the death of Alice and called "The Present and the Past," reads as follows:

How sad it is to think that they
    Whose kindness we have known,
Should die, and leave us mourning here
    In this bleak world alone;
That those bland accents which we loved
    To-day should only live
In the faint visions of the past,
    That memory can give;
That those whose fond smiles greeted us
    In childhood's earlier years,
Should need *so soon* the poor return
    Of fruitless sighs and tears;
And that our dearest wishes thus
    Should unregarded lie,
Like flowers growing round a tomb,
    That blossom but to die.

But happily, soon Pleasure's sun
    Dispels the cloud of pain,
And hopes, although they wither yet,
    They blossom soon again.
Although the lips that boyhood pressed
    Are faded now and cold,
Yet still *another* face may beam
    As bright as those of old.
This world is but an April world,
    Where sunshine blent with tears
Awaits each moment of our life,
    And chequers all our years;
But still one maxim teaches us
    The source of true delight,
And makes us own "whatever is"
    Infallibly "*is right!*"

(228–29)

In this sense the only constancy that endures is that beyond life. But what we have in this novelistic structure is an example of comprehensiveness that is based on polarities that make history a mystery. While insisting on the importance of individual decision and of individual moral action, the story makes apparent the unconscious personal drives and the accidents of nature and society in shaping behavior. In this respect the narrative reverses not only the ballad conclusion, but that of the tragedy as well. For in the ballad it was Barnwell who escaped to Poland and Millwood who was apprehended, whereas in this novel it is Barnwell who is apprehended and Milwood who is freed. Theoretically, suicide is discounted in the previous narratives because it is forbidden by religious edict, but here Barnwell tries to commit suicide and Milwood succeeds. Structurally the narrative deals with the aristocracy—the Otways, with the merchant, his daughter and apprentices—and with the London gang. It thus constitutes a combination of high life and low life combined with astrology and with comments on industrial development and stable nature. But there are neither workers nor farmers in the book and the merchant is himself a successful speculator. What the novel does is erase the distinction that exists between the orders and thus between high and low life, establishing a ready commerce between them. The chapbooks based on the *Memoirs* continue to be published in the urban centers, but in the second half of the nineteenth century imprints in London disappear. This historical novel does not possess historical causation, and it is responsible, in the final analysis, for subordinating the Barnwell narrative to that of Trueman and the Otways.

In all the generic instances that I have studied, it is apparent that the generic selection has determined what is to be told, not because there is any particular absolute governing each genre but because the generic selection is a historical decision. It is significant that the chapbook of 1700 based on the ballad and the chapbook based on *The London Merchant* should resemble each other more than they resemble their sources. And historically it is important that the early chapbook should include the ballad and that at least the original audience of *The London Merchant* should bring the ballad to the performance. Genre consciousness is a way of tracing connections and defining identity for a historical moment. But in another sense it presents what history asserts. Inset stories are in no way dependent upon the Barnwell narrative, but they are characteristic of the novel of the eighteenth and nineteenth centuries. So too, thematically, the death of the father, which becomes foremost in the Blanchard novel, signals as its subtext the freedom from authority as well as the search of authority. And this is connected with the stories of youth and childhood, the periods of innocence. Only Alice and Clara have fathers but no mothers, and we have no knowledge of their childhood. What indeed can we expect of a history that is based on memory rather than perception and memory?

NOTES

1. Edward Lytton Blanchard, *The Life of George Barnwell; or, The London apprentice of the last century* (London: Thomas White, 1830), 5; hereafter cited in text. [I have used a facsimile of the original from Gale Digital Collections and The British Library. Editor.]
2. Clement Scott and Cecil Howard, *The Life and Reminiscences of E. L. Blanchard, with notes from the diary of W. M. Blanchard*, 2 vols. (London: Hutchinson & Co., 1891), vol. 1, 45. The origin of the novel is given as follows in a note: "the journalist [Blanchard] met a small printer and publisher of Holywell Street, a Mr. Olinthus Bostock. 'Good-day, Mr. Blanchard.' The salutation was returned, and after some conversation the publisher said, 'I often wonder you waste so much time on newspapers and sporting prints. Why don't you try a novel, sir—something cutting and moral?' As Bostock averred that by writing a work of this description its author's fortune would be made, Blanchard spend some days in Holywell Street, devising a story, at once thrilling and didactic, on the career of George Barnwell, the London apprentice."
3. Edward Lytton Blanchard, ed., *Chamber's London Journal* 1, no. 1 (1841): 1.
4. Kathleen Tillotson, *Novels of the Eighteen-forties* (Oxford: Clarendon Press, 1954), 88.

Ballad Criticism, Genre Theory, and the Dismantling of Rhetoric

What I wish to open up in drawing this study to a close are the historical transformations that take place when the discipline of rhetoric is dispersed and its explanatory power displaced by other procedures, by the kind of explanations that rhetoric could not make. To do this I shall take a problem that involves persuasion and examine how persuasion is accomplished. The problem is the elevation of one kind of writing to a kind respected by the learned—popular ballads to a recognized literary genre. The dismantling of rhetoric as a discipline and the elevation of the ballad to literary status can be seen as complementary phenomena: the decline of a discipline which systematized oral communication and the rise of an oral poetic form that became divorced from orality, became a written rather than oral genre. I want to trace the forces, the alternatives to rhetoric that shaped a new consciousness for writing, that initiated a new view of the individual, a new audience for popular poetry, a new concept of writing as private in contrast to public communication.

Up to the eighteenth century the ballad—though known as a type of writing from the Middle Ages—had never been studied as were the epic and tragedy. Rather, though sung by the common people inside and outside their homes, ballads were considered beneath the study of the learned. However, in May 1711 there was published the first prose criticism of ballads in English—"Chevy-Chase" and "Two Children in the Wood"— written by the critic Joseph Addison for his *Spectator,* a periodical paper.[1]

R. Cohen, J. L. Rowlett, *Transformations of a Genre*, Palgrave Studies in the Enlightenment, Romanticism and Cultures of Print, https://doi.org/10.1007/978-3-030-89668-3_12

The initiation of ballad criticism in a periodical paper constituted an important generic gesture. On the one hand the periodical paper was only beginning to make its way as an accepted form of publication, and on the other this publication identifying one ballad as an epic or heroic poem (No. 70) and the other as "a plain, simple Copy of Nature, destitute of all the Helps of Ornaments of Art" (No. 85) was part of a process in the elevation of the ballad as a valued literary genre. Addison named some of the collectors and admirers of ballads—Sidney, Jonson, Dryden, Dorset—but none had attempted a "critick."

Why did this attempt to elevate the ballad as proper for literary study occur at this time? Why undertake to persuade one's contemporaries that they were mistaken in ignoring a popular form? The line Addison took was that a poem, which the multitude approved, had to possess a special aptness to please and gratify the minds of men. He put it this way: "it is impossible that any thing should be universally tasted and approved by a Multitude, tho' they are only the Rabble of a Nation, which hath not in it some peculiar Aptness to please and gratifie the Mind of Man. Human Nature is the same in all reasonable Creatures; and whatever falls in with it, will meet with Admirers amongst Readers of all Qualities and Conditions" (No. 70).

Now it is apparent to us as it was to many of Addison's contemporaries that pleasing the "multitude" or "rabble" is no indication of quality, especially since the attempt to judge poetry requires knowledge of what poetry is. To argue that human nature is the same in all human creatures does not imply that such persons have the same understanding of poetic value. Still, the remnant of rhetorical strategy that Addison employed was to match the sentiments, thoughts, heroes, and heroic action of "Chevy-Chase" with that of the *Aeneid*.

In answer to the question, why did there occur at this time an effort to elevate the ballads, I begin by referring to Addison's nationalistic aim. Addison compared "Chevy-Chase" to the *Aeneid*: a strategy that implied a conjunction of an anonymous ballad of the people with a Latin masterpiece. It suggested the existence of a great English literary tradition no less important than the Latin. The process by which Addison managed this gesture can be identified as a rhetorical technique of generic matching: the matching of a low ballad genre with one of the highest—the epic or heroic poem—in order to make them level—to attribute to the lower the same literary and social status as the higher. But more was involved. Addison compared the anonymous author of the ballad to Virgil in not possessing critical knowledge of epic composition; in relying on "nature" the ballad author achieved through his talent what the rules of epic specified. Addison thus claimed for the anonymous ballad author what his contemporaries claimed for Virgil. For example, in 1711, the year of Addison's essay, Alexander Pope expressed this very view of Virgil in *An Essay on Criticism*:

> When first young *Maro* in his boundless Mind
> A Work t' outlast Immortal *Rome* design'd.
> Perhaps he seem'd *above* the Critick's Law,
> And but from *Nature's Fountains* scorn'd to draw:
> But when t'examine ev'ry Part he came,
> *Nature* and *Homer* were, he found, the *same*[2]:   (130–135)

Since Addison wanted to give to the English literary tradition the same status that the Latin classics had, he argued that the ballad author was not governed by guides; nevertheless the ballad demonstrated the very principles that have come to guide the greatest epics. The strategy was to point to an absence that revealed a presence: the absence of a guide for the ballad writer did not prevent his writing from being tested by and consistent with the rules that came to describe the structure of the classical epic.

This historical strategy is familiar to us; it has been used in our time to elevate slave narratives, women's journal writing, children's stories and other works by minorities or women that have no place in the literary canon. One of the claims of those who seek to elevate literary genres is that those which have no place in the curriculum nevertheless possess qualities of literature that prejudiced scholars do not, or do not want, to see. Addison knew that many of his learned contemporaries held the ballad of "Chevy-Chase" in little or no regard. And he commented upon those critics who mocked the epic device of cataloguing in the ballad with the words: "your little buffoon readers (who have seen the passage ridiculed in *Hudibras*) will not be able to take the beauty of it" (No. 74). And they couldn't take the beauty of it because they clung to their prejudices.

The rhetorical issue is not so simple as it seems. Any effort to persuade readers to accept the previously unaccepted importance of a genre connects the persuasion with social or political values. This is clear in the example of the persistent disregard of American Black writers of the nineteenth century no less than it is of women writers like Rebecca Harding Davis and Kate Chopin who had to wait for *The Norton Anthology of Literature by Women* to enter the canon. Political issues of democratic representation, of equality, of authority, are intimately connected with the problem of genre elevation.

Addison sought to elevate the low and unliterary ballad genre by claiming its thoughts and sentiments to be universal. It was thus possible for him to elevate as well the makers, receivers, and continuators of the ballad, the common people, into the realm of the audience that possessed reliable literary judgment by linking their taste with that of the educated. In fact, this political and literary claim was a rhetorical strategy aimed at attacking the writing of the metaphysical poets of whom Addison chose Abraham Cowley as the vicious model, calling his writing "Gothic," a term that implied, for Addison, the un-British character of such writing. "Gothic" was a derogatory term that brought with it the implication of forced poetic conceits, disunifying and inharmonious conceits in contrast to the simple and natural beauty and sentiment of the ancient writers. Addison's attack on metaphysical poetry, on a poetry of strained images whether by Martial or Cowley, was countered by his approbation of an ordinary song or ballad. His choice of these low genres makes clear the importance of hierarchical generic distinctions for his argument. Genre classification permitted him to argue that the received classification of poetry—lyric, ode, epic, tragedy, satire, and so on—had omitted ballads that belonged with the highest of them; and such argument permitted him to imply—whether he intended to or not—that current theory did not need to be revised; it had merely to include what it had overlooked. Addison was not seeking to revolutionize poetic theory, but rather to make it accommodate nationalistic aims.

Actually Addison was involved in a contradiction he did not recognize. Historically he wished to make the accepted poetic theory include what it was constructed to exclude. By extending the definition of "Chevy-Chase" so that it could be considered an epic or a heroic poem, the concept of heroic poetry became a basis for its own disuse because the examples included within it rendered it ineffective in making the distinctions for which it originally served.

When I use the term "rhetorical strategy" to characterize Addison's arguments, I mean that he embraces some of the persuasive techniques that rhetoricians used. But his whole enterprise of elevating a popular and unlearned type of writing was contrary to the types of discourse to which rhetoric as a discipline referred. Addison incorporated a dismantled element of the discipline and used it so that it undermined the practice of rhetoric. Rhetorical elements, in other words, came to be used to imply continuity of procedure while the very use of these elements supported the rejection of the discipline.

Addison's example was but part of the generic changes in English writing that were taking place at the beginning of the eighteenth century and Addison permits us to see how changes in the general literary hierarchy were analogous to explanations of social change. At the same time, his example reveals that rhetoric was not appropriate to describe these very changes. Rhetoric related to individual discourses, not to the way in which discourses underwent changes. Addison, however, linked literary with social change. In the essay immediately preceding his argument for the elevation of the ballad, Addison published an essay discussing and praising the new place that was being occupied by the merchant class. His effort to support the elevated status of his class served as a subtext for the rising status of the ballad.

Just as he praised the elevation of the merchant because of the private and public harmony the merchant created, Addison pointed to the actual elevation of the ballad because it harmonized the sentiment and taste of the rabble and the best critics: "If this Song had been written in the *Gothic* Manner, which is the Delight of all our little wits, whether Writers or Readers, it would not have hit the taste of so many Ages, and have pleased the Readers of all Ranks and Conditions" (*Spectator* 74). The universality of the ballad was based on that aspect of human nature that revealed an "essential and inherent Perfection of Simplicity of Thought" (No. 70).

But assumptions about simplicity of thought were not shared by many of Addison's fellow critics. Neither was the elevation of the ballad nor its nationalistic function. The rhetoric that devalued ballads was not readily overturned or made obsolete by Addison's commentary. On the contrary, Addison's arguments were substantively defeated. John Dennis objected to Addison's assumption about universality of judgment between uneducated and educated human beings, and he argued further that one ought not to separate simplicity of thought from simplicity of expression since it was art that joined them. Addison's readiness to justify the thought of a ballad in spite of "a despicable simplicity in the Verse" confirmed the validity of Dennis's attack. In fact, the reception of Addison's essays on the ballads was marked by numerous parodies by contemporaries; these critics were unimpressed by the inadequacies of an argument that sought to apply the contemporary critical criteria of a heroic poem to ballads that dealt with a local battle or a betrayal of family obligation.

It is necessary to acknowledge, therefore, that Addison's effort to elevate popular ballads into the domain of the highest literary genre by matching them with the classical epics had no critical support; in fact, his arguments were effectively refuted and created no immediate followers. But refutation of criticism is often irrelevant if a genre engages poets, dramatists, and novelists. Despite the inadequacy of Addison's criticism, the incorporation of ballads into the literary hierarchy was achieved.

How was this done? The first procedure to note is that Addison's argument that invoked rhetorical techniques was met by opposition which stressed the traditional moral and hierarchical element in rhetorical analysis. I do not need to stress that resistance to including popular romances or detective stories in the modern university curriculum is met by the same strategy—the argument that only great writing should be taught though decisions about "greatness" or "aesthetic quality" are made by the very same group that derides so-called minor writing.

Addison's assertions about the universality of response in the rabble were ridiculed in numerous parodies. One of his contemporaries declared ironically that "if we were to apply our selves, instead of the Classicks, to the Study of Ballads and other ingenious Composures of that Nature, in such Periods of our Lives, when we are arriv'd to a Maturity of Judgment, it is impossible to say what Improvement might be made to Wit in general, and the Art of Poetry in particular," and he proceeded to analyze "The History of Tom Thumb" mimicking Addison's comparisons.[3] Addison's claim was disavowed but it lived in its refutations. Addison's arguments existed insofar as they were entertained as a possibility that needed refutation. Addison's eminence as a critic merited replies; it did not account for the triumph of ballads as an elevated literary genre. What did account for it?

What happened in the years following Addison's essays was the introduction of ballads into the writing of established genres. Nicholas Rowe converted the ballad of Jane Shore into *The Tragedy of Jane Shore* in 1714; a collection of ballads was published in 1723; *The Beggar's Opera* introduced ballads into a new comic form in 1728; George Lillo wrote a ballad opera in 1730 and converted the ballad of George Barnwell into a tragedy, *The London Merchant*, in 1731. There were numerous ballad operas performed between 1728 and 1760.

The importation of ballads into other genres or their use as the basis for other genres is a significant aspect of literary history and an unnoted aspect of rhetorical change. For the issue is to recognize the relation between a changing society and the inadequacy of old rhetorical arguments to accommodate or explain this change. In these circumstances non-critical forms of writing—poems, plays, novels—become vehicles of elevation. By making ballads part of the existing and respected genres, the latter become events of social no less than literary change. Tragedy, for example, considered in the eighteenth century one of the highest genres, elevated the ballad of Jane Shore by making it the basis for a tragic narrative. In this procedure, the ballad story became a constituent of tragedy. When eighteenth-century poets imitated ballads, they provided the ballad form with a legitimate status it did not previously have. The consequence of these literary procedures was that, historically, poems and tragedies and other literary texts could and did function as critical illustrations and persuasive examples. They demonstrate by their production that ballads did form part of the current literary hierarchy.

Even before the ballad became a recognized genre in its own right with a theoretical rationale for its independence—and that was in 1765 in Percy's *Reliques of Ancient English Poetry*—it became a part of established genres, or was converted into established genres, or was parodied and ridiculed as a literary form.

What I wish to suggest is that the merging, incorporation, and transportation that took place—placing ballads together with contemporary poems, incorporating them in comedy or domestic drama, using ballads as subject matter for tragedy—departed from rhetoric altogether. The validity of ballads as a genre was demonstrated by their interaction with received literary genres. Thus we can observe that the decline of rhetoric was enforced by having literary genres function in a rhetorical manner. They were examples that were persuasive. They addressed audiences that accepted ballads without a prose argument that urged their acceptance. The alteration of a traditional genre could thus be accepted by readers and audiences as giving literary status to a previously declassed form.

The reshaping of these genres reshaped the way in which writing portrayed the lower and the upper classes; the novel, for example, initiated the self-consciousness of the individual author as he identified the nature of his writing (*Tom Jones*); it also reconceived the relation of writing to the private self (Richardson's *Clarissa Harlowe*), and altered the relation of the changing genres to the changing social and economic groups. In this respect Addison's interrelations of descriptions of class change with arguments for literary change were profoundly insightful even if his use of rhetorical strategies trivialized these very insights.

I wish to offer one example of genre change that might be called the Jonah technique—the ingestion of ballads in the form of ballad opera to illustrate the force of fictive works in changing audience responses not merely to ballads but to an understanding of one's society. The example is the new genre called ballad opera, first acted in 1728. This genre ingests a number of ballads, puts new words to their music, and makes them part of a comic or serious drama. The ballads are moved from the streets to the stage and their elevation is self-evident since they become part of a formal performance. In *The Beggar's Opera*, for example, the incorporation of ballads into the comic drama enacts the same leveling that Addison sought in comparing the ballad with the epic. Here the leveling makes ballads part of comedy; in other ballad operas they become part of domestic drama. The ballads of *The Beggar's Opera* are converted to social commentary just as the actions of the criminals and prostitutes are a parody of the actions of the upper classes. This ballad opera satirizes the narratives of social history, showing the merchant as a self-interested exploiter so that the Addisonian image of the benevolent merchant is mocked by a counter-image in a different genre. But at the same time, Addison's aim to elevate the ballad is achieved by incorporation.

Critics and theorists sometimes ask: "Which comes first in the elevation and change of the ballad genre—the social and economic conditions or the literary revision?" The answer is that such a question of origins is misconceived. And it is misconceived not because origins are, as we have been persuaded, multiple but because explanation and social condition are not comparable, only explanations and explanations of conditions are. Conditions, like poems, come to be described in textual explanations, just as textual explanations can become conditions and events (realism, Quixotism, declaration of independence, etc.). In trying to explain, to shape, to control our actions and the events in our society, we write in various genres. We can understand that what is the surface text in one genre (Addison's commercial essay) becomes a subtext for another genre (his critical essay). One of the aims of John Gay's joining the ballad to comedy in *The Beggar's Opera* is to level the behavior of the low (ballad) with that of the accepted high (comedy), to suggest that the merchant mediators are the exploiters and betrayers, the makers of fake harmonies.

The Beggar's Opera demonstrates the possibility of the ballad as a literary form and at the same time mixes and levels popular and polite genres.

The romance ending, the assurance that no serious consequence is intended by the social analogy, defuses the political power of *The Beggar's Opera*. The characters thus remain within the domain of the unpunished and unserious. The conclusion, by making justice an act of romance, retreats from the seriousness, from the consequences of justice that is bought and sold.

Writers who take a genre like the ballad and incorporate instances of it into a comedy to create a ballad opera are engaged in an interpretive process. They change the words and make the ballads part of a consistent narrative. This procedure identifies the writers as critics rather than rhetoricians and their works as implicit analyses of the interrelation of song and narrative. And when a ballad is rewritten into a tragedy there can be little question of the interpretive involvement of the dominant genre with the ballad subject matter.

Three years after *The Beggar's Opera,* the seventeenth-century ballad of George Barnwell was rewritten by George Lillo as a tragedy, *The London Merchant*. In the ballad, an apprentice, seduced by a prostitute, robs his merchant master and eventually murders his rich uncle. When the prostitute throws him out, he betrays her to the authorities and she is apprehended and hanged. He escapes to Poland and is hanged for a murder he claims he did not commit. The rewriting of this criminal, confessional first-person ballad into a tragedy constitutes a reinterpretation of the characters and events; the absent character of the merchant in the ballad becomes the model figure of the tragedy. Characters unmentioned become physical presences, places undescribed become identified on the stage.

Lillo's project linked tragedy to genres from which it had previously been separated; his change of protagonists included classes previously considered unfit for tragedy; his change of the effect of tragedy from the purgation of emotions through pity and terror to the exciting of passions in order to correct those that are criminal altered its social and literary aims. Tragedy became connected with stories about criminals, treatises of law, sermons about commerce. Ballads dealing with criminals and murder became the basis for high art.

By mid-century the elevation of ballads had been achieved, and Shenstone and other poets were writing ballads. The generic procedures of ballad inclusion, ballad mergers, ballad transformation established the status of these poems. The social analogy with the status of the merchant was no longer appropriate, for the merchant had himself become an accepted part of commercial and social activity. When Bishop Thomas Percy published his *Reliques of Ancient English Poetry* in 1765, more than a half-century after Addison's essays, this act was no longer an effort at elevation. Percy saw as his chief issues the historical relation of ballads to modern poetry and the need to insist on the valuable and authentic texts of his chosen poems. Percy declared that his object "was to please both the judicious Antiquary, and the Reader of Taste; and he hath endeavoured to gratify both without offending either."[4]

The concern for authenticity represented a desire to preserve the artifacts of the past. Commerce that had previously been considered the valuable interchange for use between countries in which manufactured goods were exchanged for raw materials had become, in addition, a type of exploitation in which items were valued not for use but for scarcity. A few eccentric collectors of ballads were found in the seventeenth century but the value of authenticity was now formalized in the collections of antiquarians. Old ballads were especially valuable if they were the trusted expressions of an earlier British society. As originators of a British literary tradition, ballads no longer needed the *Aeneid* to illustrate their literary value. Rather, their value lay in the thoughts and sentiments of a primitive time that revealed some of the virtues still possessed by the moderns.

Percy wished to please not merely the antiquarians but "readers of taste." For him one value of the ballads as a literary genre was to demonstrate the evolutionary tradition in English poetry. He thus included a number of contemporary poems in his collection of old ballads in order to illustrate that poetry had not attained its "highest beauties." For him, the model was the modern.

Percy was attacked because his notion of "authenticity" did not prevent him from rewriting or editing the ballads to conform to the beautiful taste of the modern. His notion of "authenticity" had to be reconciled with the sophisticated needs of men of taste, and his revisions were intended as necessary mediations. But this behavior introduced questions and problems that were primarily historical. How could authenticity be made palatable to an audience that despised the diction of authentic ballads? What kind of value did authentic artifacts possess? How could one mediate between past authenticity and modern beauty?

To these questions, the remnants of the rhetorical discipline could offer no answers. These were questions that demanded the reconsideration of literature in the light of history; it was not the oral ballad performance that was important, but the written or printed artifact. The dispersion of the elements of rhetoric was thus accomplished by raising questions about change that elements of rhetoric could not address. I have thus traced for you the increasingly limited role that rhetorical elements came to have in persuading audiences that ballads deserved elevation to formal literary genres.

I have shown that Addison used rhetorical elements to urge ballad elevation but that he failed to persuade the learned. I have shown that his procedures were parodied indicating the misuses of rhetoric. But the composition of literary genres became themselves forms of persuasion by merging lowly ballads with established genres, by rewriting the subjects of ballads in received terms, by moving the idea of ballad performance from the street to the playhouse. Thus the art of persuasion attributed to rhetoric was achieved by various genres of fictive narration. This dismantling I have referred to as "the fictions of rhetoric."

In conclusion I return to my beginning. Why has the term "rhetoric" been resurrected in our time to describe the strategies of persuasion in presidential addresses, in poems, plays, or discourses of any kind? I believe we can now point out that individual discourses have come to be analyzed as discrete objects, as ideological entities, as interpretive expressions. If, for Percy, artifacts raised historical issues, for us texts raise interpretive rather than historical problems. Moreover, "rhetoric" functions for us as an alternative to explanations modeled on so-called scientific method; insofar as texts are open, ambiguous constructions not satisfactorily deciphered by quantitative or a priori "methods," rhetorical analysis reveals the unstated as well as stated assumptions. The very notion of communication implies for us the possibility of its opposite non-communication— or its use to deceive or conceal. "Rhetoric" returns us to the moral issues of the discipline, to needs, aims, and values connected with discourse.

But even as critics and theorists seek to reassemble "rhetoric" into a discipline, then merely use it as a set of techniques, it is apparent that the historical questions that "rhetoric" avoids and has avoided will have to be confronted. Whether "rhetoric" can do this remains to be seen. Meanwhile, other kinds of criticism and theory seem able to include rhetorical strategies without neglecting the historical dimension so crucial to an understanding of the discourses in which we engage.

Notes

1. Addison, Joseph, and Richard Steele, *The Spectator*, ed. Donald F. Bond, 5 vols., 1: No. 85. My citations are by number.
2. *The Poems of Alexander Pope*, ed. John Butt (New Haven, CT: Yale Univ. Press, 1963), 148.
3. William Wagstaffe, *A Comment upon the History of Tom Thumb, in Miscellaneous Works of Dr. William Wagstaffe*, 2nd ed. (London: Printed for Jonah Bowyer, 1726), 4.
4. Thomas Percy, *Reliques of Ancient English Poetry*, 4th ed., 3 vols. (London: John Nichols, 1794), 1:xvii.

The Regeneration of Genre

In this study I have proposed a process theory of genre in which every text is considered a member of one or more genres, and I have suggested that a genre system itself undergoes continuous change with each new text. Here I mean to sum up as well as open up the final chapter of my study by reiterating and expanding upon what I see as the value of the regeneration of genre theory for literary study in hopes that my proposal for a new literary history will prove inclusive and collaborative.

Why undertake to regenerate genre theory when we have numerous other theories to explain literature? What are the aims of this particular genre theory? The aims are to explain the nature of the literary universe in which we live and to make it possible for us more adequately to support, resist, revise, or oppose this universe. The choice of any kind of criticism—genre, deconstructive, psychoanalytical, phenomenological, and so on—rests on literary value propositions each critic holds. These may be latent or overt, may be expressed in the text or the subtext, in textual statements, ruptures, or gaps. Still, any text a *critic* writes is committed to and involved with one or more genres and is itself a contribution to genre. No other literary theory can be as comprehensively inclusive as genre theory; without denying the values of deconstruction or other theories, it reveals both how and why these theories came to be; it reveals, too, why they are part of a process of continuity and change. Even texts that deny genre theory are themselves instances of genre. For example, the current term

R. Cohen, J. L. Rowlett, *Transformations of a Genre*, Palgrave Studies in the Enlightenment, Romanticism and Cultures of Print, https://doi.org/10.1007/978-3-030-89668-3_13

"écriture" or "writing" deprives a text of its generic identity; it substitutes for analyses of generic continuity and discontinuity analyses of discrete linguistic elements. But it does so in a critical text modeled on other such texts of the genres we call criticism and theory. I do not deny the value of non-generic analysis in illustrating the density of the discrete text, perhaps even the contradictions such texts may reveal. Deconstructive analysis offers a cautionary warning about language or the depiction of its social and political implications. But it does not deal with historical transformations; it simply ignores them. So, too, analysis of selected discursive formations makes discussions of change and persistence untenable, even though it provides insights into how literary structures exercise control and power. My genre theory is not offered as still another theory. Rather it seeks to explain how such theories are developed and why they develop along particular lines since theory is itself a genre.

I urge the regeneration of genre theory because more adequately than any current critical hypotheses it engages the problems of textual continuity and change without excluding the phenomena of contradictions, dispersals, and disposals. Genre theory need not avoid analysis of particulars; in fact, it contributes insights that cannot be made without it. To demonstrate the possibilities of this kind of criticism has been the purpose of this study—the literary history of a narrative that is a generic Proteus. It was first composed as a ballad and then rewritten as a life-history, a tragedy, a novel, a history, and so on. If it appears marginal, I urge that you keep in mind its applicability to the rewriting of creation myths, the narratives of Venus and Adonis, of Jesus, of Faustus, of the very construction of our literary history. With this in mind, let me rehearse some of the issues and dilemmas.

The broadside ballad of George Barnwell, composed between 1600 and 1624, was entitled "An Excellent Ballad of George Barnwel, An Apprentice of London, who was undone by a Strumpet; who having thrice robbed his Master and Murdered his Uncle in Ludlow, was hanged in Chains in Polonia, and by means of a Letter sent by his own Hand to the Mayor of London, [she] was hanged at Ludlow." An abstract of the narrative is as follows:

1. George Barnwel, a youth apprenticed to a merchant is accosted by a woman.
2. She is an experienced harlot and seduces him.

3. As a result of his infatuation and seeking to satisfy her needs and pleasures, he embezzles his master's money.
4. When accounting time comes he flees to her for protection.
5. During a drunken debauch, he offers, and she encourages him, to murder and rob his good uncle, and he does so.
6. When the money is spent, she betrays him to the authorities.
7. He escapes and betrays her to the authorities in turn and she is hanged.
8. He flees to Poland where he is hanged for an unrelated murder (which he claims not to have committed).

Here are the first twelve lines of the ballad:

> All youth of fair *England*, that dwell both far and near,
> Regard my story that I tell, and to my song give ear:
> A *London* Lad I was, a Merchant's Prentice bound,
> My name *George Barnwel*, who did spend my master many a pound.
> Take heed of Harlots then, and their inticing trains,
> For by that means I have been brought, to hang alive in chains.
>
> As I upon a day walking through the street,
> About my master's business, I did a wanton meet:
> A dainty gallant Dame, and sumptuous in attire,
> With smiling looks she greeted me and did my name require.
> Which when I had declar'd, she gave me then a kiss,
> And said, if I would come to her, I should have more than this.

I present my abstract and the words of the ballad to illustrate how differently the two genres sound. Any attempt on the part of a critic to discuss a literary text inevitably involves him in his own genre more closely than in that of the text he discusses. In this respect Pope's versified *Essay on Criticism* resembles Boileau's *L'Art Poétique* more than it does Virgil's *Aeneid* to which it refers.

When at the end of the seventeenth century (ca. 1700) the ballad was published together with a brief prose life of George Barnwell called *The 'Prentice's Tragedy: or, the History of George Barnwell: Being a fair Warning to Young Men to avoid the Company of Lewd Women*,[1] the prose fiction was written as the history of a brief life, and it began as such popular lives did with the protagonist's birthplace and parentage, even though the original ballad did not mention Barnwell's place of birth or the family of the merchant: "*George Barnwell*, a Youth descended of rich and honest Parentage, in the County of *Hereford*, being by his industrious Parents put Apprentice to a Merchant in *London*, behaved himself so well, that he gained not only the Love and good Opinion of his Master, but of all the Family, and all that knew him" (3–4).

The question, therefore, is not of the reworking of the ballad into prose but of the reworking of the ballad into a particular prose genre, the brief (true or false) life history. Thus, even though writers like John Dennis in 1701 insisted on distinguishing poetry from prose—"Poetry therefore is Poetry, because it is more passionate and sensual than Prose"[2]—their examples were drawn from specific poetic genres and specific prose genres, not poetry or prose in general. Life histories in chapbooks represented positive or negative examples, and the importance of such examples at the end of the seventeenth century lay in the social possibilities of rising or falling in society.

An example of the shaping force of genre can be noted in the tragedy that was written in 1731, based on the George Barnwell ballad. Tragedy traditionally dealt with affairs of state and with those who conducted such affairs. When George Lillo wrote a tragedy, *The London Merchant; or, The History of George Barnwell* (1731) based on the seduction of a merchant's apprentice by a harlot and the murder for money of the apprentice's uncle, he sought to make the characters worthy of high and traditional art. He had, therefore, to alter the characters and to make the narrative worthy of the status which tragedy possessed. Lillo did this by relating the role of the merchant (and that of his apprentice) to national interests. Here is the merchant speaking to one of his apprentices:

> you may learn how honest merchants,
> as such, may sometimes contribute to the safety
> of their country as they do at all times to its happiness;
> that if hereafter you should be tempted to any action that
> has the appearance of vice or meanness in it, upon
> reflecting on the dignity of our profession, you may
> with honest scorn reject whatever is unworthy of it.[3]   [I.i.16–22]

My point is that generic considerations control the method of narration; they can reshape the narrators and the incidents in the plot. A genre inevitably is related to earlier members of the genre as can be seen in *Youth's Warning-Piece; or, The Tragical History of George Barnwell*, the brief prose life written soon after the performance of *The London*

Merchant in 1732. Lillo's tragedy makes no reference to Barnwell's parents and begins with a scene discussing the merchant's role as a financial power in the reign of Elizabeth. The prose fiction however begins in a manner similar to that of the 1700 prose fiction:

> GEORGE BARNWELL, was the son of Mr. William Barnwell, a very eminent and wealthy Goldsmith in Lombard Street. George's father dying whilst he was very young, he was left to the Care of an Uncle, who lived in a Village near London. This Gentleman had a great affection for George, and having no Child of his own, treated him in all Respects as a son, giving him a very liberal Education, and when he was old enough, put him Apprentice to Mr. Thoroughgood, a Merchant, with whom he lived three or four Years, behaving himself in such a Manner, as endeared him to the whole family.[4]

The significance of birth, parentage, and place is that these provide a basis for the kind of life cycle the individual reveals. They indicate a generic continuity that is gradually formalized. In the ballad, Barnwell's reference to his father occurs in the drunken exchange with Millwood, the harlot, but in the prose version the reference to Barnwell's father begins the narrative; it is an originating gesture characteristic of the life histories at this time. Examples of the controlling force of the prose life history in shaping a narrative are evident in the making of Defoe's *Moll Flanders* into this genre. The novel does not reveal the discovery of Moll's mother until deep in the novel, but the chapbook, *The History of Moll Flanders*, begins with her birth.

The Barnwell ballad begins as a first-person narrative, but it has other narrators in addition to the autobiographical voice. Consider the following passage in the ballad in which Millwood feigns great financial need. There is a shift from first-person narrator-confessor to third-person commentator to first-person confessor. Barnwell speaks:

> "But tell to me, my dearest friend, what may thy woes amend,
> And thou shalt lack no means of help, though forty pound I spend."
> With that she turn'd her head, and sickly thus did say,
> "O my sweet *George*, my grief is great, ten pounds I have to pay,
> Unto a cruel wretch, and God he knows," quoth she,
> "I have it not." "Tush, rise," quoth I, "and take it here of me":
>
> "Ten pounds, nor ten times ten, shall make my love decay."
> Then from his bag into her lap, he cast ten pounds straight way.
> All blith and pleasant then, to banqueting they go,
> She proffered him to lye with her, and said it should be so.

And after that same time, I gave her store of coyn,
Yea, sometimes fifty pound at once, all which I did purloyn: (77–88)

These changes indicate some of the disorder in the very presentation as well as in the subject of the narration. The shift of narrator exemplifies the carelessness with which Barnwell treats his responsibility as apprentice and is a commentary upon readiness to be debauched. The 1700 prose version, however, provides a single omniscient narrator, and the intertextual linkages are with prose genres. It not only has the generic feature of parental descent, but it connects the narrative with a passage from Proverbs: "Certainly there is nothing more destructive to Youth, than to be ensnared by a Harlot; it is an Entrance into all manner of Miseries; ... *for her House enclineth unto Death, and her Paths unto the Dead*" (3).

The quotation stresses the symbolic role of the house, drawing attention, as does the prose fiction, to the importance—the danger—of place. Millwood's house is not only a sexual symbol, but it is also an entrance to diverse types of debauchery and exploitation. In this prose genre the role of place is connected with the gang that Millwood controls; so that the notion of "community" is that of the corrupted and corrupting group.

Since the prose fiction genre is a life "history," it concerns itself with one of the characteristic late seventeenth-century problems, pertinent to a "history": that of literacy, the effect of reading upon youths. Despite the commercial narrative—a merchant's apprentice and a harlot who connives for his master's money—the fiction deals with the false views imposed on a reader by romances. For Barnwell misinterprets Millwood, identifying her, in all her artificiality, as an angel. The fictive life history becomes self-reflexive because it raises the question: how can reading without experience avoid misinterpretation and how can experience be attained without moral contamination? In this fiction and in that of numerous contemporary romances, the reader is confronted with the problem of how to identify true from false values. Here we can note that the implied answer is avoidance: avoid lewd women. The reading that the text offers, however, is itself a temptation to indulge in reading other than the Bible. But even if the Bible is read, how can one who has never seen a holy cherub or a whore know how to distinguish between them?

Now this discussion is related to genre in terms of defining kinds of writing. The prose fiction serves to define itself by reference to the ballad narrative, by introducing the problem of perception, by including sermonizing and the passage from Proverbs, and by adding an episode that is a

fabliau. The prose genre remains linear; indeed, it removes the disjunctions that characterize the ballad narration. Since the ballad and prose life
history were published together, they offer an example of generic competition. The prose writing filled some of the gaps of the poem—for example, the reasons for Barnwell's sudden infatuation and the kinds of wiles
Millwood practiced. It supplemented others and added new episodes. In
the ballad, it is the debauched Barnwell who suggests the robbing and
killing of his uncle:

> Whilst I was in her company, in joy and merriment,
> And all too little I did think, that I upon her spent.
>
> "A fig for care or careful thought, when all my gold is gone,
> In faith, my girl, we will have more, whoever it light upon:
> My father's rich, why then," quoth I, "should I want any gold?"
> "With a [rich] father indeed" (quoth she), "A Son may well be bold."
> "I have a Sister, richly wed, that I'le rob e're I'le want;"
> "Why then," quo' *Sara*, "They may well consider of your scant."
>
> "Nay more than this, an Uncle I have, at *Ludlow* he doth dwell,
> He is a Grazier, which in wealth, doth all the rest excell.
> E're I will live in lack" (quoth he) "And have no coyn for thee,
> I'le rob the churl and murder him!" "Why should you not?" (quoth she).
>   (139–50)

In the prose fiction, it is criminal harmony—the plot spun by Millwood
and Barnwell together—that accounts for the murder.

> After this manner of riotous Living, this 20 Pound lasted not long, and then
> growing weary of him again, she began to put him on other Projects, but
> they not being practicable, and he telling her he had a great many Rich
> Kindred in *Herefordshire* especially a rich Uncle at *Ludlow*, they agreed to go
> down, she being to personate the Merchant's Wife, with whom he was
> Apprentice; … they had wickedly laid a Plot against his Life, which was to
> go with him to a Market, where he was to sell his Cattle, under pretence of
> seeing the Fashion of it, and so in his return to Murther him. (15)

The 'Prentice's Tragedy does not rewrite the ballad by creating some
abstract world of its own; it converts the *narrative* into a series of explanations the aims of which are to control the readers' responses to the

narrative. In the ballad, for example, when Barnwell decides to stay for supper, he describes the situation as follows:

> I supt with her that night, with joys that did abound,
> And for the same paid presently, in money twice three pound.   (61–62)

But in the chapbook, Millwood tells him about her (feigned) passion for him: "going on with a long Story of her Passion for him, she so bewitched him that he was no longer Master of himself thinking that being courted by so fine a Woman, he had the World in a string, he looked on her as an Angel" (8).

What the quotation makes clear is the narrator's commentary on Millwood's story: "she so bewitched him." The purpose of her story was to control Barnwell and manipulate him, and the narrator's aim is to make certain that the reader is not deceived as well. This procedure arises in consequence of the possibilities of misinterpreting narratives, a phenomenon that results from shifts in values. The desire to retain traditional values in an environment in which literary competition offered new dress for traditional thoughts and sometimes concealed thoughts by dress created a situation in which the genres came to have power to manipulate readers in different ways. Texts came to describe varieties of experience by criminals and aristocrats, and this variety created ideological dilemmas. On the one hand, the life history stressed moral religious values, but on the other, the experiences of an innocent youth involved in illicit sexual pleasures could serve as a negative model. The assumption that audiences knew how to take these texts is surely questionable; among the more famous of ambiguous responses are Defoe's injunction to his readers in *Moll Flanders* and Fielding's treatment of Richardson's *Pamela* as a form of sexual economics. Defoe declared: "this Work is chiefly recommended to those who know how to Read it, and how to make the good Uses of it, which the Story all along recommends to them; so it is to be hop'd that such Readers will be much more pleas'd with the Moral than the Fable, with the Application than with the Relation, and with the End of the Writer than with the Life of the Person written of" ("The Preface," 4).

I have been characterizing *The 'Prentice's Tragedy* by comparing the prose narrative with that in the ballad, and I have pointed to its formal beginning. I have compared the relation of narrator and the varied types of narration to the ballad, the sermon, Proverbs, fabliau. I have shown that the prose narrative is presented in a linear manner although within the single story of Barnwell there are several stories of Millwood and her supposed victimization.

The two texts—the ballad and the fictive life history—illustrate the historical continuity of specific narrative actions, but discontinuity in rhyme, diction, and narrative method. The ballad deals with an apprentice who becomes debauched and enjoys the pleasure of sex and immorality until he is betrayed. The prose text indicates that the basis for his debauchery is the reading of romances; these turn his head and lead him to misinterpret the world around him. *The generic issue* is the interrelation of different texts in understanding a genre at any one time. The broadside ballad that was sung in the streets of London was related to actual events—though the Barnwell ballad events have not been identified. This ballad, moreover, was related to other criminal ballads and, musically, its tune was based on that of Thomas Deloney's ballad, "The Rich Merchant Man." Its tune, moreover, was identical with that of two other seventeenth-century ballads—"The Unfaithful Servant" and "The Kentish Miracle." Generically, we have here four ballads that have a single tune but different subjects. This cluster of ballads, therefore, suggests a closer relation between these texts than discrete analysis might warrant: all of them deal with fidelity or betrayal and their shared tune indicates an underlying identity among contrary actions.

Inherent in the different ballad subjects with the same tune was the leveling of religious and high subjects with low. This leveling indicated the possibility of parody, of mixing the fantastic with the real, the merry with the mad. The grounds for this variation in the seventeenth century can be identified with the tactic of play, for there are songs sung in the streets as well as those sung at home. But this is a special kind of folk play; it belongs to the principle of pleasing different groups within the populace. Thus the stable tune and the unstable words can be the occasion of authentic variety as well as variety that could be used to cozen or manipulate the buyer.

This clustering of ballads is part of an irregular but persistent procedure in the history of literature. The sonnet becomes in Petrarch a sonnet sequence; individual poetic fictions are grouped together in *The Canterbury Tales*; a single embracing prose fiction, *Don Quixote*, includes a number of shorter fictions; a number of individual ballads are gathered together to form a ballad opera. This phenomenon of individual texts that become part of a sequence or a single text that incorporates them is a procedure that characterizes literary history. Group texts such as the sonnet sequence, the periodical essay, or the ballad opera may be defined as new genres and the reasons for their initiations are historical and varied. In view of the fact that I am using a ballad as my generic model, it is appropriate to consider the initiation of the ballad opera which ingests or incorporates ballads, particularly since the ballad opera was initiated in the early eighteenth century—a time when the Barnwell ballad was being rewritten as a tragedy. In the ballad opera, the tune of a ballad is paired with new lyrics and made part of a drama. The pairing serves as an element in the narrative dialogue and it is addressed to an audience in the theater. The ballad opera parodied the songs of the newly imported Italian opera; it thus stressed the importance of English-made songs, and critics recognize this.

But the ballad opera is also characteristic of a complicated generic process. Broadside ballads were street literature, and we note in the ballad opera the shifting generic status of broadsides. The ballad opera is a genre which includes within comedy such genres as parody of opera and of satire on romances. The new genre creates a mixture that results in audience responses different from those accorded individual ballads or non-musical comedies. What takes place is the elevation of a popular genre into a sophisticated one, and the compromising of the higher genre by having it include the lower. This hierarchical reshifting of genres is not confined to the late seventeenth and early eighteenth centuries. It is characteristic of the process of generic absorption or transformation. It is at this time that generic reshifting is taking place in the role of the mock-epic, periodical essay, satire, the georgic, the ballad opera, and the novel. Such reshifting is intertwined with social and economic changes. The procedure of relating higher to lower units and the reverse—lower to higher—is especially pertinent to the early eighteenth century, for the origin of ballads was then identified with primitive authorship; the procedure is analogous to the new commercial enterprises of bringing "civilization" to uncivilized countries and taking raw material from them. The justification of this commercial procedure is that high culture—manufactures—is brought to primitive countries, and that primitive countries provide energy—raw materials— for the high culture. It is an argument for intermixture in which exploitation is concealed by the language of public benefits. It thus indicates the possibilities for satire and irony of the interaction of low generic forms with high generic forms. This exploitative "commerce" for self-interest is what Pope satirizes in a passage in *The Rape of the Lock* describing Belinda at her dressing table:

> Unnumber'd Treasures ope at once, and here
> The various Off'rings of the World appear

From each she nicely culls with curious Toil,
And decks the Goddess with the glitt'ring Spoil.
This Casket India's glowing Gems unlocks,
And all Arabia, breathes from yonder Box.
The Tortoise here and Elephant unite,
Transform'd to Combs, the speckled and the white.   (129–136)

While Pope is using commercial imagery to indicate the misuse of religious, reflective (artistic), and personal values so that comprehensiveness
becomes a personal trait of acquisitiveness, the ballad opera suggests the
internalizing and manipulation of the ballad. It becomes a song of personal expression or an allegorical reflection or a narrative within a narrative. When the ballad is absorbed by the drama, it produces a genre in
which the function of song serves to make sophisticated what was unso-
phisticated, to bring artistic unity to a street poem that was inconsistent,
even contradictory. There are other commercial aspects to this interchange. "Commerce" in the seventeenth century was a term for intellectual as well as economic exchange. The elevation of genres constituted a
process of elevating the audience's consciousness of "class" change. What
it justified, of course, was the shift in the role of the merchant who had
become important enough to be satirized. In *The Beggar's Opera* (1728)
Peachum is a merchandiser of criminals and stolen goods, and he operates
both against and for the law. He is thus held up to ridicule as the unprin-
cipled man of principle: the principle being his own self-interest. It is only
three years later (1731) that the ballad of George Barnwell is made into a
tragedy, *The London Merchant*, in which the merchant's principles are
identified with the moral and economic interests of the state: "I have
observed [says Trueman] those countries where trade is promoted and
encouraged do not make discoveries to destroy but to improve mankind—
by love and friendship to tame the fierce and polish the most savage; to
teach them the advantages of honest traffic by taking from them, with
their own consent, their useless superfluities, and giving them in return
what, from their ignorance in manual arts, their situation, or some other
accident, they stand in need of" (III.i).

The commercial narrative in the ballad, prose fiction, and tragedy demonstrates the status function of genre: the ballad can be raised to high literary status by raising the low characters to the generic assumptions of
tragedy. But this must result in changing the aims and concept of the
tragic genre. When Bishop Percy published the Barnwell ballad in his

Reliques of Ancient English Poetry (1765), together with similar poems by Ben Jonson, John Dryden, and other poets, he elevated the status of the genre by interrelating this criminal ballad with sophisticated lyrics. When Lillo extended and lowered the status of tragedy by accommodating it to "the circumstances of the generality of mankind," here a merchant's apprentice and a "fallen woman," he defended his reconceptualizing of tragedy: "tragedy is so far from losing its dignity by being accommodated to the circumstances of the generality of mankind that it is more truly august in proportion to the extent of its influence and the numbers that are properly affected by it, as it is more truly great to be the instrument of good to many who stand in need of our assistance than to a very small part of that number."[5]

Throughout this study I have sought to persuade you of the value of genre criticism for understanding the changes texts undergo. I have explained that a genre is a process for understanding a group of texts by their relation to and interconnection with other genres; I have shown how genre controls the method of narration of a text, how it alters conceptions of characters and sequences of events. I have shown that the status of a genre changes depending upon the texts with which it is identified and the constituent features that are added to it. I have shown that certain economic and social changes do not affect different genres in the same way. Such non-verbal changes become translated into generic features that contribute in significant or insignificant ways to generic change.

What is involved in generic variations? I have sought to explain how a genre like the brief life history becomes interrelated with other prose genres thus defining its own temporal identity. I have sought to show that the ballad, the prose fiction, the tragedy are not evolutionary in their functions. Rather, they supplement, contradict, continue, and compete with one another, controlled as they are by relations to earlier members of their own genres.

Why do some genres decline and disappear while others decline and are revived? I have explained the concept of clustering as a repetitive and historical pattern, but why do such clusters decline or recur? I suggest an answer to this question by referring to the sonnet. It is well known that after Milton the major poets of the late seventeenth and eighteenth centuries wrote very few sonnets—Pope and Swift wrote none, and Gray composed only one. It was not until the 1780s that sonnets began to be written in considerable numbers and, of course, Wordsworth, Coleridge, Byron, Shelley, and Keats composed in this genre. What kind of interpretative analysis of "Westminster Bridge" can we have if we do not even consider why Wordsworth chose this genre in which to compose? To consider this is, of course, to recognize that the poet functions critically when he writes, or chooses to write, an instance of a genre or genres. A genre theory compels us to recognize the poet as critic in his poetry. The sonnet represented for Wordsworth an organic universe, and he selected the image of a sphere or dew drop to characterize it. The genre written with enjambed lines connecting octave and sestet represented for him "that pervading sense of intense unity in which the excellence of the sonnet has always seemed to me mainly to consist."[6]

Wordsworth considered the sonnet as a conceptual form in opposition to the antithetical georgic or satiric poems of a Pope or Gay or Swift. These writers used a myth of nature to control the empirical disorder they found around them. They selected genres that were marked by a shifting awareness of human limits amid the mystery of God's presence in nature; inexplicable moments of grace within a metaphysical belief of true unity. They avoided using a genre that implied intense unity and harmony since it was hardly a model for *concordia discors*. John Denham's Thames verses that became the model image of the river as poetic power specified the kinds of limits within which eighteenth-century poets varied their couplets:

> O could I flow like thee, and make thy stream
> My great example, as it is my theme!
> Though deep, yet clear, though gentle, yet not dull,
> Strong without rage, without ore-flowing full.   [1655; 189–192]

Need I remind you of Wordsworth's reworking of this river image: "all good poetry is the spontaneous overflow of powerful feelings." The shift in the concept of the metaphor embodied within it a shift in the concept governing certain georgic and pastoral genres.

The Denham quote and the Wordsworth quote are constituents of larger works, the first being two couplets from *Coopers Hill*, a long georgic poem, and the second, part of a sentence in Wordsworth's 1800 preface to the *Lyrical Ballads*. The first indicates how a nationalistic river image becomes a metaphoric invocation of poetic ideals; the second indicates how a nationalistic river image becomes part of a *theory* of the nature of poetry. Such interconnections demonstrate continuity of metaphor, discontinuity of metaphoric function.

But such analyses taken from the text to which they refer *cannot* explain to us why the Thames is central to Denham's view, nor why his metaphor slips from nature to human nature, from "clear" to "dull," from "rage" to "ore-flowing." For this we need a generic analysis of the georgic structure in which man and nature, politics and economics, poetry and power are constituents. Nor is it possible to determine, in my quote from Wordsworth, his argument which relates spontaneity to regularity, good poetry to his theory of pleasure. But I trust that the case for the value of such analysis has been made.

For changes *within* a genre, in order to show how key passages are interwoven with generic analysis, it is necessary to turn to analyses of wholes, since genre members are textual entities. It is precisely this notion of "wholeness" that disturbs opponents of genre theory. Even though "wholeness" refers to a textual process of reader-text construction and to a process in which each "whole" is, as I have indicated, somewhat different from previous textual members, the assumptions of textual disintegration or discursive formations oppose "wholes" of any kind. But a generic theory that explains the process of change needs the diverse parts of a text in order to explain the types and significance of changes. Metaphors must be grasped in relation to the non-metaphoric, the stated related to the unstated, the ideal related to the actual.

To demonstrate the analysis of changes within a genre and what they imply, I shall use the examples of Collins's "Ode Occasioned by the Death of Mr. Thomson" (1749) and Wordsworth's early "Remembrance of Collins" (composed 1789, published 1798). Collins's ode is a pastoral elegy and if we wish to grasp the change that takes place between this poem and Wordsworth's elegy, we can begin by noting that both poems have a similar scene: the speaker-poet rowing on the Thames remembering the death of a poet who sang of nature poetry. Collins's poem begins with an act of sight separating the speaker from the poet spoken about. It describes a future of pastoral ceremony. Collins's elegiac relation of loss moves from imaginary pastoral to country maids and youths as guardians of the grave of the dead poet—to the speaker's "remembrance" as recollected moments of the past that lead to suspended action followed by mourning in the present. Collins's elegy, connected with imaginary eclogue scenes, illustrates the attempt to mix real with imagined time, natural cycles with progressive movement. Wordsworth's "Remembrance of Collins" begins with an invocation to the Thames and concludes with a prayer and ends with gathering darkness as a holy convocation. Wordsworth's invocation to the river sees it as a "soul" that can bestow on poets the deep and holy quietness that makes man and nature sharers of blessedness. Mourning becomes, in this elegy, a prayer for calmness and serenity in this life. Wordsworth established his continuity with Collins directly not only by establishing a similar scene but by quoting a line from Collins's stanza, Wordsworth writes:

> Remembrance oft shall haunt the shore
> When Thames in summer wreaths is dressed,
> And oft suspend the dashing oar
> To bid his gentle spirit rest!
>
> Now let us, as we float along,
> For *him* suspend the dashing oar;
> And pray that never child of song
> May know that Poet's sorrows more.
>
> How calm! how still! the only sound,
> The dripping of the oar suspended!
> —The evening darkness gathers round
> By virtue's holiest Powers attended.

Collins connects "remembrance" with Thomson's *Summer*, season of meditation and the suspension of movement, to urge Thomson's spirit to rest as well. Collins seeks an imitative effect so that the elegy is connected with empirical values of sight, memory, and imagined ceremony. Wordsworth, however, connects suspension with prayer and the single sound of the dripping of the suspended oar, an epiphany, a unity with the still, the dead, and the holy. For him, the elegy becomes connected with powers beyond the empirical. It substitutes the mystery of nature for the pastoral, mythic descriptions of nature. Wordsworth's use of the elegy is thus conceptually different from Collins's use of it. Linguistically, structurally, and philosophically, his use of elegy reveals the changes the genre undergoes.

My summary rehearsal of the Barnwell narrative and these three genres in which it was written has illustrated how a ballad initially considered "non-literary" became "literary," and how a prose fiction text of this narrative exemplified its generic identity in its rewriting. "The 'Prentice's Tragedy" or "The History of George Barnwell" reveals that self-designating genre terms like "tragedy" and "history" cannot be trusted as theoretical terms, for they in no rigid way characterize a reading text and a performance text. Nevertheless, a text does present itself as self-reflexive to the extent that it deals with the reading of prose fictions and the misperceptions these cause. *The London Merchant*, a tragedy, deals with Millwood's role-playing, a self-reflexive reference to play acting. The genres direct us, the readers or viewers, to underlying assumptions about generic differences no matter how much one genre interrelates with another, no matter how much of the narrative of the prose text interrelates with that in the tragedy.

This study has been an effort to answer the questions I asked of myself in my autobiographical introduction: Why does a particular narrative get rewritten in various genres? Why does the Barnwell narrative presented in a ballad get rewritten in a prose fiction, in a tragedy, and in another prose fiction within a hundred years? To begin with, it deals with disobedience and punishment, the archetype of man's fall. It also deals with sexual seduction and exploitation, with the crime of parricide and its punishment. The seduction is a version of youthful innocence corrupted by crafty and wicked experience. Historically the narrative deals with a reversal of values and situations: the merchant's apprentice becomes a criminal and the harlot, in her criminality, acts like a merchant. As the social roles of merchant and apprentice change, the genres in which they are rewritten provide different reasons for their behavior. The brief life history begins to individualize the youth. So, too, the function of organized criminality. Millwood's gang inverts the role of the true family, making criminal acts the basis for the receipt of immoral love. In *The London Merchant* the narrative presents contrary interpretations of the institutions of society and the role of the merchant.

The genres reshape our consciousness of the characters and events in the narrative. The genres address different audiences and keep before us our continuity with aspects of our past. The different genres reveal a history of literature that moves between audience levels. They reveal to us procedures for controlling and directing different responses. They reveal the need to undo history by redoing it in a different genre. And they demonstrate that no undoing can proceed without some continuous doing. Genre members enact the process by which a genre undergoes change so that my own chapters are themselves a contribution to literary history and critical theory.

This study of genre, narrative, ballad, and context has been an attempt to explain and regenerate genre theory, to insist on the necessity of genre. My aim has been to demonstrate the value of an embracing genre theory, a theory that explains the continuity and change in literary study. The time has come for such a theory, and I invite you to join me in giving it life.

NOTES

1. The title page states, "Printed for W. O. and sold by the Booksellers of *Pye-corner* and *London-bridge*" (n.d.; the British Library suggests 1700). Page numbers hereafter cited in text.
2. John Dennis, *The Advancement and Reformation of Modern Poetry: A Critical Discourse* (London: Printed for Rich. Parker, 1701), 24.
3. George Lillo, *The London Merchant*, ed. William H. McBurney, 11.
4. *Youth's Warning-Piece; or, The Tragical History of George Barnwell* (London: 1932), 4. Text is taken from the Gale ECCO Print Editions. Other eighteenth-century editions vary only slightly.
5. Lillo, *The London Merchant*, "Dedication," 3.
6. Wordsworth, "Letter to Dyce" (n.d.; written in 1833), in *Wordsworth's Literary Criticism*, ed. Nowell C. Smith (London: Henry Frowde, 1905), 247.

Barnwell Bibliographies

Ballad Bibliography 1660–1800

Based on a catalog search of ESTC at the British Library for the keywords "George Barnwell" and "ballad." When the publication year and/or place do not appear in the imprint, the ESTC catalog estimate is noted in brackets.

1. *An Excellent Ballad of George Barnwel, an Apprentice of London, Who Was Undone by a Strumpet, Who Having Thrice Robbed His Master, and Murdered His Uncle in Ludlow. The Tune Is, the Merchant.* Microfilm ed. [London]: Printed for F. Coles, T. Vere, and W. Gilbertson, [1658–1664].

2. *An Excellent Ballad of George Barnwel, an Apprentice of London, Who Was Undone by a Strumpet, Who Having Thrice Robbed His Master, and Murdered His Uncle in Ludlow, Was Hanged in Chains in Polonia, and by the Means of a Letter Sent from His Own Hand to the Mayor of London, She Was Hang'd at Ludlow. The Tune Is, the Rich Merchant-Man.* Microfilm ed. [London]: Printed for F[rancis]. Coles, T[homas]. Vere, J[ohn]. Wright, and J[ohn]. Clarke, [1674–1679].

3. *An Excellent Ballad of George Barnwell, an Apprentice in the City of London, Who Was Undone by a Strumpet, Who Caused Him*

© The Author(s), under exclusive license to Springer Nature Switzerland AG 2021
R. Cohen, J. L. Rowlett, *Transformations of a Genre*, Palgrave Studies in the Enlightenment, Romanticism and Cultures of Print, https://doi.org/10.1007/978-3-030-89668-3_14

Thrice to Rob His Master, and to Murder his Uncle in Ludlow,
&C. To the Tune of, the Merchant, &C. London: printed by and for
C. B[rown]. and are to be sold by J. Walter, at the Hand and Pen
in High Holbourn, [1682–1707].

4. *An Excellent Ballad of George Barnwel an Apprentice in London,*
   Who Was Undone by a Strumpet, Who Thrice Robbed His Master,
   and Murdered His Uncle in Ludlow. The Tune Is, the Merchant.
   [London]: Printed for J. Clarke, W. Thackeray, and T. Passinger,
   [1684–1686].

5. *An Excellent Ballad of George Barnwell, an Apprentice in the City of*
   London, Who Was Undone by a Strumpet, Who Caused Him Thrice
   to Rob His Master, and to Murder His Uncle in Ludlow, &C. To the
   Tune of, the Merchant, &C. London: printed by and for W[illiam].
   O[lney]. and are to be sold by the booksellers of Pye-corner and
   London brid. [sic], [1705].

6. *An Excellent Ballad of George Barnwell, an Apprentice in the City of*
   London, ... To the Tune of, the Merchant, &C. London: printed for
   M. Deacon, [1710].

7. *An Excellent Ballad of George Barnwel, an Apprentice in the City of*
   London, Who Was Undone by a Strumpet, Who Caused Him Thrice
   to Rob His Master, and to Murther His Uncle in Ludlow. [London]:
   Printed for J Hodges, on London-Bridge, [1750].

8. *An Excellent Ballad of George Barnwell, Who Was Undone by a*
   Strumpet, ... London: printed and sold by L. How, in Petticoat-
   Lane, [1760].

9. *The Cruel Lover: Or, the Credulous Maid. Being an Account of a*
   Young Man near London, Who, after He Had Courted a Young
   Maid, and Gain'd Her Consent to Lie with Him, Cruelly Murder'd
   Her, and Afterwards Threw Her into Ann-Is-So-Clear, near Shore-
   Ditch, &C. Tune, George Barnwell [London?, 1760].

10. *The Excellent Ballad of George Barnwell, Who Was Brought to an*
    Untimely End by the Allurements of a Strumpet: She Encouraged
    Him to Rob His Master and Afterwards to Murder His Uncle.
    Warrington: W. Eyres, printer, [1770].

11. *An Excellent Ballad of George Barnwell, Who Was Undone by a*
    Strumpet, Who Caused Him to Rob His Master and Murder His
    Uncle. [London?], [1775].

12. *An Excellent Ballad of George Barnwell, Who Was Undone by a Strumpet,* ... [London?]: printed and sold in Stonecutter Street, Fleet Market, [1778].
13. *The Excellent Ballad of George Barnwell, Who Was Undone by a Strumpet, Who Caused Him to Rob His Master, and Murder His Uncle.* [London]: Sold [by J. Evans] at no. 41, Long-Lane, West-Smithfield, London, [1791–1803].
14. *The Excellent Ballad of George Barnwell, Who Was Undone by a Strumpet, Who Caused Him to Rob His Master, and Murder His Uncle.* [London?], [1795].

CHAPBOOK BIBLIOGRAPHY 1690s–1840

Based on a catalog search of ESTC and OCLC for the keywords "George Barnwell," the list below includes works 8–32 pages long. Uncertain publication years, as estimated by the ESTC or OCLC catalogers are denoted by the *s* after the date (e.g., "1690s"). The rest of the dates are, according to the catalog, as they appear in the imprint of the work.

1. *The 'Prentice's tragedy: or, The history of George Barnwell: being a fair warning to young men to avoid the company of lewd women,* Printed by W. O. and sold by the booksellers of Pye-Corner and London-bridge, 1690s.
2. *Youth's warning-piece; or, The tragical history of George Barnwell who was undone by a strumpet,* London, 1750.
3. *Youth's warning-piece: the tragical history of George Barnwell, who was undone by a strumpet, who caused him to rob his master, and murder his uncle,* Printed and sold [by Timothy Green] at the printing-office in New-London, [Conn.], 1770.
4. *Youth's warning-piece; or, the tragical history of George Barnwell; who was undone by a strumpet, that caused him to rob his master, and murder his uncle,* [London]: Printed and sold in Aldermary Church Yard, Bow Lane, London, 1775.
5. *The History of George Barnwell, of London,* Norwich, Conn.: Printed by John Trumbull, 1783.
6. *The history of George Barnwell, of London,* Norwich, Conn.: Printed by John Trumbull, 1792.

7. *Youth's warning-piece; or, the tragical history of George Barnwell, who was undone by a strumpet, that cause him to rob his master, and murder his uncle,* Stockton: printed and sold by R. Christopher, 1795.

8. *The old ballad of George Barnwell,* 1800s. page 17.

9. *The pathetic and interesting history of George Barnwell, the London 'prentice: founded on facts,* London: Printed for the booksellers and for T. Deighton York [sic?], 1804.

10. *Pathetic history of George Barnwell, the London apprentice: who, by keeping company, and following the advice of a woman of the town, was reduced to the lowest pitch of infamy: detailing every particuler [sic] of his guilty career, from the robbing of his master to the most dreadful murder of his uncle! for which he was executed,* Glasgow: Printed for the booksellers, 1820.

11. *The life and history of George Barnwell; who, from the highest character and credit fell to the lowest depth,* London: Dean & Munday, 1820.

12. *The pathetic history of George Barnwell, the London apprentice,* London: Hodgson, 1820.

13. *The London apprentice; or, The melancholy history of George Barnwell, shewing the evil effects of bad company, with the untimely end & execution of this deluded young man, who was induced by an infamous prostitute, named Mary Millwood, to rob his master, and murder his uncle, which caused the death of his master's daughter, a beautiful young lady, who had placed her affections on him; intended as a warning to youth, to avoid the company of abandoned women,* London: O. Hodgson, 1820s.

14. *The Joys of Kilfane together with George Barnwell.* Dublin: R. Grace, 1820, 8 p. illus.

15. *The Tragical history of George Barnwell, the London prentice,* Falkirk: T. Johnston, 1821.

16. *The Life and history of George Barnwell: who, from the highest character and credit, fell to the lowest depth of vice through the artful stratagems of a woman of the town: detailing his love for Maria, the steps which led to his own ruin, and ultimately to the murder of his uncle, his affecting execution, and the death of Maria through a broken heart,* London: Dean and Munday, 1826.

17. *The history of George Barnwell, the London apprentice, who robbed his master and murdered his uncle to satisfy the extravagance of his mis-*

tress, Milwood, showing, to inexperienced youth, the necessity of avoiding bad company, London, 1826.

18. *The pathetic history of George Barnwell, the London apprentice; who, by keeping company, and following the advice of a woman of the town, named Milwood, was reduced to the lowest pitch of infamy; detailing every particular of his guilty career, from the robbing of his master to the dreadful murder of his uncle! With the history of Maria, his sweetheart,* London: Printed by and for Hodgson & Co., 1829.

19. *The London apprentice; or, The melancholy history of George Barnwell: showing the evil effects of bad company: with the untimely end and execution of this deluded young man, who was induced by an infamous prostitute, named Mary Millwood, to rob his master, and murder his uncle,* Derby: Thomas Richardson, 1830.

20. *History of George Barnwell, the London apprentice: who, by keeping company, and following the advice of a woman of the town, was reduced to the lowest pitch of infamy: detailing every particular of his guilty career, from the robbing of his master to the most dreadful murder of his uncle!: for which he was executed,* Belfast: Smyth Printer, 1830.

21. *The history of George Barnwell, the London apprentice, who robbed his master and murdered his uncle,* 2nd [Anon.] ed., London: Mason, 1830.

22. *The history of George Barnwell, the London apprentice; detailing every particular of his guilty career, from the robbing of his master to the dreadful murder of his uncle,* London: A. Ryle & Co. printers, 1840.

23. *Pathetic history of George Barnwell, the London apprentice,* Newcastle: W. & T. Fordyce, 1840.

INDEX

Keats, John, 161, 162
Kris, Ernst, 13
Kurz, Otto, 13

L
Language
  commercial reciprocity, 65
  conversion of nonlinguistic
    behavior, 152
  didactic, 43, 53, 78, 79
  idiomatic, 53
  of manipulation, 108
  metaphoric, 153
  multiple dimensionality, 150, 152
The Law of Genre, 4
Letters
  from correspondents, 61
  inclusion in larger genres, 22
*The Life of George Barnwell; or, The
  London Apprentice of the Last
  Century*, 19, 181, 188
  behavior in individual terms, 184
  changed concept of history, 184
  falsifying 18th-century history, 195
  industrialization, and, 183
  multiple narratives
    simultaneously, 190
  relationship between men and
    nature, 183
  sudden character changes, 184
  synchronic time frame, 190
  temporal displacement, 188
Literary criticism, 7, 11
  autobiographies, and, 11
  inclusion in larger genres, 22
Literary history, 44
  individual texts, and, 219
  use of ballads for genres, 204
Literary structures
  economic structures, homology
    between, 2

exercising control and power, 212
Literary texts, 11
  aesthetic principles, 11
  contributions to new societies, 12
  functions of, 205
  non-literary texts, differences
    between, 8
  not merely formal combinations, 26
The London Merchant, 18
  based on George Barnwell
    ballad, 80
  characters worthy of high art, 214
  conversion from ballad, 97
  couplets, 78
  Dedication, 79
  Dramatis Personae, 82
  18th-century, 18
  elevating ballad, 109
  elevation of merchant, 157
  genre transformation, as, 159
  genuine love, 97
  past and present historical
    components, 21
  personal love, and, 90
  Prologue, 84
  reader response, 129
  revised concluding scene, 101
  revisions and re-editing, 103
  rise of the merchant class, 130
  role playing, 226
  social construction, 28
  statement of intention, 83
  status of protagonists, 124
  20-th century publications, 19
  vice, reducing, 81
Lovejoy, Arthur O., 27

M
Mailer, Norman, 14, 15
Majestic simplicity, 67
Marxism, 2
Maxims, 87

McBurney, William H., 19, 83
Mead, Margaret, 3
The Memoirs of Maria Brown, 168
Memoranda
    inclusion in larger genres, 22
Mergers
    political and economic
        implications, 15
Metaphoric language, 153
Metaphysical poetry, 202
Milton, John, 30
Minstrels, 105, 113, 117
*Miscellaneous Pieces relating to the
    Chinese*, 117
Miscellanies, 105, 109, 117
Moby Dick, 23
Mode, 154
    of accommodation, 120
    of distribution, 49
    of presentation, 51, 56
Moll Flanders, 168
Multivocal text, 2

N
Nabokov, Vladimir, 15
Naive romance, 155
Narratives
    bildungsroman, 172
    commercial, 216, 221
    criminal, 37, 77, 78
    defining, 24
    disjunctions, 191
    first-person, 38, 133, 215
    first-person genres, 92
    imaginery, 170
    interpolated, 155
    misinterpreting, 218
    penitential, 166
    prose, 49, 50, 146
    rewritten in different genres, 226
    third-person, 56, 157

treatment in different genres, 2, 49
    valuable distinctions, 154
Natural poetry
    corruption of, 117
Nisbet, Robert, 151
Non-communication and, 209
Nonlinguistic behavior
    converted into language, 152
Non-literary texts, 12
    literary texts, differences between, 8
Non-textual genres, 62
Novels
    inclusion of other genres, 126
    multiple voices, 150
    numerous narratives, 133

O
Objectivity of history, 14
*Ode Occasioned by the Death of Mr
    Thompson*, 224
*Ode on a Distant Prospect of Eton
    College*, 161
Ode on Melancholy, 162
Old ballads, 108, 118, 208
*Old Ballads, Historical and Narrative,
    with some of modern date*, 119
Open systems, 20
    genre, 25
    unanticipated components, 22
Oral societies, 5

P
Pale Fire, 15
Parables
    inclusion in larger genres, 22
Parody
    defining, 70
    member of ridiculed genre, 72
    satire, intertwined with, 72
Penitential narratives, 166

Printed by Printforce, United Kingdom